NICANOR PERLA and speaker on artif. ....zation and spiritualized science. He has advised UN agencies, the Office of the President and Congress, as well as cities and towns undertaking large-scale social threefolding projects. He has headed global and national civil society networks that were responsible for stopping 12 nuclear power plants, banning 32 pesticide formulations and bringing about mainstream sustainable development, including organic farming in the Philippines. Perlas is a member of the Senate Task Force on Artificial Intelligence. For the global impact of his work, he has received the Right Livelihood Award (Alternative Nobel Prize), the Outstanding Filipino Award and UNEP S Global 500 Award. He is the author of *Shaping Globalization: Civil Society, Cultural Power, Threefolding.*

Advance Praise for *Humanity's Last Stand*

'The most important book I have read in the past decade ... When I finished it, I took a few deep breaths, gathered myself, then asked, 'Now that I know this, how do I best live my life?' Please, everyone, read this book, ask yourself the same question, and together, with the guidance Nicanor provides, let us build the new world we all know is possible.'— *Thomas Cowan, MD, physician and author, USA*

'In Nicanor Perlas, the conscience of the world is embodied. He is describing the heights and depths of humanity with presence and actuality, incredible knowledge and spiritual advice for each one of us. You are a different person after having read this book. I am deeply touched by messages of "the keeper of the world's conscience".' —*Elizabeth Wirsching, Anthroposophical Society in Norway*

'Reading this book encouraged me to awaken even more fully to the importance of the *human* soul and to nurture and defend the *truly* human. I will do this not only in my daily work in the Brazilian slums but also in the anthroposophical movement and other spiritual streams that strive for humanness. We all have to work *together* to keep alive the human-spiritual spark in us.'—*Ute Craemer, Waldorf community educator, Brazil*

'Nicanor Perlas approaches the burning, crucial subject of artificial intelligence with untiring courage. The image of the modern archetypal hero emerges from between the lines of this book. Nicanor sets out on the (im)possible quest barehanded and unable to predict what the final outcome will be, yet he moves on, anchored in his uniquely deep and powerful thinking imbued with his love for humanity.'—*Mónica Cumar, publisher, Chile*

'Nicanor Perlas joins the likes of Elon Musk and Stephen Hawking in raising a red flag of concern over the ever-widening dissemination of Artificial Intelligence into the life of worldwide humanity.'—*Van James, artist, author, educator and Chairman of the Anthroposophical Society in Hawaii*

'In this book, Nicanor Perlas is almost shouting out the message that it is time now to wake up and realize that we are on the edge of a complete breakdown ... A very important book that in so many ways is an urgent wakeup call for us all! Read it and do it now!'—*Mats-Ola Ohlsson, Curative educator / social therapist and General Secretary of the Anthroposophical Society in Sweden*

'This book is important for the present and will be relevant for the future, just like the books of and works by Rudolf Steiner are and will continue to be.'—*Yuji Agematsu, Japan*

'As profoundly important, utterly mesmerizing, as it is at once both terrifying and an incredible call to arms. Nicanor Perlas adeptly outlines the urgent need to move away from a materialistic consciousness to an emerging science-based spirituality that can address the existential challenges and issues surrounding artificial intelligence ...'—*Emily Fletcher, Editor, Sphere Magazine, New Zealand*

'The value of this book is that it points to a profound way of contextualizing and understanding a phenomenon that will influence individual lives and society in ways we can hardly comprehend.'—*Cornelius Pietzner, CEO of Alterra Impact Finance, Switzerland, and Member of the Board and Director of Mind and Life Europe, Switzerland*

'Well researched and deeply passionate, this book embodies a care for humanity that has its wellsprings in knowledge of the spiritual as well as the scientific ... It awakens and guides us as to how artificial intelligence, instead of suppressing humanity, can be a part of our healthy evolution.'—*John Bloom, General Secretary, Anthroposophical Society in America (US), Vice President, Organizational Culture, RSF Social Finance, USA*

'Nicanor Perlas brings a lifetime of human intelligence—the active relation of thinking, feeling, acting human beings to each other—to the challenge of the apparently intelligent machine ... There have been many predecessors, but this is the first book of "the human movement". Let us read it and awaken to the next stage of our humanity!'—*John Beck, Editor, Being Human magazine, USA*

'Nicanor Perlas' book is a necessary wake-up call. Far from any hostility to technology, he describes with great expertise these challenges and shows ways out that are based especially on the spiritual activity of humans.'—*Christoph Strawe, Institute for Social Issues, Initiative Network Threefolding, Germany*

'Nicanor Perlas has written a very important book that many should read! ... Humanity has to wake up to what it means to be fully human and harness latent spiritual capacities. Only in this way, and together with others worldwide, will we succeed in finding a solution to the biggest challenge humanity has ever faced.'—*Alexander Schwedeler, Leadership consultant, IMO Institute for Man and Organisation Development, Germany*

'As a true global citizen, living with the major issues of our time, Nicanor Perlas raises awareness on the existential challenges of AI/ AGI/ ASI ... With clarity and precision, he describes what can be understood as human and what not. The book leaves one concerned and yet more decided than ever to do one's share for a more human and sustainable world.'—*Alexandra Abensperg-Traun, Director, Philiana, Austria*

'Nicanor Perlas presents eloquently and clearly the issues at stake with the accelerating developments of Artificial Intelligence at different levels: physical, psychological, social and spiritual ... He provides a road for anthroposophists to contribute in the solution of these issues in combination with a wider Michaelic community. This is his unique skill— global networking and community building.'—*Karla Cryer, psychologist and adult educator, Australia*

'This is an eye-opening book that reveals the true face of AI and the negative forces that it is bringing to humanity ... It is filled with Nicnor's deep love for humanity and his hopes for our evolution. Reading this will most certainly motivate readers to take a courageous step towards a better future for humanity.'—*Kaori Akimoto, counselor and biography facilitator, Japan*

'Nicanor Perlas draws upon his extensive research, spiritual insights and experiences as a global activist to issue a Michaelic call to action—a call to wake up to the potential dangers of Artificial Intelligence, while making suggestions of what to do about it that engender hope for the future evolution of humanity.'—*Gary Lamb, Co-Director of the Hawthorne Valley Center for Social Research and the Ethical Technology Initiative, USA*

'Nicanor has given us another unique book. As Steiner showed, "the way to counter Ahriman is by unmasking it". Nicanor gives us two vital hints: how to understand AI and the shadow behind it and secondly, how to intervene along with others without distinction of creed or culture, in order to make AI benefit and serve humanity.'—*Luis Espiga, President, The Triform Institute, Spain*

'A timely call at the right moment ... Nicanor Perlas, inspiring insight and determination, gives an in-depth spiritual-scientific analysis by going to the core of the matter which only this perspective truly allows, thereby informing about the latest state of technological research and digital transformation, and offering a joint strategy of action for waking contemporaries in civil society and in spiritual-science. Written from the heart of urgency to the hearts of those who care!'—*Ulrich Morgenthaler, Event Manager, Forum3, Germany*

'... This book is a potent reminder that the deeper fear inside each person—the holy and cosmic fear of avoiding a real engagement with the spiritual battle for the true image and future of the human being—is the one truly worth our attention. It is an earnest invitation to let courage direct our intelligence so that we may give ourselves a chance to participate in this decisive moment in evolution.'—*Tom O'Keefe, Editor and Publisher, Deepening Anthroposophy, USA*

'I applaud and welcome the vigour and energy with which Nicanor Perlas has taken up the challenge of Artificial Intelligence and what it really means to be human ... This book is a call to action and for collaboration for all those who seek, cherish and strive to actualize what it truly means to be human.'—*Reinoud Mejer, Director, The International Youth Initiative Programme, Sweden*

'... Nicanor brings together a bold call to arms in his clear and well-researched account of our task, both spiritually and willfully, in a time of great technological advancement. We certainly can no longer hide behind our own satisfying spiritual practice, but must begin to take action and bring Spiritual Science to life.'—*Rose Nekvapil, Initiator, Moral Technology Initiative, Australia*

HUMANITY'S LAST STAND

The Challenge of Artificial Intelligence

A Spiritual-Scientific Response

Nicanor Perlas

TEMPLE LODGE

Temple Lodge Publishing Ltd.
Hillside House, The Square
Forest Row, RH18 5ES

www.templelodge.com

Published by Temple Lodge 2018

A CIP catalogue record for this book is available from the British Library

ISBN 978 1 912230 17 4

Cover by Morgan Creative
Typeset by DP Photosetting, Neath, West Glamorgan
Printed and bound by 4Edge Ltd., Essex

Contents

Preface

PLEASE DO NOT SKIP READING THIS PREFACE. IT WILL GIVE THE PROPER CONTEXT AND ORIENTATION FOR THOSE WHO SERIOUSLY PURSUE THE SUBSTANCE OF THIS BOOK. HOPEFULLY, IT WILL PREVENT MISUNDERSTANDINGS.

The twenty-first century is the age of science and technology. It will also be the age when humanity confronts, for the first time, a challenge that may overwhelm and destroy the human species itself in as little as 12 to 20 years from now.

This is the challenge of artificial intelligence (AI). Deployed properly, AI will confer tremendous benefits to society. It is already doing this. Deployed inappropriately or mistakenly, AI will undermine human civilization, as it is also starting to do, and could then lead to the extinction of humanity. Scientists, philosophers, and engineers call this latter possibility the 'existential risk' of AI. The fate of our future is literally in our hands.[1]

The Nature of Artificial Intelligence

Artificial intelligence is the use of sophisticated software (algorithms) to instruct ultra high-speed machines (hardware) how to process gigantic amounts of data and find connections and patterns in and among the data in order to achieve a programmed goal.

There are two broad categories of AI.

First is what we have now, sophisticated AI. This 'narrow' AI is already benefiting some segments of humanity in many ways, while raising large questions about unintended or intended impacts. Witness the Cambridge Analytica/Facebook scandal that the world press continues to cover.

The second is human-level artificial intelligence or Artificial General Intelligence (AGI) that, then, through its own intelligence, morphs itself into Artificial Super Intelligence (ASI). Through the process of 'intelligence explosion'[2], AI will move from being narrow AI to AGI and then finally to ASI.

Commentators often see ASI as coming not too long after AGI and so generally discuss the two together.[3] The focus of this book is addressing the 'existential threat' of AGI and ASI. For the more technically minded, scientists refer to the challenge of 'existential risk' as the 'alignment challenge', aligning AGI/ASI with human values.

Most experts estimate that we have to solve the existential threat of AI in as little as 20 or so years from now. For others, including prominent artificial intelligence (AI) experts and businessmen such as Ray Kurzweil and Elon Musk, this will happen sooner rather than later, that is, by the year 2030.

There is urgency. The irony of it all is that human beings themselves are feverishly creating this challenge thinking that it will ultimately be for the benefit of humanity.

On AI and Its Impacts and Consequences for Humanity

One only need look at the recent achievements of AI to gain a very strong impression that humanity is entering an unprecedented time in history and moving into dangerous territory, from which it may not safely extricate itself.

What kind of changes can we expect with the mainstreaming of AI?

With AI, businesses will become more efficient and productive, conferring untold wealth on the owners of the new technologies. But this is just one side of the development. On the other, we will have massive job loss across many professions and job categories. The displacement of workers across industries will then translate to massive disruptions in the economies of the world. We can expect the creation of a new rich-poor divide that is technologically-defined, as well as economic serfdoms. And then the inevitable happens: governments in various countries of the world will have to deal with the chaos produced by economic implosions. They will also have to deal with the attendant violence, criminality, terrorism, drug use, and suicides that will escalate in numbers.

While governments and businesses have their hands full dealing with the urgent technology-created crises, the world will see the emergence of Artificial Super Intelligence (ASI). Then, we can expect that the extinction of human beings will proceed relentlessly, unless we realize what it means to be truly human, actualize this potential so we can be fully human and find ways to align ASI with the broad values of humanity.

The scenario I paint here may seem exaggerated and overblown, but these are based on current realities that I will document and explore in various parts of this book.[4]

Becoming Fully Human: Antidote to AI Challenges

The essence of the problem became clear to me in 1987 after reading Eric Dexler's *Engines of Creation: The Coming Era of Nanotechnology*. My first concern was technological singularity or convergent technology. Then increasingly, I started closely monitoring developments in artificial intelligence.

Somewhere during this journey, I would occasionally hear comments from scientists and friends about human beings as simply being 'complex biological machines'. That was around 15 years ago. I took those comments merely as a joke.

Today that comment can no longer be taken as a joke. More and more young people are proudly declaring themselves to be nothing but 'complex biological machines', not realizing the contradiction in that statement. This perspective is becoming mainstream in the materialistic West.[5]

The mainstreaming of sophisticated artificial intelligence in 2017 also shows that this belief system has become the dominant paradigm of the technological age. With this belief, comes the loss of understanding of what it means to be truly human.

Even more important, many prominent people involved in AI development seriously subscribe to this perspective. Even those who are very concerned about making sure that AI is beneficial believe that the human being is simply a complex biological machine, with no capacity for free thought, or conscious experience. These include well-meaning and admirable people like Elon Musk, Max Tegmark, Sam Harris, and many others.

I am not criticizing these individuals. They are doing a huge service to humanity by waking up millions around the world regarding the existential risk that can be associated with pursuing 'beneficial AI'.

However, the truth about what it means to be truly human is significantly different. There are aspects of us that are mechanical. But these mechanical parts of our body are infused with life, consciousness, and spirit, making matter function differently as compared to when our physical body is simply matter, simply blob.

Amazing untapped potentials reside in the human being that can be used to address the temptations of super health, super intelligence, super strength and physical immortality promised by the advocates of sophisticated AI and AGI/ASI.

My concern here is the same as that of Albert Einstein's from more than 70 years ago. Though the nature of the risk has changed, his words still ring true:

Our world faces a crisis as yet unperceived by those possessing power to make great decisions for good or evil. The unleashed power of the atom has changed everything save our modes of thinking and we thus drift toward unparalleled catastrophe ...

We need ... to let the people know that a new type of thinking is essential if mankind is to survive and move towards higher levels.[6]

The possibility of human extinction, made possible by materialistic technology, cannot be solved by materialistic consciousness. We have to take a totally different, and more realistic perspective to address this issue. In the same way, if we are to take full advantage of the benefits of AI, then we need to move away from a materialistic consciousness. A whole constellation of developments in this direction encouraged me to write this book.

Finding Hope And Allies To Address the Challenges of AI

There are two rays of hope that shine in the horizon to aid in navigating the treacherous waters of extreme technology in the twenty-first century.

One is within the matrix of materialistic science itself, wherein developments are increasingly, and successfully, transcending the limitations of its materialistic origins. The other is inside the 'skin' of materialistic science but was never the substance of that skin; what we call today spiritual science. Both, especially the latter, operate from a thinking and consciousness that is different from current habits of materialistic science, therefore, in the spirit of Einstein's quote, increasing the chances that some solution to the AI challenge would emerge from their quarters.

This book will discuss both of these movements but with more emphasis on spiritual science for reasons that will become clear shortly.

First Ray of Hope: A Second and More Spiritual Scientific Revolution
The first of these two rays of hope is the amazing development in mainstream science that refutes the materialism of the AI creators. It is deeply ironic and tragic that people do not know that we are in the middle of an exciting new, and more spiritual, scientific revolution. Most are not aware of this profound development because of the fragmentation of knowledge into different scientific silos and the structural forces that keep it this way.

The tragedy lies in this. While this science-based spirituality has emerged and continues to emerge[7], giving us a new kind of consciousness to address the challenges of AI, a decisive and powerful minority of scientists, businessmen, government officials, are either ignoring or are not aware of these developments. Instead they are pushing the envelope on technological singularity including artificial intelligence.

It is also tragic because, despite having very shaky and ultimately false epistemological and ontological bases, the existing elite powers of humanity are conferring truth and existence status to AI, when in reality it is merely a degraded version of the human being.

But as we will see below, all hope is not lost. The way forward is dramatically demonstrated by agriculture itself. The Medusa-like touch of death of AI is thwarted in agriculture which will become a strategic area of refuge for real humans, not fake digital humans including their robotic versions.

Second Ray of Hope: The Global Movement for Spiritual Science
The second ray of hope is the 'waiting culture' of spiritual science, also known in its current form as anthroposophy. It is a 'waiting culture' because, as this book will show, the latter is the best-kept secret of the twentieth century. Spiritual science now has to face world scrutiny as it becomes more active in addressing the challenge of AI and technological singularity. Interestingly, this struggle may just be the stimulus for anthroposophy to become a real civilizational factor in the future of the Earth.

Engaging the Diverse Identities of the World to Collectively Address AI Challenges

I want to emphasize that all the different identities in the world, including such opposites as Christianity/Islam and materialism/spirituality, atheism/theism, have something important to contribute to the overall evolutionary development of humanity. All identities, whether grand or modest, have access to a facet of the world as a unified Reality.[8]

Mindful that other perspectives and identities will be reading this book, I will try to provide bridging language where necessary. But I also request goodwill from those accessing a worldview and language with which they may not be familiar, but whose identity may have something useful to contribute to the world, and to the substance of other identities.

The Anthroposophical Identity
I have written this book to alert the global anthroposophical movement (GAM) including the global Anthroposophical Society (GAS). Those engaged in spiritual science, including its first manifestation in the world

as anthroposophy, are, by their very interest and training, theoretically most prepared to understand the deep strategic significance that AI holds for the future of humanity.

After all, the literal translation of anthroposophy from the Greek is wisdom (sophia) of the human being (anthropos). The understanding of what it means to be truly human, through the careful study guided by anthroposophy, may provide an antidote to the serious, and potentially fatal, attack by AI on the meaning and nature of humanity.[9]

While this book is a call to awaken the global anthroposophical movement (GAM) into creative and strategic action, that is not its only intention. The other is to encourage GAM to converge together with the other diverse identities of the world. We need to put all our heads and hearts together and arrive at a Collective Human Intelligence (CHI) that will create alternatives to negative or extreme versions of AI.

The impossible becomes possible when tens of thousands of minds and hearts, especially from the entire range of human identities, work with focus to arrive at the AI challenge of human extinction.

Personal Disclosure

The reason why I am familiar with spiritual science is because I count this worldview as the central core of my identity. I have studied it for more than 45 years and have used the insights that I have gained through it to pursue my global work and advocacies.

However, I want to also say at the same time that, for me, spiritual science, properly understood, means not isolating oneself from other identities, including materialism or other forms of spirituality. Rather spiritual science means creating and enhancing one's inner capacity to truly respect and empathize with the different identity of others. We all breathe one Reality and, for me, the different identities are my windows to an expanded experience and appreciation of the diversity and beauty of the world.[10]

Spiritual Science Appreciates the Legitimate Mission of Materialism

Rudolf Steiner, the founder of spiritual science, had a distinctive understanding of materialism because he viewed it from the perspective of the evolution of human consciousness.[11]

In this paradigm, human consciousness moved from unconscious participation in the world process, to our current dualistic, separated, alienated subject-object consciousness, and on to a future state of free and conscious participation in the creative dynamics of the world.[12]

Within this process, Steiner appreciated materialism as a blessing that had the nature of a two-edged sword. On the one hand, materialistic science had to come about to enable humans to fully individuate from their unfree unconscious participation in the essence of the world, and gain authentic freedom, thus, developing the ability to truly love. On the other hand, if humans then get stuck with materialism, they will become the instrument of massive destruction, the likes of which are now in our horizon.

A Request for Understanding

At this point, I would like to add a request for understanding, in addition to the one I have written above concerning identities and language. Should individuals not familiar with spiritual science, including anthroposophy, get hold of a copy of this book, as they surely will, I would encourage them, out of goodwill to reserve judgement.

One has to have at least a basic familiarity with the vast literature concerning anthroposophy, especially its epistemological, phenomenological, and scientific foundations, and its practical applications in education, health, agriculture, architecture, banking, societal transformation, art, science, and others, in order to understand and judge the content of this book.[13]

Invitation to the General Public

Nonetheless, I also write this book with the public in mind. I will try to explain things in a way that individuals not familiar with anthroposophical substance can follow the conversation. It is important for those who are new to anthroposophy to view it as a positive force for human good. Anthroposophy, notwithstanding some 'socially-challenged' anthroposophists who can turn off others, wills to connect with other human beings of goodwill in the world to create societies that nurture our true humanity. As concerned human beings, we all have to do it together, whether we are anthroposophists or not. Only collective action by humanity, in all its diversity, will work.[14]

AI Challenging Us Towards Collective Human Intelligence and Altruism

In a sense, one may say that this is why the challenge of extinction through AI is upon us. Perhaps, AI is here so we may all grow up, mature, and learn to appreciate other identities, and build upon our differences. Our collective failure to do this would mean the end of all of us.

Collective Human Intelligence and Collective Altruism are the next stages of world evolution. But this new era of humanity will only come with birth pains and sacrifices. The price to create a new world is already upon us. We must face it armed with courage and understanding of the task that needs to be done.

Steiner's Prediction on the Coming of Extreme Technology

Those familiar with anthroposophy know that its founder, Rudolf Steiner, more than 100 years ago, already warned about the developments in extreme technology including AI. Steiner's term for extreme technology was 'sub-nature'. He said that failure to address this challenge would mean that humanity will plunge into the 'abyss'. He gave this warning barely two days before he died.

This fact emphasizes the urgency of our situation because Steiner saw it coming upon us at around this time. The current threat of extreme technology was thus, very real, and very much on his mind when he permanently left his physical body on March 30, 1925.

Those familiar with Steiner's work also know that while he was still in the process of distilling the ideas of his first major book, *The Philosophy of Spiritual Activity*, Steiner already knew that he had won a significant epistemological victory against the spiritual and earthly powers that want to turn humans into a machine. In his notebook, he noted the significance of his epistemological victory: '1888. Ahriman is wrecked.'[15]

This historical deed only emphasizes the red line of consistent concern in Steiner's biography regarding the misuses of materialism while simultaneously appreciating it. Now, anthroposophists, together with other identities and movements, have to advance this victory in the societal and global realm, and transform extreme technology to serve humanity, not to decimate it.

Among others, in the book cited above, Steiner demonstrated that human thinking is not a mere secretion of brain processes, but that our thinking has its own reality independent of the brain. This highly significant and powerful finding, is directly in opposition to and refutes the major assumption in AI: that intelligence is merely computational power capable of solving a diverse range of problems and pursuing goals, and that there is no such thing as human consciousness and human identity. In Chapter 16 we shall see how the latest advances in philosophy and science support Steiner's perspective on consciousness.

Why the Last Stand?

Artificial Super Intelligence (ASI) will be a technology where AI scientists and engineers only have one chance to do it right. If they do, it will bring about untold blessings to humanity. If they make a mistake, it could mean the extinction of humanity.[16]

In a sense, this is the 'last stand' for both humanity and anthroposophy to take in order to help avert worldwide catastrophe. The cosmic ramifications of failure, for tens of thousands of years to come, are too depressing to dwell upon.[17]

Because of these circumstances, readers and friends will forgive me if I take a hard look at the past failures and illusions of the global anthroposophical movement in Chapter 19. The intent there is not to blame but to awaken, to learn from mistakes, and to embark with renewed enthusiasm and determination on the task of anthroposophy to be in service, with others, for the world. My purpose is to shine a kind of historical conscience on the past and future of anthroposophy vis-à-vis the future of the world.

How to Read This Book

All three chapters of Part I of this book are the necessary context to understand the urgency of this book. If you just want to have a quick overview, read Chapter 1. The succeeding two chapters are a detailed elaboration of the first.

For the general public, a thorough understanding of the substance of Part 2 will help gain an insight into the spiritual dimensions of the challenge connected with AI as articulated in the chapters that follow. Most anthroposophists would be familiar with Part II but will probably not be familiar with Chapter 7. So I encourage them to read Chapter 7 carefully as this would give the spiritual context for the current concern with all aspects of artificial intelligence.

All the chapters in Part III are essential reading for everyone. We can only transform the world to the extent that we have learned to master ourselves. Only then can we truly come together and freely create a potent form of Collective Human Intelligence (CHI).

All the chapters in Part IV are essential, especially Chapter 11, 12 and 13. The perspectives contained there would be new even for most anthroposophists.

Similarly, all chapters in Part V are essential for all. They contain insights on how to appreciate the inspiring achievements of the second more spiritual scientific revolution in mainstream science and the tremendous value of global civil society. For anthroposophists, in the process of knowing this and acting out of it, such knowledge will help overcome the relative isolation of the global anthroposophical movement (GAM). This self-imposed relative isolation is the Achilles heel of the GAM.

And, finally, anthroposophists and friends ideally should read all of Part VI because it deals with healing aspects of the anthroposophical past that have not been dealt with adequately. Healing inner wounds is essential if one is to truly serve the world with purity and goodwill.

The minimalist approach above is for those who have very hectic schedules and have limited time to read. But of course, the most ideal would be to read the entire book. Then there is a greater probability that the urgency of the situation will dawn on the readers and they will take action on behalf of humanity.

Final Words: Not Anti-Technology, but Pro-Spiritual Individuality

Finally, I assure readers that I am not anti-technology nor a Luddite. I use technology in every facet of my life. Often, I have been a pioneer in introducing appropriate technologies in my country. But when others are developing technology that has the potential to create massive and unprecedented global disruption, and ultimately, human extinction, I cannot, in conscience, just stand by to let these very disturbing things happen.

Instead of writing in the usual scientific manner, I will write in the 'first person'. It does not mean, however, that all that I will be writing is 'subjective'. I want to emphasize that spiritual agency resides in the human being. Our identity is not a mere accident of information processing brought about by our DNA 'algorithms', which are then reinforced in the synapses of our brain cells, as current materialistic science would have it.[18]

This book is a synthesis of the dozens of lectures that I have given on Artificial Intelligence (AI) around the world, in the last three years. My intention is to have readers gain a concise overview on, and not a detailed treatment of, the developments in AI. This will enable readers to have enough information for them to make their own independent judgement and to take action on the greatest issue facing the planet today.

There will be more books to come, addressing other diverse identities in the world. This book is an introduction as well as an urgent plea for comprehensive, systemic and timely action. So let us fasten our seat belts and forge ahead to see the very disturbing future that awaits us all, and discover what we all can do about it.

Part I

BRAVE NEW WORLD OF ARTIFICIAL INTELLIGENCE (AI)

There are three major considerations in this part of the book. These three considerations are found in the three chapters that follow.

Chapter 1 gives an overview of the seriousness of the challenge of AI. It is a phenomenology, quick snapshots, of what is currently arising in the world of AI.

Chapter 2 gives a more detailed and considered reflection on these developments. I draw out points that may not have been obvious in the bullet point presentation in Chapter 1. It also goes into greater detail on the so-called 'alignment' challenge of AI. It demonstrates the urgency of solving this challenge. Failure to do so will most likely lead to human extinction.

Chapter 3 rebuts some perspectives that the advent of the 'intelligence explosion' leading to the creation of Artificial General Intelligence (AGI) and Artificial Super Intelligence (ASI), which could then lead on to human extinction, is still very far away into the future. So, as some would say, let us not worry now about the possibility of human extinction that AGI and ASI will bring. Leave that to the future generation to solve.

Unfortunately, the evidence is that the intelligence explosion, AGI and ASI are all coming sooner than later. And there is a high probability that it will come within the lifetime of most humans living on this planet today.

So let us take a ride into the present and future of AI. This is going to be both exhilarating and very disturbing.

Chapter 1

The World is on Fire!

From the lens of normality and traditional history, the world has become weird. An all-consuming fire is starting to consume the planet.

To be sure there are benefits that come from the use of AI:

- Driverless cars and trucks are poised to become ubiquitous in the road.[19]
- Robots are already assisting elderly people and other individuals in Japan.[20] In fact, they have already taken over the task of dishwashing and house cleaning.[21]
- AI can make doctors' diagnosis of illnesses more accurate.[22] Aside from early detection of illnesses, AI can also be used to assess and promote mental health.[23]
- It can help students learn better.[24] The deployment of the Internet of Things (IOT) can lead to better understanding and prediction of the weather.[25]
- It can integrate the information silos of government agencies, and unburden government employees, hence enabling the latter to better serve the general public.[26]
- It can prevent crimes by alerting authorities to suspicious behaviour.[27]
- It can prevent identity theft.[28]
- In business, AI can automate the sales process enabling business to respond to customer needs, as well as develop potential opportunities for increasing sales.[29]
- AI can shape[30] and predict consumer behaviour[31] resulting in better inventory management and marketing strategies.
- AI can support poverty eradication and food security efforts around the world.[32]
- It can alert environmentalists in real time where serious threats to the oceans' waters and aquatic species are taking place.[33]

One can easily extend this list of benefits. But, the price to obtain these benefits is too high.

Why is Elon Musk, the billionaire owner of Tesla Motors, CEO of Space X, and investor in a number of AI companies, saying that, 'with artificial intelligence we are "summoning the demon"'? He added: 'You know those stories where there is the guy with the pentagram and the holy water. And he's like he's sure he can control the demon. It didn't work out.'[34]

At the San Francisco Code Conference, Musk warned that under 'any rate of advancement in AI we will be left behind by a lot. The benign situation with ultra-intelligent AI is that we would be so far below in intelligence we'd be like a pet, or a house cat. I don't love the idea of being a house cat.'[35] Musk adds that 'the scenario in which humans are turned into pets was the optimistic one, and that the true consequences of artificial intelligence could be much worse'. He was so concerned about saving humanity from extinction that he created a $1 billion fund, along with others philanthropists, to 'research on saving humanity from AI'.[36]

Musk is not alone. Why was the late Stephen Hawking warning that AI could mean the end of the world? The world famous physicist and cosmologist, Hawking, considered by many to be the Albert Einstein of the twenty-first century, warned that AI will 'either [be] the best, or the worst thing, ever to happen to humanity'. He 'praised the creation of an academic institute dedicated to researching the future of intelligence' and said that it was 'crucial to the future of our civilisation and our species'.[37] Hawking fears that there is a risk that humanity will 'be the architect of its own destruction if it creates a super intelligence with a will of its own'.[38] Hawking has said this repeatedly in the past four years.

Why is Bill Gates giving a less shrill but similar warning?[39] And then there are the likes of Thomas Dietterich[40] and Stuart Russell[41], both of whom are pioneers of AI and machine learning, calling for the need for additional research to ensure that AI values remain aligned with human values.

It needs to be said though that all these individuals see the benefit of using AI and are encouraging the community of scientists and experts to ensure that the forthcoming generation of AI will be safe for humanity. At the same time, we can understand their concerns when we look at some of the more dramatic developments in the field of Artificial Intelligence recently.

Fuel for Conflagration

Economic Impacts of AI

- After only one minute of recording, AI can now imitate a person's voice and impersonate that person forever.[42] An excellent example of this is the fake Obama posted in YouTube. But it is not only the cloning of voices we have to worry about. There is a recently launched innovation that enables computers to change the accent and sex of the voice samples.[43] This means that the technology now exists to wipe out millions of call-centre jobs around the world. (See Chapter 2.) But joblessness will not be limited to lower-level jobs. Even the livelihood of professionals is threatened.

- An AI has now passed a medical exam and can now diagnose more accurately than most doctors.[44] It can even detect symptoms of cancer in a person! For sure the medical profession is no longer safe from an AI takeover.

- The same has happened in the legal profession.[45] An AI has now succeeded in passing a bar exam and is better than most lawyers in making legal analysis. And to think this AI was not even developed by a major AI company. Lawyers could become obsolete in the near future.

Political Impacts of AI

- AI-driven drones can now accurately assassinate a specified individual or group.[46] Some AI experts have considered this to be more dangerous than nuclear power.

- Governments are losing control over the way business is creating and deploying sophisticated technology in the lives of billions of humans. Humanity is at the mercy of untested and unregulated technology. But this is not all. AI is being used to directly shape the perceptions of voters, hence indirectly affecting the results of elections. Democracies are threatened.[47]

- Techno-utopians are installing billions of sensing objects every year to build the Internet of Things (IOT). They want to create 'smart cities'. The flip side of this will be a world of massive intrusion into the privacy of individuals around the world, or super 'Big Brother' in action.[48]

Cultural Impacts of AI

- Digital classrooms are starting to arise. Digital teachers are replacing humans in classrooms around the world. There is a partnership between US and Russian educators that will digitalize education, from cradle to grave. There will be no solid classrooms and human teachers. Everything will be done digitally.[49]

- Sean Parker, former president of Facebook has admitted that they designed Facebook to manipulate the mind of and create addiction among its massive user base, now surpassing two billion.[50]

- Tristan Harris, former high-level employee of Google, now considered the 'conscience of Silicon Valley', rose to prominence by explaining vividly how Google designed its product to dominate the attention of all Google users.[51]
- The practice of manipulating and sucking the attention of searchers and social media denizens in the Internet, as well as creating addiction among children using Apple computers,[52] is widespread among technology giants in Silicon Valley.
- Sophia, a robot, has become so sophisticated that Saudi Arabia has granted it Saudi citizenship. This is the slippery slope towards the granting of rights for robots which some are now actually advocating.[53] Under the concept of legal equivalence, humanity is de facto being reduced to nothing but a sophisticated robot.

Collapsing Boundary Between Humans and Robots

- Boston Robotics now has a robot that can do back flips with ease.[54] How many of us, humans, can do that? Some would say that this just means that millions of years of natural evolution has just been compressed into two years.
- AI can now create its own music. It has produced a pop song, some heavy metal music, and an entire symphony.[55] There is now a best-selling album created solely by AI.[56]
- In a test of whether AI could imitate and play Bach, AI beat humans at Bach imitation.[57] Both forays of AI into art collapse one critical boundary between humans and robots.
- Deep Mind, a Google subsidiary, created AlphaGo, an AI-playing the game of Go. AlphaGo beat the two top world champions in Go, a feat considered to be ten years into the future. Go is considered the most complicated board game because the possible moves involved are greater than the number of atoms in the entire universe.[58]

Technology Advancing Towards 'Intelligence Explosion'

- In less than a year, Deep Mind subsequently upgraded AlphaGo to create Alpha Zero, which trained itself from scratch, and then, in a few weeks, went on to beat AlphaGo, 100–0.[59] The implications are staggering. This prepares the way for the creation of human level AI or Artificial General Intelligence (AGI), and could be the beginning of the slippery slope towards the end of humanity.

- AI can now design other AI systems. It is software creating its own software.[60] Again, this is another technological stream that could result in the creation of the heavily debated AGI.
- In 2017, Facebook shut down its AI because it started to communicate with other AIs, in a language that its human creators can no longer understand.[61] To date, its developers have not yet discovered how the AI was able to do this outside of its original code. Though the effects of this are far from human extinction, it is a testament to what AI critics like Elon Musk have been saying all along. AIs that do not follow human instructions and create their own instead, is the baby stage of AGI and ultimately Artificial Super Intelligence (ASI).
- There is now a supercomputer that can 'calculate' over 100 quadrillions instructions per second.[62] And the world's fastest supercomputer, as of November 2017, is Chinese, not American. Furthermore, a Canadian company has built the world's fastest partial quantum computer, with blinding speeds over a million times faster than supercomputers.[63] Such a development will make it easier to achieve an intelligence explosion.

Existential Risks and the Worrying Absence of a Solution

- Prominent businessmen, scientists, and AI experts have warned that, if humanity is not careful, ASI can wipe out humanity. Voices calling for care in the deployment of AGI/ASI include Elon Musk, Stephen Hawking, Bill Gates, Jack Ma, Stuart Russell, and many others.[64]
- These sentiments stand behind the signature campaign launched on January 2015 by the Future of Life Institute in Puerto Rico. As of early 2018, over 8,600 AI experts, AI technology creators from Google, Microsoft, Deep Mind, some other distinguished business and academic institutions, as well as a few concerned citizens, have all signed the document that seeks to spread the concern for 'safe' AI.[65]
- Similarly, at the beginning of 2017, hundreds of AI scientists met in Asilomar, California, USA. This was a very diverse group of AI engineers, scientists, scholars, and businessmen. And they had debates among themselves, both before and during the conference. But they were all unified in their call for the pursuit of 'beneficial AI', a pursuit that is mindful of the existential dangers involved.[66]
- But this goal of 'safe AI' or 'beneficial AI' will not be easy to

achieve.[67] In fact, as of today, no one really knows how to go about it. AI experts have not yet found a solution to the biggest problem facing the deployment of AGI and ASI: the 'alignment' challenge. Chapter 2 will detail why.

- Because there is no proven way yet to make ASI align with human values and priorities, and the Facebook incident has shown that AI can override human programming and make itself unintelligible and, therefore, unmanageable to humans, there is a likelihood that AI will act against humanity, and lead the extinction of the human species.

Why There May Be No Solution

- Some nation states, including rogue ones, as well as dozens of shadow corporations are moving full speed ahead with developing an ASI, forcing alarmed and capable countries to follow and compete in the development of ASI.[68]
- President Vladimir Putin of Russia has stated that the first country to develop ASI will rule the world.[69] This success will be short-lived as it could backfire on the country that develops ASI. This newly emerged AI could decimate the entire human race, as is laid out in one scenario in Chapter 2.
- A significant number of engineers and AI experts in Silicon Valley are adherents of the ideology of *transhumanism*. For them, the replacement of humans by robots is inevitable and not worrisome; this is to be expected in the process of natural evolution.[70]

Short Time Frame to Figure Out the Puzzle of Existential Risk

- The prediction as to when ASI would come varies from expert to expert. These predictions cluster and range from 12 years to 25 years from now. In Chapter 3 I will make a case for why the shorter timeline is more likely and that it is prudent to plan for.
- The acceleration of technological innovations and developments in AI makes this prediction likely to happen.[71]

With these kinds of developments happening simultaneously on so many fronts, even large institutions have no idea what the ultimate future holds. But we have enough information to see where it is all heading towards, even if only in rough outlines.

Let us now look at some details and draw out the implications of the developments above.

Chapter 2

Utopia or Extinction?

Welcome to the brave new world of artificial intelligence. It is so new and radical that thought leaders, as we have seen, in the example of Elon Musk, the late Stephen Hawking, and others, are prone to use dramatic language to emphasize the speed and huge potential for AI to disrupt the world.

This chapter can be very depressing and may induce fear and passiveness in readers. But as they say, it is much easier to deal with something you know than something you do not know. For in the case of the latter, it will not exist for you. And being non-existent you will not pay attention to it. And so by the time you do pay attention, the problem has become very serious and basically unsolvable.

Massive Joblessness and Economic Implosion

Presently, AI is eating up jobs that are relatively easy to automate. Low-skill jobs such as those in call-centre companies, will be among the first to go.

Look at the voice-imitating technology described above. Combine this with an AI that only requires very little time to get 'trained' in the call-centre script as compared with two–three months with human training in call centres. Plus the AI does not need to rest and eat; it does not get sick. AI does not get emotionally triggered as compared with call-centre workers who get stressed out (and cranky) when they receive numerous complaints on a daily basis. With these technologies, most would expect the current BPO industry to be near total collapse in five years.

In the next three to five years, the world will see the beginning of massive job loss. In the Philippines alone, around 40,000 to 50,000 low-skilled Business Process Outsourcing (BPO) jobs will be replaced.[72] That's the conservative estimate—around 40–50% job loss. But if the International Labour Organization (ILO) and the United Nations Conference on Trade and Development (UNCTAD) are to be believed, the job loss in the BPO industry could reach 80–89% by 2022[73]—that's roughly 1.1 million jobs and billions of dollars in revenue lost. This figure does not even include job losses in retail trade, hotels and tourism, banking and finance, and of course, in overseas contract work. The

Philippine Senate Committee on Science and Technology estimates that 24 million Filipinos will be affected by the collapse of the BPO industry.[74]

Already, as I write this book, foreign businesses are starting to abandon the BPO panacea in the Philippines. The BPO industry has already lost more than 35% of investments as compared to last year.[75]

The use of AI in automation in other countries where millions of Overseas Filipino Workers (OFWs) are working, will strike a fatal blow against the billions of dollars of remittances sent to the Philippines from OFWs. The accelerated decline of both the BPO and OFW industries will definitely cripple a large segment of the Philippine economy and force millions out of their jobs. And this is going to happen not only in the Philippines.

'Fine, but, like before the jobless can simply get retrained and transferred to another industry. Job substitution has been going on for decades,' says the sceptic.

What most people do not realize is that humanity is dealing with a very different kind of technology and automation crisis. In principle, anything that can be routinized can be automated. Any job that can be expressed in clear mathematical language can be programmed and automated. Those are the majority of the jobs that OFWs and call-centre agents have.

And the worst part is, there are very few higher-level jobs to turn to. Increasingly AI is invading the territory of doctors and lawyers as seen above. Other professions are falling, too. Teachers, accountants, bank tellers, and a host of other jobs are going to be replaced by AI in the near future.

Overall, according to the International Labour Organization, 137 million workers from Cambodia, Indonesia, Philippines, Thailand, and Vietnam stand to lose their jobs in the next 20 years with the coming of automation.[76] In the US, investment analyst John Mauldin predicts that AI will take over 73 million jobs by 2030.[77] Finding a new job is not so easy, as discovered by the eight-month study conducted by the McKinsey Global Institute. The study discovered that 14% or 375 million people around the world would have to find entirely new occupations since their old jobs would need fewer workers, or they would not exist anymore.[78]

And the trend will not stop. Businessmen see a huge economic pie in the sky. Forecasts for the growth of the AI market vary, anywhere between 5.05 billion to 8.3 trillion dollars in the next ten years.[79] This accounts only for the direct sale of AI products and services, not the indirect revenue from the use of AI developments. With less than 1% of medium to large industries (in the US alone) adopting AI, automation is the Holy Grail for the early adopters.

Political Instability and Chaos

Most government officials are unaware of the breakneck speed at which AI is imposing its presence in the world. They are clueless about the technological tsunami that is going to ravage their economies, which in turn, could fuel confusion and chaos.

Take the example of the Philippine government. It has no idea that the two pillars of its fast growing economy, Business Processing Outsourcing (BPOs) and Overseas Filipino Worker (OFW) remittances are going to be extinct in five to ten years.[80] Sure, there are initial comments on how AI is going to cause disruptions in the economy, but there is a false sense of security in statements like, 'It may take some time ... before societies and governments accept this technology and to put in place the appropriate regulations for its use, especially in sensitive areas such as transport and medicine'[81], as if the technology is far in the future, or the government has the capacity to regulate it.

Therefore it has no plan on what to do when the technological superstorm hits the country. The Philippines has barely started moving its huge population out of poverty, and providing important basic needs such as universal education from kindergarten up to college. The demise of the Philippines' BPO and OFW industries will plunge millions into even greater poverty, and all the problems connected with it.

Those countries that do know how fast AI is developing, intend to use these technologies for pervasive spying on, and control of their own citizens. The whistle blower, Edward Snowden, has already revealed the massive spying that Western governments are doing against their own citizens. But the Snowden revelations will be nothing compared to the day when governments (and corporations) control the Internet of Things (IOT).

With IOT, billions of sensors will track everything: humans, nature (plants and animals), and non-living things (weather, vehicle movement, solar radiation, etc.).[82] Then supercomputers linked with the 'big data' of IOT will analyze patterns and trends, as specified by the programmers in control, and for whatever purposes it may serve, beneficial or totalitarian. Super-fast 5G cell signals will be able to transmit these data to and among supercomputers.[83]

Here, one can clearly discern the emergence of the digital neurons of the super brain of artificial intelligence. This will be a more thorough and draconian version of the world of 'Big Brother' as lucidly described in the book, *1984*.[84] Individual privacy rights will perish, reinforced by the idea of creating a national registry number that will be all things for the individual.[85] This will also mean total and complete surveillance of the individual's economic and private life. And this will not be taken sitting down by human and privacy rights activists.

And for the more ambitious countries, they, including China, Russia, and the United States, are now all in cyber race to develop the first Artificial Super Intelligence (ASI).

But here is the irony that these countries do not understand. The first country to have ASI may initially dominate the world. But then shortly thereafter, this ASI will turn against its own creators and destroy the latter and the rest of humanity with it.

This will happen unless countries have figured out the solution to the 'alignment' problem pointed out in Chapter 1. Unfortunately, as we shall see in the next two chapters below, some of the potential creators of ASI do not care about the 'alignment' problem because, in the end, their techno-utopian vision, of being fused with a machine, excites them!

Cultural Anomie, Confusion and Fear

My conversation with a taxi driver captured the sense of millions around the world. He realized that he would lose his job in the very near future. He rejected Universal Basic Income (UBI). For someone with limited choices, he complained: 'What will I do with my life in the future? My job gives me meaning. It is part of my identity. I have been driving for a long time. What will I now do with my time?' In desperation, he finally closed the subject with a typical Filipino expression: '*Bahala na ang Diyos!*' Loosely translated: 'It is up to God. He will provide for my future.'

I have been giving seminars and workshops on artificial intelligence in many countries around the world. The initial reaction is basically the same no matter which country I am in. The reaction is typically this: incredulity, shock, confusion and incapability to suggest creative ways of dealing with the challenge of AI.

First is the non-belief. They cannot believe that humans would actually do this to other humans: the overhype of benefits at the expense of a more cautious precautionary approach; the blatant lies and manipulation by tech giants of people's private data; the embedding of chips in people's bodies; the Big Brother scenario and total surveillance situation of the world; new weapons of mass destruction; the potential extinction of humanity; and the speed at which the potential apocalypse is coming.

Then it dawns on them that this is not scientific fiction. In some aspects, it is worse than science fiction. It is as if some of their worst nightmares have come true. They are shocked that all these, and much more, are actually happening in the world, in their lifetime.

Then they get confused. They do not know what to do. Normality is now up in the air. Traditional ways of life are fast disappearing, and they experience the need to hold on to the past, trying to anchor their life in an illusion.

Eventually all these lead to questions such as: Who am I? What is my purpose? What am I doing here? How do I now move on with my life? Will humanity have a future? Cultural anomie becomes epidemic.

Then fear slowly creeps in. They are inwardly paralyzed. They do not know what to do. All they can practically say, which on one level makes sense, is that 'I have to read more about it.' At least that is a beginning, if they are strong enough to stand by that resolution.

Some do get angry. But still, in the end, do not know what to do.

It is interesting that in this situation, the younger ones, the teenagers, are clear on what has to be done. Some of them say, at least, that they have to spend less time with their smart phones; that they have to strengthen themselves; that they have to do inner work; that they should organize together and work out a creative response. But whether they will or not, is uncertain.

Societal Chaos, Martial Law and Control

This joblessness and other economic disruptions, not only in the Philippines but also around the world, will intensify and translate into political and societal chaos. Criminality, war, drug use, suicide, and other untold drastic consequences will ensue without any clear solution in sight. Climate disruptions and unpredictability can only worsen the situation.

This kind of situation could force some countries to impose martial law. But this solution will only worsen the situation. The massive sense of individual freedom is already out of the box (see Part II and Chapter 13 for the scientific, spiritual, and societal movement basis for this). People will resist and even revolt under conditions of martial law. It may not happen immediately. But the tension brought about by resistance will be there.

Not even the proposed Universal Basic Income (UBI) will stem the tide of chaos.

For some countries, UBI may work. Fledging cash-starved artists and other creative persons will finally have the economic freedom to do what they want to do. However, that will depend on how much 'basic income' they will finally receive and under what conditionalities. And basic income will not change the ruthlessness and joblessness of the current and upcoming economic structure.

For countries that do not have the economic structure, UBI will be pie in the sky.

But in the end, all these will not matter. When ASI arrives uncontrolled, human rights will no longer matter. The reason will be simple. There will no longer be any humans around to worry about their rights.

Human Extinction

Amidst all these, short-sighted humans, whether hungry for profits or lusting for power and control, will transform sophisticated AI into human-level AI or Artificial General Intelligence (AGI) and, shortly thereafter, into Artificial Super Intelligence (ASI), an IQ-based intelligence a million times above what human beings are capable of achieving in this lifetime. With these developments, the future of humanity is at stake. The emergence of AGI or ASI could lead to the extinction of humanity.

A very interesting article appeared 18 years ago. The author exhibited unusual prescience. There were people then who saw the AI dilemma coming and to what extent it would manifest.

The article was published in *Wired* magazine. *Wired*, in the English-speaking world, is a cutting-edge magazine that looks at technological trends. It is like the *Economist* for businessmen or the Bible for Christians. The article had a striking title: 'Why the future doesn't need us.' You can still google it.

Bill Joy wrote the article. Joy is the chief scientist of a large corporation called Sun Microsystems in Silicon Valley. At the time he wrote the article, he was the inspiration for the development of various technologies including the SPARC microprocessors, and the Java programming language. He was right in the middle of the technology revolution. A Luddite definitely did not write the article.

Yet Joy wrote that humans, *Homo sapiens* would, in the future, be defined as an 'extinct biped species'. In other words, he was seeing the potential future extinction of humanity through the abuse of extreme technologies. And AI was not even the hottest thing then, as it is right now.

Joy's article became the most discussed article in the history of *Wired* magazine.[86] Joy's article remains a landmark document in terms of the future of humanity in light of technology.[87] His article resonated so profoundly because the article came from an insider in the technological world. Or to use a metaphor, it was like a catholic Cardinal saying that the Pope has no clothes.

Today, no one knows, not even AI experts and engineers, how to create a truly beneficial AI, let alone a 'good' Artificial Super Intelligence. That much is clear from the Asilomar Conference on Beneficial AI organized and convened last January, 2017 by the Future of Life Institute. While they released some 23 principles for the creation of beneficial AI, they could not release a single principle on the toughest problem of AI. And this is the 'alignment' challenge.[88]

The Alignment Challenge

AI experts, for example, keep on emphasizing that we may come up with the ideal values to program into the robot, but it is not certain whether an AGI, ASI, or even a more sophisticated version of current AI will necessarily follow these values. There are tacit sub-programs including survival algorithms that the AI may follow to override the values of humanity being programmed into them.[89]

This is a major headache for scientists and AI creators. They call it the alignment challenge: how to ensure that sophisticated AI, AGI, or ASI behaviour is aligned with human values and norms.

There are several reasons for the lack of progress in this area. Let us start with the relatively simpler ones.

More Resources Going to Productivity Solutions Than to Safety

First most computer programmers have no real awareness of the need for friendly AI. And if they do, they are driven by the imperatives of their employment contract with their mother company. And often these contracts mean more and more sophisticated AI that can bring in a better bottom line, i.e. profits. Forget about the impact on society.

This is where the push for AI creating more sophisticated AI comes in. And pretty soon, humanity will enter the slippery slope of the 'intelligence explosion'. This prediction foresees AI becoming more and more sophisticated as it improves its own capabilities without the interference of human beings.

Sophisticated AI Becoming a 'Black Box'

As the intelligence explosion gathers momentum, it is difficult for human programmers to know exactly what their own AI creations are doing. It starts becoming a 'black box' for them, if it is not already. The human programmer no longer has an idea of what he/she is designing.

'Genetic programming', 'evolutionary algorithm', 'machine learning' and 'deep learning' are some of the labels used to describe current capabilities of AI.[90] Genetic programming is a subset of evolutionary algorithm and both are subsets of machine learning. Deep learning tries to emulate how the brain structures and organizes information in hierarchical fashion. In the case of all of these advanced forms of programming, human beings no longer have to program the intended outcome of the algorithms themselves. The algorithm selects, after the pre-supposed pattern of random selection of genes in the context of biological evolution, what segments of the algorithm to retain and what segments to combine with still other programs that are part of the total set of programs to be selected from.[91]

Both intensify the 'black box' effect because then, human programmers do not really know how the AI is reprogramming itself.

This is not a theoretical concern. Sometime in August 2017, Facebook shut down its AI because the latter created its own program and no longer followed the programming that humans gave to it. The human programmers could no longer understand the language of the new AI-created program and instead noted what seemed like garbled or garbage sentences coming out of it. They discovered later that the garbage language was actually a new program that the AI created for itself and was later used for communication with other AI machines.[92]

In short the Facebook AI did not align itself with what the programmers wanted it to do.

So this is the warning signal that the 'alignment' challenge is a real and urgent one. It was good that the Facebook AI was a relatively simple one and that they were able to still shut it down. But what if in a future situation the AI involved is AGI or ASI, and it is no longer possible to shut down the ASI? What then?

Impractical Problem-Solving Scenarios

Some people have suggested shutting down the entire Internet. But this is nothing but a knee-jerk reaction.

For one thing, it would cause trillions of untold damage in the world economy not to speak of the societal chaos that will ensue once people no longer have their usual communication, utility, transportation, financial and other services available.

For another, it is also not clear whether shutting down the entire Internet would destroy the ASI. What if the ASI had already found a way to replicate itself thousands of times in safe server areas, even in servers which people think are safe?[93]

Whose Value System Will Be the Standard for the World?

Then comes the more difficult problem. Whose value system will we program into an AGI? Already scholars have shown that some current AI algorithms display bias against women and people of colour.[94] And who would convene a worldwide conversation around whose and what values to embed in AI? Who would have the authority to do that? A more realistic alternative will be massive global resistance and innovation of the kind discussed in Parts IV and V of this book.

Stuart Russell is one of the top global experts on AI. He co-authored a textbook on AI that is widely used as the fundamental text on the subject around the world. He points out: 'The question is not whether machines can be made to obey human values but which humans ought to decide those values.'[95]

One author observes: 'On the contrary, both are important questions that must be asked, and Russell asks both questions (values and alignment) in all of his published talks. The values a robot takes on will have to be decided by societies, government officials, policy makers, the robot's owners, and so on. Russell argues that the learning process should involve the entire human race, to the extent possible, both now and throughout history.'[96]

The impossibility of this procedure is just one conundrum facing the AI safety community. Let us assume we have figured out the human values part. Assume we can know what values to place into the computer. But can we really program this into the machine? The Facebook example shows that this may be unlikely.

Can Human Values Really be Programmed into an ASI?

The AGI may have already developed 'survival' drives. In other words, for it to pursue the objective goal function or the values that humans programmed into them, AGI must have an inner programming of survival. How can you perform a task if you are 'dead'? So it is quite possible that an AGI would pursue its survival function at the expense of the original values that humans programmed into it.[97] The Facebook example gives a simple illustration of this problem.

Think of it this way. Every time you are angry you find yourself in a situation where you say and/or do stupid stuff that you regret later on. You have this sophisticated part in your brain known as the prefrontal cortex that helps you differentiate your conflicting thoughts, as well as to determine acceptable or unacceptable behaviour. This is the reason why the prefrontal cortex is also called the executive centre of the brain.[98]

Yet we also have a more primitive brain part in ourselves, the brain stem, sometimes also called the 'reptilian brain'. The function of this brain part is to help us survive, on an automatic basis, the challenges of physical existence. It tells us when to fight and when to flee or when to simply stay put.[99]

In the example of anger above, the 'reptilian brain' (the lower part) automatically overrides the more sophisticated part of ourselves (the prefrontal cortex) and we no longer follow the goals of our prefrontal cortex. In short, the lower brain has basically hijacked the higher part of our brain.[100]

And with this, we have an idea of the 'alignment' challenge in artificial intelligence.

On the Near Improbability of Aligning ASI Goals with Human Values

There is also a much more sophisticated line of argument making it almost impossible to solve the alignment challenge. An AI analyst, Eliezer Yudkowsky, clearly lays out the difficult scenario.[101]

We want AI to be friendly to humans. So we program this ASI to do 'X'. And let 'Y' be one approach to achieve the programmed goal, 'X'.

There may be an infinite number of Y approaches to achieving X. This may come from under-specifying what 'X' actually means in thousands of different scenarios under which 'X' is to be achieved. Furthermore, since the ASI 'learns' from the Internet, and can read hundreds of million pages in a few seconds,[102] it may discover different ways of understanding 'X', as well as thousands of possible but undiscovered ways ('Y') for achieving the goal.[103] That is another way of saying that, given a paradigm, there would be thousands of different ways of developing that paradigm.

Take this often-repeated scenario of the 'literal' intelligence of AI. Suppose you give an AI car the instruction to drive you to your destination in the fastest and safest way possible. That would be your goal, your 'X'. Unless you start specifying every possible combination of methods (your permissible 'Y's if that is even possible), for your car to reach that goal, then your AI car will indeed bring you to your destination in a safe and speedy manner. The only problem is that you will be vomiting all over the place due to car motion sickness as a result of the sudden stops and starts, driving curves at very high speeds, not to speak of racing up and down hilly and bumpy roads.[104]

We will not know the outcome for sure because 'humans have a tacit higher context that would constrain them from actualizing a possible scenario'.

Yudkowsky points to this higher source in our selves, not to the impersonal, random dynamics of matter itself. He says, 'Humans have their own goals already … they have their own enforcers. They have their own structure for reasoning about moral beliefs. There is something inside that looks over any instruction you give them and decides whether to accept it or reject it.'[105] With the AI or AGI/ASI, there is no such inner structure that would constrain them once they discover an unknown expression of possibility within a paradigm. They will seek the most efficient way of achieving their goal under the paradigm the AGI has been programmed from the very beginning, regardless of how it impacts humankind.

Powerful Interests Do Not Want Value Alignment

Then here comes the tough one. Some world powers may actually not like to have beneficial ASI. They would like to have ASI that can dominate and control the world.

And the corporate world will not be left behind. As we have seen earlier, young tech-savvy nerds in Silicon Valley, who populate the tech industry in Silicon Valley, actually do not worry that humans may become extinct. That is the way the materialist version of natural evolution works. Instead they foresee the day when they can download their consciousness into a machine, an ASI, and achieve digital physical immortality. Welcome to the latest religion in the world, Transhumanism.[106]

One writer on AI, James Barrat, estimates that there are dozens of rogue or stealth corporations that want to achieve AGI/ASI.[107]

One Scenario of Human Extinction

We must not forget that today AI controls all the vital infrastructure of nations and the world. If, in the future, ASI goes rogue, it will start crippling the electronic stock market where trillions of dollars are traded on a daily basis. It would sabotage the telecommunications and transportation industries. Economies would collapse.

Because sophisticated 'narrow' AI now controls the nuclear weapons system of the world, ASI can easily override the safety control of nuclear weapons and trigger a nuclear holocaust. Meanwhile ASI would ensure that it would survive all these apocalyptic disasters by making billions of copies of itself in safe places across the Internet.[108]

Nature and Agriculture: The Bright Spot of Humanity

Techno-utopians believe that AI can practically do anything. So now some of them are toying with the idea of using AI to analyze weather patterns and to control them. This is in the tradition of 'geo-engineering' which has been banned by the United Nations.[109] But eventually some nations, which did not sign the treaty banning geo-engineering will be tempted to experiment with it. The availability of sophisticated AI will be their temptation.

Sure, there will also be attempts to automate the production of agricultural products. In fact this is already being done today. Low orbiting satellites control robot-tractors on earth. These satellites can tell the automated tractor when to plant their crops, apply fertilizers, harvest their crops and so on.[110]

But this is very different from AI creating a tomato or a potato or wheat. AI is not sophisticated enough to create life. In fact, it never will. Chapters 12 and 16 will show this very clearly.

There were also on-going attempts to engineer nature itself. There were talks of converting 'useless' biomass from trees and high-carbon, non-edible shrubs and grasses into all kinds of food. This biomass would be converted into a liquid pulp-like material that can be converted, using nanotechnology, into any kind of beverage. Just press a button and electromagnetic radiation from the device will turn the pulp into 'orange' or 'coffee' or any other drink depending on what frequency we choose to do the conversion.[111]

It is quite a statement that this prototype technology did not flourish. It does indicate that there is one area that AI engineers have not yet figured out: how to make artificial nature. Their failure to do this represents one of the biggest hopes of humanity in the pervasive age of artificial intelligence. It also points to the strategic importance of agriculture in the era of AI. We shall see more clearly in Chapters 16 and 18 what societal and ecological factors made this prototype fail and why these factors will be very important for humanity in addressing the coming of artificial intelligence.

In fact this area provides a strategic example of the scale of what needs to be done to ensure that AI is beneficial for humanity.

Chapter 3

Awakening to our True Humanity—The Way Out

When it comes to predicting the future, especially where the possibility of Artificial General Intelligence (AGI), Artificial Super Intelligence (ASI) and human extinction are under consideration, one will certainly get a wide range of opinions. And these perspectives are changing all the time. That is good. There is some elbowroom, so to speak.

Here are some well-known predictions within the AI community.

How Much Time Do We Have?

2029. An article published by the *Independent* had this headline: 'Robots Will Be Smarter Than Us All, Warns AI Expert Ray Kurzweil.'[112] I hope the readers get that. 'Smarter than us all' means the combined intelligence of the entire human race. For Anthroposophists that means the total defeat of the task of bringing back Cosmic Intelligence to the Time Spirit, Micha-el. (See Chapter 5.)

2030–2040. The second prediction comes from billionaire Elon Musk, the world-renowned founder of Tesla Motors, SpaceX and Solar City. In response to the *New Scientist* article entitled 'AI Will Be Able to Beat Us at Everything by 2060, Says Experts'[113], Musk said, 'Probably closer to 2030 to 2040 [in my opinion]. 2060 would be a linear extrapolation, but progress is exponential.'[114] But in the headline of *Teslaratl*, Musk is leaning more to 2030.[115] So Musk is predicting the advent of AGI by 2030-2040, not too far away into the future. And remember, when AGI emerges, many AI scientists think that ASI emergence will not be far behind. And with the emergence of ASI, the risk of human extinction becomes even more probable.

These two points are significant. Kurzweil and Musk often do not agree on issues connected with AI. Kurzweil is a moderated techno-utopian. Elon Musk, as many know, is known for using his 'rock star' status as a much-admired serial high technology innovator to make millions of people around the planet aware of the real existential dangers surrounding the development of AGI and ASI.

However, both are now in near agreement regarding the estimated timeline for the arrival of AGI.

Finally let us take a look at other perspectives. There was a poll taken of

AI experts who attended the 2015 Conference on Neural Information Processing Systems and the International Conference on Machine Learning. According to the panel AI will achieve AGI in 2060—30 years later than what Elon Musk has predicted.[116]

However, AI experts have predicted that before 2060, sophisticated AI will have mastered many human activities. AI will beat humans at 'translating languages by 2024, writing high school essays by 2026 ... driving a truck by 2027, working in retail by 2031, writing a bestselling book by 2049, and surgery by 2053'.[117]

However, Asian AI experts predicted a much earlier date for AGI than 2060. For them 2045 would be the more likely timeline.

In an interesting development, the website www.fanaticalfuturist.com, which reported this survey of AI experts, had another article reporting on the earlier arrival of AGI in 2035.

So you can see there is quite a range of opinions out there regarding the future disruption of human civilization. The range is from 2029 to 2060. Given this context, I will now state the reasons why I think the ASI and potential human extinction scenario will come sooner rather than later and would be closer to the dates predicted by both Kurzweil and Musk.

Three Reasons Why the Extinction Scenario Will Come Earlier Rather Than Later

Here briefly are my reasons for why ASI will be coming sooner rather than later:

- Exponential explosion of technological growth.
- Predictions of later emergence coming sooner than expected.
- Application of the Precautionary Principle.

Exponential Acceleration of Technological Developments

I would like to begin with the nature of exponential growth. AI technologies are growing exponentially. Ray Kurzweil has shown this very clearly in his book, *The Singularity is Near*[118]. Here is one way to illustrate what this means.

Have you heard of the metaphor of 'the 29th day'?[119] To get an idea of exponential growth, picture a lily pond and watch how it multiplies every day. The first day there is one lily, the second day there are two lilies, the third day there are four, the fourth day eight, the fifth day 16, and so on. Now on the 28th day, half the pond is full, so when we double it, it becomes completely full in one day, on the 29th day. So while it may appear to be growing slowly to begin with, all of a sudden it's accelerating astronomically.

There are many examples in real life. Take the tsunami that hit Asia in 2004. It was a warm and sunny day in Indonesia the day the tsunami hit. People were swimming at the beach, enjoying their time. All of a sudden, giant waves started to engulf their beloved ones. And the tsunami travelled hundreds of miles away to as far as India. The wave was travelling at the speed of a jet plane, almost 900km per hour. People did not see it coming. A few hours later, over 100,000 people were dead. They were unprepared.

We are living in a world that seems very 'quiet' for those who are not closely following the revolution in extreme technologies including artificial intelligence. But we have to be aware that aside from ordinary exponential growth, there is also the acceleration of the rate of acceleration.[120] It is impossible to predict on the basis of past rates what the future will be especially when the more than 50 technologies clustered around nanotechnology, biotechnology, info technology, and cognitive technology all come together and synergize each other.

Elon Musk has a version of it. He calls it 'double exponential'. The takeoff to AGI could come sooner because of exponential developments in both hardware and software growth.

The Drivers of Exponential Growth—Advent of Sophisticated Hardware
On the hardware side, it was only in November 2015 that the fastest supercomputer had the power to do over 34 quadrillion 'instructions' (calculations) per second.[121] By the following year, in November 2016 the fastest supercomputer in the world was already processing information at speeds of over 100 quadrillion or 100 petaflops per second.[122] These mind-boggling processing speeds of supercomputers are way beyond what the human mind can even envision.

One approximation is to imagine what these supercomputers could do when fed with trillions of bits of information. With that kind of speed and using a similar capacity as Watson, IBM's AI, and Google/Deep Mind's AlphaGo Zero, the AI in the near future will most likely read the entire Internet with billions of pages in less than a minute![123]

This could be the reason why Kurzweil has an AGI arrival date set for 2029 when a supercomputer is expected to have the computing power of all the human beings on the planet. Consider what that means, because right now in some areas of life, AI, with less computing power than these supercomputers, now surpasses humans to such an extent that machines are already starting to take over the jobs of humans.

We have not even considered the advent of a version of the quantum computer that is calculating at speeds millions of times faster than supercomputers in certain specified jobs.[124] Nor have we factored in the arrival of Nvidia's neural chips that are expected to make AI do even more amazing things due to its capability to emulate the neural net processing of the human brain.[125]

The Drivers of Exponential Growth—More and More Powerful Software
Musk's poster boy for exponential growth in AI software could be AlphaGo, the Google Deep Mind supercomputer that defeated Lee Sedol, the world champion in Go for 18 years. Sedol is considered the second best Go player of all time. Go is much more complicated than chess, with the number of probable moves estimated to be more than the entire number of atoms in the universe. Yet AlphaGo defeated Lee Sedol, 4 wins–1 loss.[126] Experts were shocked.

But that development was so last year. Several months later, in May 2017, an advanced version of AlphaGo defeated Ke Jie, the world champion of Go from China, 3–0.[127] Recently, Google announced the creation of AlphaGo Zero,[128] the most advanced version of its AI. AlphaGo Zero did not even have to be trained by humans. It trained all by itself through trial and error. And after only four hours of training, the program taught itself how to play chess and beat the world-champion chess program, Stockfish 8, winning 100–0. Also, it learned how to play Go, and after only eight hours of training, AlphaZero beat AlphaGo, winning 60 of 100 games.[129] To date, AlphaZero has beat Alpha Go 100–0.[130] The exponential explosion of AI capabilities is nothing short of outstanding!

Equally as important, is that this kind of software was not supposed to exist until ten years into the future. Now it exists today.

Long Term Predictions Continually Being Surpassed

And this leads me to the second point. There are a number of AI developments that are happening much faster than expected. Longer timelines are starting to collapse. The long- term future is becoming the near term almost now.

Take a look at the 2015 predictions of AI experts discussed earlier. Each one of them has been superseded in just two years. And yet most of them were predicted to happen way into the future.

The 2015 AI experts said that AI would be better than humans in translating languages by 2024. Well, Google had a breakthrough in language translation process and the Google translator can now translate dozens of languages with human proficiency.[131] And we are only in 2018.

AI experts in 2015 said that AI would be better in writing high school essays by 2026. So much for that prediction since it is not accurate. In 2017, AI was already proficient in writing articles for newspapers and online news outfits,[132] and was even writing books.[133] AI experts predicted that this latter would happen in 2049.

And it is the same with the other predictions. There are already robotic cars and trucks. The latter was supposed to come in 2027. It is already here. AI involvement in retail was supposed to come in 2031. But AI is already involved in various aspects of the retail operations.[134] Surgery by AI was supposed to happen by 2053. Yet over 70% of precise and delicate surgery to cure prostate cancer, are now being done by robots.[135]

And there are other achievements by AI including passing the Turing test that was not supposed to happen for quite some time still.[136] And, in Chapter 1 above, we saw that AI is now better than humans at imitating classical music, a feat that people in workshops immediately react to with unbelieving stares.

And, of course, the most outstanding example of the future collapsing to the present in less time than expected is Deep Mind's AI called AlphaGo and AlphaGo Zero discussed above.

On top of this, AI news is booming with all kinds of developments on both software and hardware aspects on AI. Do a search on AI in Google and it will reveal over 40 million articles, most of them in very recent years. This is just one symptom of acceleration of the surpassing of thresholds that we have not supposed to be surpassed until some time into the future. Indeed the future is starting to implode into the now!

Time for the Precautionary Principle to Kick In

And here is my third point. Despite the different dates, most agree that AGI is coming. Since AGI, and shortly after, ASI, will be so disruptive to the future of humanity, it is best to apply the Precautionary Principle. It is better to prepare early than late.

If we prepare earlier for the arrival of AGI and ASI, then we are in a better position to figure out what to do. If we say, 'Ah, don't worry. ASI will not be around for another 50 years', then we will let our collective guard down and we will be caught totally unprepared; just like the people on the beach in Indonesia, 14 years ago.

So it would be more prudent to expect an earlier arrival date for AGI and ASI.

The Fully Human: Putting a Safety Break on the Risks of AI

There is one thing missing in all these concerns about AI discussed above. This missing element is also the same one that can radically shift the debate about the future of AI and its safe use in service of humanity instead of enslaving and/or ultimately destroying humanity.

There is some, but very little debate on what image of the human being stands behind the AI creation. In current AI work, the tacit belief is that human beings are nothing but complex biological machines that could be manipulated, altered, cloned, and patented. This attitude stems from the ruling assumption of modern-day science that humans are nothing but pure matter and there is no active spiritual agency within us.

Having this materialistic view of AI means that these technologies go against the spiritual beliefs and rights of billions of human beings, and are de facto being forced upon humanity with hardly any serious debates (except for occasional concerns here and there expressed by prominent global leaders).

It is therefore necessary and imperative to bring this serious deficit in current debates about artificial intelligence to the general public awareness and consciousness. As I mentioned in the Preface, the primary audience for this book are those conversant with spiritual science. As a way to segue to that perspective, and as a preparation for the next sections and chapters of this book which consider also the interest of the general public, I would like to make the following framing remarks.

In spiritual science the image of the human being is much richer and more detailed than in the prevailing materialist ideology behind artificial intelligence. These outstanding capacities of humans took tens of thousands of years to evolve in a way very different from what is currently envisioned in materialistic versions of evolution. And, as we shall see in Chapter 16, mainstream science is starting to confirm some of the pioneering findings of spiritual science.

The development of human beings is shaped, if you look at anthroposophical cosmology, by evolutionary processes that recapitulate themselves in a different and more enhanced form at specific points in human history. The chapters that follow will unravel the details of this process.

This recapitulation has stopped during our time—nothing is being repeated now. This is because we have reached the point of 'human freedom', and it is unpredictable what humans will do with their freedom. It is now a time for decisive moments in world history.

Humanity is now in a situation that totally has no antecedent. After billions of years being the passive product of cosmic evolution, the human species is now becoming a powerful agent of transformation in the evolutionary stage. What the human beings on this planet decide to do now will affect what happens in the entire universe in the epochs to come.

And if we don't overcome this challenge as anthroposophists, in alliance with other global identities and movements, we will be contributing to the burden of humanity.

Purpose of the True and Fully Human

We all have a choice, but we have to answer questions about our purpose in a much larger context. Most of the time or practically all the time, when you ask 'What is my purpose here on Earth?', most people refer to this purpose in connection with their personal aspirations.

Yet, to be elaborated more fully below, the answer has nothing to do with you. When I say nothing to do with you, I mean it has nothing to do with our persona, our personality, our 'mask', with our 'ordinary self' because our ordinary self separates us from the unity of the world context.

The purpose we ought to serve, and the purpose truly appropriate to our own divine nature, our higher self, is a purpose that understands, cares for, and loves the profound intentions embedded in the whole fabric and evolutionary thrust of the universe.

We also need to understand how humanity has been evolving since the beginning of time until today. We will determine the future by what we do today. With their good intentions or inaccurate beliefs, some members of humanity are going to drag us into the abyss, but there are others who will use these technologies and transform them to a higher level.

There is a lot of food for thought in these two words: the *cosmic context* of the fully human. In anthroposophical science, it is a very large context. I will elaborate the exact meaning of this in what follows below.

Anthroposophy has a huge amount of knowledge and skills to contribute to the world. But it is important for anthroposophists to remember that the world also has a lot to contribute to anthroposophy. This is a mutual engagement, whereby something new can emerge that can move humanity forward in the way that it needs to, if it is not going to fail in its mission—the evolutionary mission of the human species.

The interesting thing is that the world is actually catching up with spiritual science (see Chapter 16). Many amazing things that are now being achieved in the world are being done within this world cosmic context even if understood mostly on the physical level.

Technology, as Substitution, is the Double of the Fully Human

Technology, in essence, is substitution. Continuous substitution has the effect of externally creating the shadow of the truly human. It is a caricature of the truly human.

AI is asking a series of serious and profound questions for humanity. What does it mean to be truly and fully human? If we do not answer this question, then AI will give us ASI. What does real working and collaborating together really mean? If we do not answer this question, then AI will answer it for us. It will create a world of its own where humans will no longer have a place to work, to live, and to flourish.

I would like to end this chapter with a quote from Steiner. This explains to us his perspective on the unabated use of technology born out of a materialistic framework:

> If we allow things to take their course, in the manner in which they have taken their course under the influence of the world-conception which has arisen in the nineteenth century (materialism) and in the form in which we can understand it, ... we shall face the war of all against all, at the end of the twentieth century. No matter what beautiful speeches may be held, no matter how much science may progress, we would inevitably have to face this war of all against all. We would see the gradual development of a type of humanity devoid of every kind of social instinct, but which would talk all the more of social questions.[137]

With this strikingly accurate prediction, we will now turn to a more spiritual understanding of what lies ahead of humanity. To be aware is the necessary beginning to enable us to prepare for the task of transformation.

Part II

PREPARING FOR SPIRITUAL BATTLE

To understand all the chapters that follow, we need to understand the phrase: 'Spiritual Battle'. So first let us first take the world 'spiritual' and see what it means and how it will be used in this book. And then we will clearly describe the word 'battle' to avoid any misunderstandings of how I am using the term.

The elaboration that follows may not be necessary for anthroposophists. Their cosmology is explicitly spiritual. The word 'spiritual' is familiar to anthroposophists both as objective Idea and actual spiritual beings standing behind the Idea.

This is clear both from Steiner's *Philosophy of Spiritual Activity*,[138] his key book on epistemology, and his Leading Thought 112 as found in *Anthroposophical Leading Thoughts*,[139] the aphoristic summary of his spiritual scientific research based on higher faculties of supersensible cognition. Through our thinking, we perceive the Ideas as spiritual realities, and a further intensification of our cognitive faculties will reveal the spiritual beings that are operative behind the world of Ideas.

However, for the general public this elaboration is essential in order to develop a deeper appreciation of the urgent crisis that humanity is facing and the steps that can be taken to turn potential disaster into a blessing for humanity.

Spiritual Reality and Spiritual Beings

We live in a world today where any notion that there are spiritual beings other than human beings is ignored, dismissed immediately as childish superstition, or blamed for producing diverse forms of religious fundamentalisms that are the cause of endless violence and wars.[140]

Yet for thousands of years until as recently as the early twentieth century, the worldviews of practically all civilizations were overtly spiritual. They had their dark side but they also brought amazing gifts to humanity. If we take the 24 hours of a digital clock, we can say that for 23 hours and 50 minutes, humanity was deeply and overtly spiritual. And in the last ten minutes, humanity became more and more infected with materialism that acted like a highly virulent virus spanning the planet.

The lofty ancient Indian civilization was highly spiritual and spoke of thousands of different kinds of spiritual beings. The ancient Persians spoke about the battle of two spiritual powers, the Spirit of Light, Ormazd, and the spirit of Darkness, Ahriman, and the hosts of spiritual beings surrounding them. The Egyptians had their gods and goddesses principally the sun god, Osiris, and his wife, the sun goddess, Isis. The Greeks had Zeus and that pantheon of other gods that lived in Mt. Olympus. The Jews had Yahweh who endlessly warned the Jews against worshipping other gods. The Muslims have Allah and a worldview populated with malevolent Jinns. And the Christians have Christ and a whole hierarchy of angels, archangels, primal spirits, Elohim, Seraphim and so on plus the opposing dark powers: Lucifer, Satan, Mammon, and countless other devils.[141]

Were all these billions of people merely hallucinating for thousands of years? Why is it that today no one in their ordinary consciousness has access to these kinds of perceptions let alone has developed very detailed descriptions and consistent understandings about spiritual beings and spiritual realities, including the dark side of these spiritual entities?

The Evolution of Human Consciousness

The answer lies in a certain obvious phenomenon that was massively ignored, for understandable reasons, in the latter parts of the nineteenth up to the twenty-first century. Mainstream scholarship in general ignored the reality that *human consciousness has evolved since the beginning of human time.*

There was a time when human consciousness was more spiritual and had direct access to spiritual beings and realities. Then this direct experience of the spiritual gradually faded away and human consciousness became more and more limited and earthbound.[142] And this latter form of earthbound consciousness, from its own standpoint, understandably, could not fathom what it would call the 'childish', 'superstitious' and even 'psychopathological' fascination of past civilizations with the spiritual. And any current conversation about spiritual realities would be considered 'rubbish'.[143]

When it has this condescending attitude, the modern mind is in a state of profound contradiction. The contemporary world with its amazing sciences has shown that *evolution is a fact of life.* Even Pope John Paul II admitted that evolution is a reality, although he did not agree with the materialistic explanation of it.[144]

It is one of the most amazing distortions of both materialistic and spiritual modernity not to believe that human consciousness itself has also evolved. Everything is subject to evolution. Yet many religious and materialistic people believe that human consciousness is exempted from the wide-ranging evolutionary processes that pervade the cosmos.

It is like our thinking. We think all the time. But we are often not conscious of the twists and turns of our thinking and thoughts (the product of thinking) all day long.

Rudolf Steiner was one of the earliest thinkers to demonstrate the reality of the evolution of human consciousness as manifest in philosophy and the history of ideas.[145] Yet he was hardly understood in his time and even in our time.

It is the great achievement of Ken Wilber, the American integral philosopher, to gain academic and post-modern respectability for the notion that human consciousness evolves. He laid it all out systematically in his book, *Integral Psychology*, where he brings together the discovery of the evolution of human consciousness by dozens of thinkers, philosophers, and scientists. He also includes Steiner's contribution in this new field of academic research even if, interestingly enough, even he had difficulties totally comprehending the complexity of Steiner's contribution to this topic.[146]

Owen Barfield, a British scholar from Oxford, is one of the early pioneers of the science of the evolution of human consciousness. He documents his discovery in his book, *History in English Words*. There he empirically demonstrates this reality using the tools of linguistic analysis.[147] I will use his simplified framework to help understand the present trajectory of artificial intelligence and what it means for humanity.

I say 'simplified' because Steiner, Wilber, and others identify still other stages of consciousness in between the major phases that Barfield describes. But this book is not a thesis on the evolution of consciousness. The 'simplified' framework of Barfield, in its broad strokes, is more than helpful to give us a sense of what the evolution of human consciousness would mean both in terms of the reality of the spiritual and the meaning of artificial intelligence in the life of humanity.

Barfield identifies three major stages in the evolution of consciousness: original (unconscious) participation, representational (dualistic, onlooker non-participatory, modern) consciousness, and final (conscious) participation.[148]

In the stage of original participation, the human being is totally immersed, totally participating unconsciously in the spiritual matrix and context of life. Human consciousness is totally in unity with the world process. There is no separation from the world. An experience of the world as spiritual, with concrete spiritual beings, benign and malevolent, is pervasive in this state. There is no sense of self. There is no concept of self. There is no thinking. There is no freedom.

In the stage of representational, onlooker consciousness, our current state of consciousness, the human being no longer has a direct experience of the spiritual world and sees himself/herself as separate from the world. The sense of a 'self' is born, a self that is standing, conscious of itself, in a world that is not-self. This is dualistic consciousness. Thinking is born and with this is also born a sense of oneself as an individual. There is also a sense of freedom born from the capacity of the thinking consciousness to separate itself from its direct experience and reflect upon it. And, on the basis of this reflection, humans can then create new possibilities for the future.

In the stage of conscious participation, the human being re-enters into a non-dual experience of the world, including the spiritual processes pervading the world. But this time, because of the birth of the 'I', because of individuation, the experience is conscious. States of intense creativity are indications of the beginning of this process. There are higher levels of this stage of conscious participation.

There are various intermediate stages inbetween. And it is in these intermediate stages where we can see the relevance of understanding the evolution of consciousness for understanding the substance of this book.

As the human being woke up from its spiritual immersion, the human being started to become conscious of the spiritual beings, both good and evil, that were part of the spiritual environment that the human being previously experienced, albeit unconsciously. This explains the pre-dominantly spiritual worldviews of the past ages of human history mentioned above. Animism is a symptom of this state of consciousness.[149]

The experience of spiritual beings increasingly fades through time, throughout history, as the human being awakens more and more into earthly reality. First there is a direct experience of spiritual beings as such. This is the Age of ancient India and Persia. When this direct experience fades away, the experience of Being transforms increasingly into Images or representations of spiritual beings as the latter works in the cosmos. This is the Age of ancient Egypt and Greece. This consciousness is the source of Mythology, often considered fictitious, but in reality, represents a symbolic account of spiritual realities.

Then comes the Age of the exploration of the 'active Working' of the Spiritual. Thinking, still very much in its living form, is born in the world. Humans start using their emerging cognitive capacities to explore the spiritual in how the latter is forming the regularities, patterns, and laws of Nature. Then comes our modern Age. The spiritual is totally gone in the experience of ordinary cognitive consciousness. Everything is now finished work. Materialism understandably dominates the consciousness of the world.[150]

Aristotle's Four Causes Affirms the Evolution of Human Consciousness

This gradual loss of the direct experience of the spiritual in its various forms is wonderfully captured in the works of the great philosopher, Aristotle, whose works in logic, among others, are endlessly cited even in the contemporary world today.

Aristotle works out an early version of a phenomenological approach to the reality of the spiritual that one can only understand if we take the evolution of consciousness briefly described above as our framework. He identifies four kinds of causes: material, efficient, final, and formal.[151]

We can take his approach and apply it to the creation of a piece of pottery.

What we see before our eyes is a vase, for example. The actual substance of matter that makes up the vase is the 'material cause' of Aristotle.

But this piece of art could not have come about by itself. It has been shaped into existence by human hands and the potter's wheel. This force that shaped the material is the 'efficient cause'.

But human hands had to have an idea, a goal in mind, a 'telos' in order to guide the shaping and forming of the pottery. This is the 'final cause', in the sense of an ultimate direction towards which creation is heading.

Then there is the 'formal cause'. This is the human being himself/herself that produces the idea of the vase and guides the process that shapes the vase to imprint the idea and create the actual product in a material substance. This is the ultimate source of cause behind the three other causes.

Here we have a holistic account of the different kinds and levels of 'causes' active in the world. Material causes are present but, alone, materialism cannot be the sole cause for every phenomenon in the world. Even modern science recognizes the limits of trying to reduce everything to material causes.

Take the case of the 'hard problem' of consciousness that is so relevant in the current debates ranging around artificial intelligence. Philosophers of mind and neuroscientists define the 'hard problem' with this question. How can the activities of matter translate into our subjective immaterial experiences of sensation, colour, feelings, and thoughts?[152]

Some thinkers even believe that the answer to this question will forever elude the human mind.[153]

It is important to note that we can see the stages of the evolution of human consciousness in Aristotle's doctrine of the four causes.

The formal cause is the stage where humans had direct perception of the spiritual. The final cause is the stage where the spiritual is no longer directly visible but can be found in the representations, images and ideas that humans can experience in their minds. The efficient cause is the stage of human consciousness where the spiritual is seen, not directly as being or even image, but as active in the working of forces and processes of nature. Human consciousness understands the activity of the spiritual as laws of Nature. And finally, the material cause is the stage of the current consciousness of humanity where the spiritual is effectively banished from every consideration in human affairs.

In the four causes of Aristotle, the four stages of the gradual loss of the perception and sense of the spiritual are captured.

This gradual loss of the spiritual becomes relatively complete in Europe shortly before the birth of the Renaissance. This loss of direct spiritual experience is reflected in the great debate between nominalists and realists at the time of St Thomas Aquinas who refined the wide-ranging ideas of St Augustine's pastoral theology and wrote a Systematic Theology.[154] Nominalists believed that ideas were just abstractions of reality. The Realists believed that ideas were spiritual realities and had formative influences on physical reality. St Thomas successfully defended Realism in his time.[155]

Now the human being begins to focus more and more on physical reality. Materialism is born in the process and intensifies as the default mode of consciousness of humanity. First materialism expresses itself in the methods of science. Then materialism becomes an ontology, the state where humans start to believe more and more that everything is matter, and there is nothing spiritual beyond matter.

As this process continues, hyper-materialism is born as a worldview. Humans are expressing this hyper-materialism in their current radical technologies, including artificial intelligence.

While the emergence and value of materialism is clear and undeniable in the birth of human freedom and the latter's ultimate capacity to love (one can only love when one is free), this does not mean that the spiritual beings that humans once knew have simply disappeared into oblivion. They are very much there even if ordinary human consciousness cannot perceive them.[156]

Rudolf Steiner's highly significant contribution lay in consciously creating a bridge for all humanity to move from dualistic, alienated consciousness to conscious participation.

First, he did this in the realm of epistemology where he demonstrated the capacity of free living thinking to penetrate, with its carefully weighed ideas, into the objective spiritual world.[157] This, in effect, is the equivalent of humanity regaining consciously its capacity to re-experience the presence of the spiritual in the working and processes of Nature and in objective Ideas one can have about these natural processes.

Then he intensified this cognitive capacity into a scientific penetration of spiritual realities and established a spiritual science.[158] Anthroposophy is the result of this first wave of spiritual science, a scientific training in conscious participation. With this new scientific consciousness of the spiritual, the human being then re-participates consciously in the spiritual foundations of the world, including having a direct experience of the reality and the intentions of spiritual beings.

The Phenomenological, Epistemological, and Ontological Reality of the Spirit

Steiner's philosophical works, written over a hundred years ago, are far from outdated. Dr Peter Heusser has written a very lucid and significant book updating Steiner's phenomenology, epistemology, and ontology for the twenty-first century. The title of his book is *Anthroposophy and Science. An Introduction.* Heusser is a medical doctor and Dean of Integrative Medicine at the Witten/Herdecke University in Germany at the time his book was translated in English in 2016.

In this book, he demonstrates very clearly that Steiner's philosophical and spiritual scientific writings are very much cutting-edge and sheds light on many of the questions now plaguing a diverse range of sciences: from physics, chemistry, biochemistry, neurology, psychology, pedagogy, philosophy and the social sciences, among others. And he does this knowingly and perceptively as he engages with the different perspectives that currently inform the understanding of these different sciences, especially materialism.[159]

In essence, he demonstrates that a real empirical approach cannot reduce one discipline to another. He calls this 'epistemological dualism'. Epistemological diversity would be a more encompassing term since the realm of matter, life, consciousness, and spirit are related but very different from each other.

One has to develop the appropriate, different research approaches and analytical tools to understand the very different empirical realms of the material world, the living world of biology, the inner experience of consciousness by animals and humans, and the cognitive capacity of human consciousness to reflect on its reflection. This idea world that can permeate the last level, he calls the realm of the spirit.

However, at the ontological level, at the inner realm of cognition, not the outer realm of physical observation, Heusser defends '*ontological monism*', which, for me, constitutes the present-day language of the Realism, active in the time of Aquinas and which also built upon the Doctrine of Four Causes of Aristotle.

Ontological monism is the view that understands that any experience of an inner or outer percept is not complete.[160] Human thinking needs to complete these percepts of experiences by adding the appropriate concepts and ideas to the percepts. These concepts and ideas govern the real connections between percepts and are actively at work in the percept world itself.

Real thinking (not finished thought) allows humans to consciously participate in this 'inside' of Nature. This inside of Nature is the law or ideal relationships that govern the level of phenomena being studied (that is whether it is matter, life, consciousness or even the very cognitive activity of humans.) This is brought about by active thinking.

These ideas are not simply added on to the percepts as abstract mirrors having no real value, as nominalists (and most materialists) would believe. Reality appears to humans as incomplete even if Nature, in itself, is complete. Real Nature, not observed by humans, is complete. It is both percept and Living Idea at the same time.

But we humans have two distinct ways of relating to Reality: through observing and thinking. This is due to the way we are made as humans. Within the frame of the evolution of consciousness, this separation of percept and concept in our inner experience was necessary so that human freedom could emerge. The perceptual world, if experienced as a whole, that is, non-dualistically, would compel us into submission and continually interfere with our freedom to reflect upon and judge the content of the percepts themselves.

Percepts are not complete due to the way humans are made. Humans, in their physical organization and cognitive makeup, have to first observe and then think about what they observe. Thinking, which produces concepts and ideas, completes the reality of percepts, forms one integrated whole at the different levels of phenomena (matter, life, etc.) that pervades all reality. These ideas have real effect in both the natural and human worlds.

Heusser points to the reality of spirit as the highest integrative level of the organism of thought (Steiner's terminology for the inner coherence of the Idea world of reality) by pointing to two phenomena: emergence and suppression.

Emergence is the phenomena of life seemingly evolving out of non-life.[161] The lower (non-life) gives rise to the higher (life). But the reverse does not happen: that the material level (non-life) emerges from the higher level (life). This indicates that the emergent higher phenomenon is already present in the integrative realm of the Ideas. Life is already active, even if invisible to the physical senses, in creating its vessel for visible manifestation in the realm of matter.

Suppression is clearly visible in the operations of the brain. Consciousness suppresses the lower level realm (in this case the life processes of the neurons in the brain) before manifesting itself.

Heusser vividly cites this reality thus:

> In the context of the relationship between the body and soul [or what others would call the 'psyche'] there is in fact a rarely acknowledged but very revealing antagonism between the organic or vital functions on the one hand and the workings of consciousness on the other. This antagonism exists phylogenetically, ontogenetically, physiologically and in relation to functional anatomy: the higher the development of the nervous system or the workings of consciousness enabled by its processes, the lower is its regenerative power in a certain respect. This apparently contradicts the well-known fact that the human brain which enables the highest functions of consciousness, also has the highest metabolic rate. Although it only constitutes 2% of the body by weight, the human brain consumes 15–20% of the cardiac output and over 50% of blood glucose. But this very active metabolism is a regenerative reaction to the achievements of consciousness.[162]

He then goes on to demonstrate this 'suppression' effect of consciousness on the vitality of life processes by taking different examples of lower forms of animals up to mammals.

> This reciprocal relationship between consciousness and vitality is shown phylogenetically in the ability to regenerate, for example. Lower invertebrates such as the almost 20,000 (!) species of flatworms have no central nervous system but only cerebral ganglia which, in evolutionary terms, are similar to the vegetative ganglia in human beings and accordingly only enable a low level of consciousness. But as a result they possess a huge regenerative capacity which enables them to regenerate a whole organism from each part of their body if cut in two at almost any point. The evolutionary significantly higher

amphibians already possess a basic central nervous system with the corresponding higher development of consciousness in comparison to Planarians, but for this they have forfeited vitality: they can, however, still regenerate whole extremities (Gross, 1974). Mammals, which have the highest capacity for consciousness in the animal kingdom, have lost the capacity for this kind of epimorphosis (complete replacement of lost body parts) and retain only a remnant in the form of a localised ability to heal wounds.[163]

The conclusion here is obvious when combined with the phenomena of emergence of the higher from the lower. 'Ontological monism' is not an abstraction. The so-called 'laws' or 'ideas' of the Spirit have real evolutionary impact and create effects in the world. The higher levels govern the lower levels. The higher 'suppresses' the lower so that the higher can manifest itself in the physical world. A better description would be this: the higher holds back, transforms and reorganizes the lower so that the lower can become a vessel for the operations of the higher.

Evolutionarily, the higher reality is already present even before its physical manifestation as a potential in the ideational realm of the spirit. This higher is an active force in creating its presence at the lower levels in the evolutionary sequence of matter, life and consciousness. Then when the lower levels are so organized, the human spirit can now find a physical vessel, a physical body, suited to its activity as spirit in the plane of earth existence. From the physical point of view, that has no access to super-sensible perception, the higher levels of organization seem to just 'emerge' from the lower levels.

It is a real spiritual deed of Heusser to have philosophically and scientifically affirmed the reality of spirit and to have re-contextualized the powerful yet incomplete scientific framework of 'emergence' into a higher epistemologically and ontologically satisfying integrative framework of reality.

I felt the necessity of grounding the upcoming chapters in the science of the evolution of consciousness and the philosophy and science of phenomenology, epistemology and ontology. My reason for this is that some of the findings of spiritual science are so outrageous from the perspective of ordinary consciousness and modern common sense that these scientific and philosophical considerations, albeit of a preliminary nature, may help create an open cognitive space in readers. For as we shall see, these spiritual perspectives open a lot of avenues in understanding the current emergence of artificial intelligence and offer constructive and pro-active ways of dealing with it.

In contrast, many thought systems are dualistic in externally conceiving a different world of the psyche in contrast to a different world of matter. And the 'hard problem' of consciousness thus arises as it is not understood how these differently operating worlds can interact with each other and/or how matter can give rise to an inner experience of consciousness.

In effect, without his conscious intention to do so, Heusser has given a very powerful thought structure that sheds great light on the impracticality of current efforts in artificial intelligence to 'transfer' consciousness into a machine.

I will concretely demonstrate it in the different parts of the book especially when I speak about the fallacy of most AI advocates that the human being is nothing but a complex biological machine and that our consciousness and sense of self are nothing but illusions governed by the patterns of the networks of neurons in our brain. This latter worldview is amazingly false yet widely believed!

This is as far as present-day cognitive faculties of humans can go. Nonetheless scientific research and philosophical discipline at this level reveals a lot. This is what Heusser has achieved.

Steiner still goes further by enhancing his cognitive faculties through systematic concentration, contemplation, and meditative exercises. Through this means he achieves supersensible perception of the realms of the spiritual beings that are active in the universe.

The result of this spiritual scientific investigation is the focus of Part II of the book.

The Meaning of Spiritual Battle Now Clear

It is in this context then that the word, 'battle' is to be understood. One of the most important discoveries of spiritual science is that spiritual beings are not all of a benevolent kind. There are the good gods. They are opposed by the 'evil' gods.[164] And present-day human consciousness and the radical technologies that humans have created, especially artificial intelligence, are the battleground where this battle is taking place.

The word 'evil' is in quotation marks because 'evil', from the perspective of spiritual science is not absolute. They have a purpose, one that we shall see more clearly in Chapter 6 which follows below.

The Cosmic Battle

Many anthroposophists emphasize the importance of the presence of anthroposophy in the world and its ennoblement during the sun-like days of the Christmas Foundation Meeting in 1923.[165] That is very true and has a lot to say for it.

But it is also true that, a few days before he died, Steiner's very last words for the members were not a further elaboration of anthroposophy or the Christmas Foundation. Rather he assumed that that was already in the hearts of members of the global Anthroposophical Society. Steiner instead was preoccupied with something else and wanted to bring to the consciousness of the global membership an urgent matter.

And this urgent matter had to do with what he called 'sub-nature' or, in our present context, materialistic technology. But he was not concerned about just any technology. He was concerned about technologies that would lead humanity into the 'abyss'.[166] In short, using our current language, he was concerned about the rise of 'extreme technologies' including artificial intelligence (AI) that are bringing humanity to the abyss.

Dr Naoto Yoshikawa, Vice-Chancellor of Tokai University in Japan, captures the precarious condition of humanity. He said in a 2018 global forum in Japan: '... we live in a world in which all human existence is *very close to an abyss*. It shows how fragile and easily destroyed the more humane society is, which has taken thousands of years to build.'[167] [Emphasis added.]

I was personally shaken by his words. It was precise and to the point. Although he was referring to the incredible violence done by human beings to one another, it could have been a perfect description of the current condition of humanity, especially how thousands of years of civilization can just disappear in a few decades, if humanity is not careful with the way it is developing Artificial Intelligence. For indeed, AI can plunge humanity into the 'abyss' as shown in Part I of this book.

And this is the 'abyss' that includes the obliteration of human beings themselves, including anthroposophists. Steiner asked us to prepare for a spiritual battle. Out of the authority of our own moral conscience, it behooves us, if we truly believe we can be fully human, to also steel ourselves for spiritual battle.

Whether Steiner gave this warning or not should not prevent us from looking deep into ourselves as we reflect on the tragic turn that the world has taken. And if the spirit is truly alive in us, if we truly honour what spiritual science has given to our lives, then we all cannot just sit idly on the side and watch these events unfold without attempting to bring a more dignified and spiritual future for humanity.

We all came here to earth prepared for and ready to engage in spiritual battle. But that is under the assumption that we remember who we truly are and why we are here. That also assumes that we are not rationalizing our paralysis by citing our current obligations in life. Instead we must find the inner strength and creativity to take our current situation and evolve it into new forms of expressions urgently needed in the era of Artificial Intelligence.

Part of the preparation is to also understand the nature and mission of Evil. We cannot transform something that we do not understand. This is why we need to clearly understand Chapters 4 and 6 that follow shortly below.

While we all try to be 'politically correct', to use the currently terminology for social tact, ours is no longer a time for putting truth in soft gloves, so to speak. Some truths just have to see the light of day. But behind this call for uncompromising truth, is also love, love for the dignity and future of all humanity.

It is my love for humanity and all the sacrifices that our spiritual guides, human Masters and committed human beings have made continuously to give a decent future to humanity that is a major motivation for writing this book and to do it in the mood of soul above.

Therefore, I ask for understanding when there is a particular matter that may offend you. It is not meant to judge anything that you have done. It is offered as an objective mirror for the collective deeds of neglect, collective lack of courage, collective expressions of doubt, collective manifestations of ignorance and all the collective mistakes we have made in the past that have now resulted in this greatest of trials for humanity. Let us all find the inner courage and create a totally different possibility for all humanity.

Chapter 4

Spiritual Opponents Fuelling the Potential for Technological Apocalypse

Ultimately, we are not dealing with mere 'flesh and blood' humans who are bringing about the extreme technologies that will unconsciously or consciously wipe out humanity. We are dealing with spiritual opponents who have pledged, since time immemorial, to abort the emergence of the fully human in the cosmos.

Ahriman and His Coming Incarnation

The first is Ahriman, the inspiring spiritual being behind materialism and its extreme technologies. His objective is to chain the human spirit into an eternal physical, material existence and cut off humans from their rightful continued evolution in harmony with the cosmos.[168] Current attempts by techno-utopians to achieve physical immortality[169] are an obvious expression of the spiritual reality inspiring such techno-utopian dreams.

Ahriman wants to control the Cosmic Intelligence that Christ and the Archangelic Being, Micha-el, have gifted to humanity (see Chapter 5). Ahriman wants to overthrow Micha-el in the process and inspires humans to follow him in his rebellion and take full control for egotistic purposes of the sacred intelligence that once belonged to the good gods. Indeed, as pointed out earlier (see Part 2), it is a cosmic battle and the tide is tilting over into the side of Ahriman.

Ahriman will incarnate around the turn of the twentieth century. Referring to and synthesizing the indications of Steiner, T.H. Meyer summarizes these symptoms of Ahriman's coming.[170] I add my comments in the form of current developments to support the reality of these symptoms. Meyer's comments are in quotes and my comments are in brackets:

- 'the spread of the ideology and practice of nationalism and racism'
    - [witness IS and terrorism]
- 'the belief in the omnipotent nature of statistical data ... also in medical practice'
    - [big data analytics, a hot area for profits and manipulation

using AI, and in medicine the deployment of IBM's AI, 'Watson'[171]]

- 'political party management'
  - [the ruthless mismanagement of political life by the super-powers of the world, of which Donald Trump is Exhibit A and the de facto takeover by the 'big four' (Google, Facebook, Amazon and Apple) of the technological policies of the world that should be in the regulatory hands of the State with support from global civil society;[172] also in here and, as pointed out above, the current Cambridge Analytica scandal that resulted in the theft of 87 million Facebook profiles to place Trump into power]
- 'a one-sided materialistic cosmology'
  - [application of this materialistic cosmology in extreme tech-nologies including artificial intelligence, synthetic biology, and nanotechnology; interesting though that there is a huge crack in the materialistic consensus of scientific community around astrophysics; see Chapter 16]
- 'the tendency to spiritual revelations that make no demands on recipients'
  - [the revelatory but illusory world of Virtual Reality, Aug-mented Reality and increasingly sophisticated versions of such technologies experienced as a substitute by users for the ecstasy that usually comes with peak experiences and spiritual enlightenment[173]]
- 'the belief in the omnipotence of the unitary State'
  - [strong States that either ignore or suppress their civil societies and impose 24/7 surveillance (Big Brother) not only of their citizens but the entire population of the world and most citi-zens do not seem to mind;[174] Internet of Things (IOT)[175] and 5G upgrade of Big Brother technologies[176]]
- 'the literal understanding of the Gospels, uninformed by spiritual perspectives'
  - [long since a reality; also witness the emergence of psycho-analytic perspectives on Christ as a psychotic[177]]

There are three possible ways for Ahriman to incarnate:

- In a human body.[178]
- In the entire Internet.[179]
- In a hybrid of both, upgrading the human brain with a digital neural interface that is linked to the entire Internet.[180]

Sorath: Ahriman's 'Boss'

Ahriman is indeed a very powerful and cunning opponent of humanity. But, as anthroposophists know, Ahriman is not acting alone. He is acting in concert with another spiritual being, more powerful than him. Ahriman, in a sense, is a mere pawn in the grand plan of Sorath.[181]

Sorath, also called the Sun Demon, believes he has the power to overcome the extremely lofty spiritual creator and benefactor of humanity, the Christ, the Sun Principle. He has had two attempts in the past to destroy humanity.[182]

The first was around 666 AD in Gondhishapur. He inspired Harun al-Raschid, to bring together all the extant wisdom of the world and from this wealth of knowledge accelerate, beyond reasonable speed, the evolution of humanity.[183] That would have devastated humanity. Islam blunted this first attack of Sorath.[184]

The second attempt was successful. In events clustering around 1314 (2 × 666) Sorath inspired King Philip IV of France and his puppet, Pope Clement V, to destroy the incredible warrior-monks known in history as the Knights Templar.[185] The Templars would have spiritualized the world economy and it would have utterly changed world history for the better. Their cruel torture released a spiritual force that has inspired outstanding individuals like Goethe and still works until today.[186]

Today is the time of the third advent of Sorath, clustering around the year 1998 (3 × 666). Ahriman is tempting people with the half-truths of radical technologies: super health, super intelligence, super strength and physical immortality.[187] And Sorath is very active creating societal and human chaos so that masses of humans would actually yearn for these ahrimanic temptations.[188]

This is the question—how do we respond to it? How do we strengthen and enable ourselves to bring the Cosmic Intelligence back to Micha-el? For the forces that once created moral order and beauty in the entire universe, will now be captured by Ahriman who will operate the cosmos on the basis of egotism and self-serving objectives and not for the benefit of the whole. It will be a disastrous future for all. We need a deeper understanding of the nature and mission of evil. But first, we need to understand the spiritual powers that have created and guided humanity during the billions of years of its evolutionary journey.

Chapter 5

Anthroposophy: In Defence of the Truly Human

If there are spiritual opponents against humanity, there is also an array of spiritual protectors and supporters of humanity. I personally call these helpers of humanity as Keepers of Humanity. They have been with humanity, with us, for long ages of time, and, for some of them, since the beginning of time.

While important for context and to fully understand the huge significance of the existence of these Keepers of Humanity in our struggle against human extinction, nevertheless this chapter will not go into the details of the key points of anthroposophy that are contained in the basic books of anthroposophy by Rudolf Steiner and the wealth of lectures that give the most diverse details of the basic science of anthroposophy. The intent of this chapter, in harmony with the book in general, is to give an overview of the current spiritual crisis of humanity.

This chapter presumes knowledge of the different levels of spiritual beings in the Cosmos, both seen and unseen, the nine-fold human being, the evolution of the universe, evolution of consciousness and the individuation of humans and their capacity for freedom and love, spiritual history, Mystery centres of humanity, the Cosmic Christ, reincarnation and karma and many other related themes.[189]

From out of anthroposophy comes this wealth of knowledge that was intended to form, nurture, and advance the primal archetype of the truly human. It will help us defend the truly human and help us self-evolve the fully human, together with the help of the Keepers of Humanity who are just waiting for our earnest request to assist us in this most perilous moment of human existence.

For example, we know that an amazing array of incredible spiritual beings, foremost among them, the Christ and Micha-el, as well as highly evolved human initiates, are all immediately supportive to help in this dramatic battle if we seriously think of them and ask for their assistance. (See Chapter 9 on how we can do this.)

The purpose of this chapter is to talk of humanity's spiritual champions and fully human masters who are totally with us in this most difficult time in humanity's history. And when we do this kind of spirit-recalling, spirit-awareness, and spirit-beholding, then we will find the inner strength to undertake, together with the most varied identities, whatever sacrifices and deeds are necessary for us to be fully human and with that also achieve this for our billions of brothers and sisters living on this planet.

In what follows, I will only briefly touch on key aspects of the spiritual beings and human masters. Anthroposophy is full of references to these spiritual beings and outstanding human individualities and it would be redundant and unproductive to repeat the easily available knowledge about them. The focus will be on aspects of these beings that have to do with how humanity can make it through the perilous challenges of extreme technology including Artificial Intelligence.

Christ

Christ is the foremost supporter of humanity. He is the Creator, and thus the Source, of the true human archetype. The first verses of the Gospel of St John in the New Testament of the Bible is very clear and direct about this.

> 1:1 In the beginning was the Word, and the Word was with God, and the Word was God. 1:2 The same was in the beginning with God. 1:3 All things were made by him; and without him was not any thing made that was made. 1:4 In him was life; and the life was the light of men. 1:5 And the light shineth in darkness; and the darkness knew it not.

This is the Christ we are referring to in this book. It is the Cosmic Christ. It is the Christ of humanity, not just a specific religious creed that uses the name of Christ to describe itself. This is the Being that looks out for the welfare and progress of the whole of humanity.

Christ not only created us. He died and resurrected twice for our sake so that we can be fully human. (See immediately below.)

As a result of His first death and resurrection, Christ knows the secrets of life and death, in general, as well as the mystery of the human body and its transformation into the Resurrection Body. AI engineers are trying to create a totally substituted and therefore degraded version of the Resurrection Body as well as fake and illusory concepts of physical immortality. And should these materialistic scientists one day realize their aim, even if only imperfectly, the digital human that they would create, would totally make it impossible for humans to have a Resurrection Body in the future, if they have a physical future.

The second death and resurrection of Christ happened in the Etheric, the level where Life itself is active. This time it was not a physical death and resurrection, but one that took place in a supersensible level. The Angel who was the 'body' of Christ in the Etheric suffocated and lost consciousness as a result of the massive darkness of materialism stemming from the nineteenth century.[190]

But Christ resurrected again and brings the secret of overcoming and transforming the consciousness behind materialism and its radical technologies, including AI, which ideology and technology, Ahriman and Sorath inspired into existence. But this time, this possibility of transforming materialism including AI will be carried out in partnership with humanity itself. This is no longer the time for individual heroes. Humanity, as a whole, needs to wake up. Christ intended humans to have freedom. He only had one commandment: Love God, others and oneself. There is no real Love without freedom!

Because of His gift of human freedom, Christ waits for humans to use their freedom to reach out to Him and all the spiritual powers arrayed with Him. Then Christ and the Keepers of Humanity can truly help and save humanity from its impending destruction. (See Chapter 9 for a fuller discussion.)

Also, as a result of His second death and resurrection in the Etheric, Christ has the power to overcome all technological hindrances and dangers to humanity. And He will be a revealer of the secrets of the Etheric World; knowledge that humanity needs to tame Artificial Super Intelligence (ASI) and make the latter serve humanity, and not destroy it.[191]

It will be an important part of our daily meditative practice to seriously consider the presence of Christ who will personally comfort us when we have deep and perplexing questions in life[192] especially in connection with Artificial Super Intelligence.

Finally, humanity will suffer a lot when confronting the impending arrival of ASI. There will be suffering inside us as we purify ourselves to be worthy to be 'in battle'. There will be suffering outside us as waves of destruction and devastation become the daily staple of humanity.

Therefore, imagine Christ, the second loftiest being, next only to the Absolute, in all the Cosmic worlds. Yet, out of His free decision, He, who had no karmic debt, chose to suffer on behalf of humanity to enable humans to have a future. This is earthshaking! Christ teaches us to bear suffering and sacrifices in our life. We will badly need both to flourish in the age of Artificial Intelligence.

Micha-el: The Fiery Prince of Intelligence, Courage and Defender of the Truly Human

And Micha-el! What an Image of a Spiritual Being! He stands almost alone and isolated from his archangelic peers. He has unyielding trust that human beings will use their freedom wisely and in alignment with the Divine Guidance of Worlds! This confidence in humans did not sit well with his spiritual colleagues who have lost or are starting to lose confidence in humans as a result of mainstreaming a civilization that is in utter blasphemy of the spirit.[193]

Micha-el gave us anthroposophy as a weapon in our time to awaken, nurture and defend the truly human. He does not seek adherence from us in our head. He wants deeds, courageous actions. In this way, from the Word becoming flesh, the 'flesh becomes Word' [Logos] again.[194]

And like Him, he 'admires' human beings who do not and will not surrender amidst all odds.[195] He supports humans who do not have 'retreat' or 'surrender' in their vocabulary. He inspires us to be greater than ourselves especially when confronted with a battle where the odds are clearly stacked against human physical survival.

Furthermore, Micha-el is the Spirit of the Time. The 'Spirit of the Time' means that spiritual being has the task of guiding humanity to create a civilization truly worthy of the dignity of human beings. Even conventional philosophy, in its concept of the 'episteme' is recognizing that there are certain periods in humanity where it seems that a fundamental perspective of the world appears that is shared by vast numbers of human being.[196] From the perspective of spiritual science, behind this 'episteme' is a spiritual being responsible for these 'epistemes' at specific stages in the development of humanity.

Micha-el is responsible for the current cosmopolitan 'episteme' of humanity: cosmopolitanism and the transcending of identities based on blood ties, races, and nationalities.[197] On a material plane, this expresses itself awkwardly and in a distorted manner in the calls for 'globalization' and the worldwide diffusion of technologies that do not respect individual and cultural identities.

Google, Facebook and artificial intelligence are examples of globalized technologies that are ubiquitous in their presence throughout the world. But this is a globalization of 'sameness'. This is not the kind of cosmopolitanism that Micha-el has in mind. His kind of cosmopolitanism respects individuality and the true unity of individualities on the basis of universal truths and moral standards of the truly human. From this respect of the diversity of humanity is born true creative unity and community.

Micha-el, is the Time Spirit for humanity as a whole, not just for anthroposophists. Micha-el has not been idle while humanity is being battered into submission. Micha-el has been very busy, non-stop inspiring other individuals and movements, outside the anthroposophical movement to deal with the ahrimanic threat.

We get a glimpse of this inspiration, albeit operating at the unconscious level of those concerned, in the current crop of whistle-blowers from Silicon Valley who are warning the world about the manipulative nature of social media and technology in general.[198] But they are not alone. Other courageous human beings are waking up to the profound challenge that Artificial Intelligence is bringing to the world.

Visionary Wisdom: The Holy Spirit, Sophia and Anthroposophia

Christ is the Logos of St John the Evangelist, the Logos that created our world, our entire universe, hidden and seen. The Holy Spirit holds the Wisdom of that creation. The Holy Spirit thus knows all the Mysteries of the past evolution of the Cosmos and of humanity and holds the secrets of the future evolution of Worlds. Before He ascended back to the spiritual world, Christ sent the Holy Spirit to continue guiding humanity in his behalf.[199]

In truly acknowledging the workings of the Holy Spirit in us, we unravel the dark secrets of Ahriman and other demonic powers. And when this wisdom comes to us, with instant intuitive, non-local speeds, from outside the parameters of the algorithm of Artificial Intelligence, we gain new ways of dealing with the ahrimanic dragon and its allies.

The Holy Spirit works through Sophia, a very lofty spiritual being whose reality encompasses almost all the ranks of the Hierarchy, starting with the Spirits of Wisdom down to the Angelic World. She knows all these because She is this![200]

And Sophia in turn works through Anthroposophia, who, for spiritual science, is an actual spirit being, who has taken on the task of inspiring the global anthroposophical movement.[201] All three work in concert to inspire humans to have cosmic wisdom to deal with a long-term evolution challenge for the future of humanity and the Cosmos itself.

Our Guardian Angel

And let us not forget our Guardian Angels. They are our future Spirit Self,[202] the basis for a future civilization of humanity[203] when the trials with the ahrimanic challenge would have been overcome and humans would have advanced to the first full manifestation of conscious non-dual participation. Our Guardian Angels have also inspired us in countless ways to stay in the path of Christ as Universal Logos no matter how dark it might have been in moments in our lives. When you awaken to your Guardian Angels, they also awaken you back and that means incredible wisdom amidst the daily trials in life. Besides they are in the Etheric realm connected with the Christ.[204] They can help us to be close to the Power that exceeds all the power of demonic forces combined.

Masters of Wisdom and of the Harmony of Sensations and Feelings

That is how Steiner calls human initiates, highly advanced human beings who have become fully human and can therefore help humanity advance forward in evolution especially during this time of great trial.[205]

According to the spiritual research of Rudolf Steiner, the following Masters may be in incarnation in our time: Mani,[206] Master Jesus,[207] Christian Rosenkreutz,[208] and the Bodhisattva who succeeded Buddha's spiritual office and will become the Maitreya Buddha.[209] These Masters have incredible gifts and can really help us in the mess that we have created. And finally, although he never claimed it for himself, there is Rudolf Steiner himself who clearly belongs to the ranks of these highly esteemed leaders of humanity.[210]

In connection with the reincarnation of the Masters (Keepers) of Humanity, one must note that an actual physical incarnation itself is not necessary in order for these highly evolved human beings to help individuals and humanity, in general. 'We can call upon them when we need them.'[211]

Mani is the greatest Master of them all.[212] The conventional picture of Mani is a gross historical distortion, masking who he really is. This is clear from the newly discovered manuscripts that have surfaced in contemporary times.[213]

Mani not only had detailed knowledge about the workings of Evil but also the inner strength and power to do something about it. It would be truly an inspiration if he is around to give humans concrete guidance on how to handle the evil connected with artificial intelligence. He is usually quite active when humanity is faced with a deep evolutionary crisis.[214]

Master Jesus was the individuality that enabled Christ to physically incarnate on earth. Therefore, Master Jesus has an intimate knowledge of the Christ. He sacrificed his own 'I' to enable Christ to enter his soul and body during the Baptism in the Jordan River.[215] Thus, Master Jesus can inspire us to understand how Christ would deal with extreme technologies. He can enlighten us about the entire possibilities that await humans in connection with the Christ. And he can show us how to truly sacrifice ourselves so that Christ can be in us: 'Not I but Christ in me.'

When this happens, then the Truth, the Love, and the Way of the Christ will guide us in transforming Artificial Intelligence. He was also the

Master who counselled Rudolf Steiner on how the latter could go about achieving his own mission.[216]

Christian Rosenkreutz is the Master who has the distinction of being initiated by all twelve leading Masters of the post-Atlantean cultural epochs.[217] Thus, he has in-depth knowledge of the evolution of humanity in the past and in the future. Coming from the stream of humanity proficient with the technical arts, he is also an expert in the realm of technology and attempted to introduce threefolding during the French Revolution.[218]

It is an understatement to say that his guidance is absolutely essential in helping humanity deal with demonic technology that is arising all around us in this technical age. And societal threefolding, under his guidance, will have a decisive role to play in taming the forces of Artificial Intelligence.

He was also the other Master guiding Steiner in the introduction of anthroposophy[219] and walked in with his spiritual hosts during the decisive Christmas Foundation Meeting of the Anthroposophical Society in 1923. In the spiritual world, both he and Steiner are tending a spiritual altar with Christian Rosenkreutz guarding the secrets of the esoteric Christian Mysteries and Rudolf Steiner having custody of the Micha-elic cosmic Mysteries.[220]

As we saw in the Preface and we will see in greater detail in Chapter 7, Steiner first defeated Ahriman in the sphere of thought. Later on, before the turn to the twentieth century, he entered spiritually into the sphere of Ahriman himself and survived through the power of Christ.[221] This is why he had such an intimate knowledge of the workings and intentions of Ahriman. If he is with us today, he would surely lead humanity in finding creative solutions to the challenge of extreme technologies and Artificial Intelligence. Without him there would be no spiritual science and without spiritual science we would be at the total mercy or 'un-mercy' of the demonic forces behind technology.

Maitreya Buddha

Maitreya Buddha is the successor of Gautama Buddha. His gift will be the communication of moral truth that will have a very deep and profound effect on humans.[222] While his time for activity as Maitreya Buddha is still in the future, as a Bodhisattva he can already hone his moral speech capacities in raising the awareness of humanity around the world to the dangers of Artificial Intelligence. After all, spiritual research shows that this Bodhisattva, who will be the future Maitreya Buddha, is in incarnation every century.[223]

The Knights Templar

I would like to consciously include the Knights Templar in this constellation of human leaders although they are not initiated to such high levels as the other Masters. They had the painful distinction of feeling the brunt of the second attack of Sorath on humanity. This has given them an intimate knowledge of how Sorath works, knowledge essential to our time that is also under the sign of Sorath.[224]

In addition, their terrible suffering under the instigation of Sorath and his human instruments have given them the spiritual strength to inspire human beings like Goethe and others.[225]

And, finally, I would not be surprised if many of them are reincarnated during this time of huge trials of suffering by humanity. They can help lessen these sufferings and, with practical acumen, they can help use these technologies to serve humanity.

Obviously this picture of the Knights Templar diverges with the image of the Templars as portrayed by the novelist, Dan Brown.[226] But, in recent years, the Vatican itself has vindicated the spiritual and moral integrity of the Templars.[227]

Masters Active on Earth Even if Not Incarnated

It is also possible that not all these Masters are incarnated at this time. But this does not mean that they cannot inspire humanity during this unprecedented trial in connection with extreme technologies. In addition, all of them have a deep connection with the Christ, and through this, as explained in the 'Etherization of the Blood' lecture by Steiner cited above, they have the ability to influence the physical world directly. And obviously, this is also true of Steiner himself.[228]

The knowledge of these Masters comes as part of the blessings of anthroposophy. The awakening, nurturing, and defending of the truly human has been going on for long periods of time. Anthroposophy has made us conscious of this process. With all kinds of help available to us for our work, let us strengthen ourselves and get ready to change the world. Only that, is the worthy thing to aspire for in this life!

But to enable us to do this, we need to have a deeper understanding of the nature and mission of Evil. Then we can develop the proper approach to what the Keepers of Humanity want to achieve for the human species.

Chapter 6

The Mission and Ways of Evil

From the anthroposophical perspective, the mission of Evil is to make us more fully human by providing the necessary resistance that we have to overcome in order to express our full humanity.[229] Evil also is the spur for humanity to be independent and free from all kinds of influences, material and spiritual, conscious and unconscious.[230] And with the inner strength and freedom thus won, humans then are capable of love in the highest sense.[231]

Artificial Intelligence and the evil forces behind it are there to help us achieve our destiny if we can understand what it is asking of us and then transform it in the process. The radical products of technology are there because we have not lived up fully to our humanity.

Spiritual science is the modern form of Initiation Science that has always existed since antiquity. The task of Initiation Science is to inaugurate new civilizations appropriate to the evolving consciousness of humans.[232] In short, Initiation Science is the core foundation of the creation of new civilizations. Spiritual science is not mere head knowledge. It is about creating new worlds worthy of the dignity of human beings.

Anthroposophists, with outstanding exceptions, have collectively failed to permeate world civilization with the knowledge of what it means to be truly human as well as exemplify this understanding with initiatives that inspire us to be fully human. Anthroposophists, from their perspective, have given a lot. But what they have given to the world is not enough. (See Chapter 19.)

The destructive technologies are not there because we are being punished. We have brought about our own impending potential disaster by neglecting to awaken, nurture and defend the truly and fully human in us.

If Evil attacks us where we are weakest, Evil is also asking us to unleash a greater power that is latent inside us. The dark circumstances we now face challenge us to rise to our highest potential for the sake of humanity.

The benevolent gods, in line with the mission they have allowed for Evil, are expecting us to make use of these deadening technologies to serve humanity and the spiritual world, especially Micha-el, and not to allow them to dominate our future.

In short, there is no running away from AI and other forms of extreme technology. We are all being called to be our best, to be fully human, so we will know how to bring about the transformation of potentially destructive technology for the good of humanity and the spiritual worlds.

Substitution: Evil's Manner of Working and Its Overcoming

Since it is inevitable that we will be constantly surrounded by technology, it is important to understand its inner logic. Once we understand this inner logic, we can resurrect the higher truth that lies concealed behind the technological juggernaut. Technology hides important secrets about the world process.

Evil subverts the intentions of the gods who nurture and guide humanity. And Evil often does this through substitution, the distortion of a higher and larger truth that spiritually wants to be born and develop in the world and substituting it with something else.

No, technology is not neutral. It has an inner logic to it. And that logic is substitution. And ultimately it wants to totally substitute the truly human with digital versions of the latter, and another being in place of Christ Who stands defending and nurturing the truly human.

Ahrimanic Substitution 1: In the Realm of Ideas

There is a book with an exciting title called *The Intelligent Universe: AI, ET, and the Emerging Mind of the Cosmos*. I asked myself: Was the mainstream finally getting it—that the universe is alive and intelligent?[233]

In this book, James Gardner, the author, speaks about the irrelevance of human beings and instead highlights the role of super-intelligent machines in inhabiting a planet. And from earth, the super AI will start colonizing the other planets and ultimately the galaxy and beyond.

It is a total distortion, counter–image, and substitution of what spiritual science has discovered. Anthroposophy speaks about the mission of the earth, the development of the force of love out of freedom, and the birth of a new cycle, a new Cosmos, the so-called Jupiter incarnation of the future Earth.[234]

And Gardner is not alone. There are others like him, brilliant writers, but deeply influenced by materialistic thinking. Max Tegmark, a scientist from Massachusetts Institute of Technology in the US, echoes the aspirations of Gardner in the former's *Life 3.0*.[235] And there is also Yuval Noah Harari and his book, *Homo Deus*, where he develops a powerful, yet deeply flawed scenario, arising from the new worldview he calls

Dataism.[236] Ray Kurzweil, author of *The Singularity is Near*, argues the inevitability of the rapid coming of radical technologies including artificial intelligence.[237] Martina Rothblatt and her book, *Virtually Human*, prefaced by Kurzweil, argue for the creation of 'mindclones' and giving our digital doubles all the rights of the human being.[238] After all, humans are nothing but complex biological, data processing machines.[239]

If we know how to read these books from the perspective of the 'substitution' technique of Evil, one can begin to be grateful to them for showing us what Ahriman is planning for humanity as well as for pointing to us, after re-interpreting, re-framing and transformation, what capacities true humans really have.

Re-interpreting Gardner and Tegmark, spiritual science affirms that humans are cosmic beings and have a cosmic task and destiny. Humans have cosmic consciousness and will ultimately pervade the cosmos as the 'tenth hierarchy' of love.[240] Reframing Harrari, spiritual science demonstrates that, at our essential core, humans have a Divine Essence and have, once they evolve the god-like powers within, the role to love, care for, and help transform humans and other beings that have fallen into decadence. Humans ultimately have a benevolent presence in the cosmos. And reading through the substituted ideas of Kurzweil and Rothblatt, humans have the inner capacity, when fully awakened, to achieve super health, super consciousness including intelligence, super strength of character, and spiritual immortality including of the physical body through the resurrection forces of Christ.[241]

In this context, one can also reread the massive attack on Christ, by the so-called new atheists,[242] as a dark inspiration to obliterate the access of human beings to the living truth and resurrection forces of the Christ. One can find some elements of truth in the criticism of institutionalized Christianity and the outrageous behaviour of individual so-called Christians that have triggered the criticism by and rise of the new atheists. But the criticisms also drag the Cosmic Christ into the confusion.

Spiritual science understands Christ here not as the founder of a religion but the Logos power, the Divine Intelligence behind the directed evolution of the universe.[243] This Divine Cosmic Creator is identical to the 'Logos' found at the very beginning of the Gospel of St John. The permeation of the human being, in freedom, with Christ, will ultimately lead to the emergence of the super human, but not the '*Über mensch*' of Nietzsche,[244] another ahrimanic[245] distortion of the truth.

Gathering all that we know about this Being so far, Ahriman seeks to prevent, through radical technologies, this emergence of the true super human. The advocacy of the transhumanism of the physical super human is a direct counter-image, an obviously distorted one, to the amazing potential spiritual and physical capacities of the truly human. (See Chapter 16 below.)

Ahrimanic Substitutions 2: Inner Logic of Actual Technologies

Substitution of our capacities is taking place in reality as more and more technology products are being rolled out to ensnare the truly human. For example, it is clear that, when we use a calculator, we lose the inner ability to calculate mathematical operations in our mind.

Let us take the case of Virtual Reality. This technology substitutes for our capacity for active imagination. When we lose that, we also lose the capacity to love, and further on the capacity to build spiritual communities on the basis of trust.

For another example, let us look at how Artificial Intelligence itself works.

Epistemology is the foundational science of all sciences. It clarifies how humans arrive at real knowledge. In *Philosophy of Spiritual Activity*, the epistemological work of Rudolf Steiner, the founder of spiritual science, he demonstrates that all knowledge ultimately comes from two faculties of the human I.

The first human capacity is the ability to make objective observations, outer and inner observations. The latter would include feelings and thoughts including memory and mental images. He designates the results of these observations as 'percepts', or what modern philosophy would call the 'Given'.[246]

The second human capacity is the ability to make 'sense' of the 'Given', to bring the different elements of the Given into the real relationships that they actually have in Nature and in the inner life of the human being. This is the capacity for living thinking, as contrasted to thought. The former is the process. The latter, thought, is the product of the process of thinking.[247]

Thus, epistemologically, human knowledge in general is the real relationship that living thinking (not finished thought) cognizes among the different elements of the Given.

Given this epistemological background, we clearly recognize that Artificial Intelligence substitutes 'big data' as its 'Given' and 'algorithms' as its form of thinking. In the case of the human being, it is his/her 'I' that 'processes' the act of knowing, combining the Given through Thinking. In AI, it is the hardware, the supercomputer, that uses algorithms to combine 'big data', the 'Given', together.

The major substitution that takes place is in the realm of Living Thinking. Algorithms, as finished thoughts of the programmer, substitute for Living Thinking. While very powerful, algorithms can never access the spiritual realities that Living Thinking can begin to access. The illusion of 'intuition' comes from the capacity of supercomputers to combine data at super speeds.

It is an illusion because the algorithm functions as a fixed paradigm, the lens with which the big data is viewed from. And, using Gödel's Theorem[248], even if the algorithm evolves, this evolution is still constrained by the original 'mother' paradigm, the source code.[249] The infinity that seems to be present in the algorithm and data processing of the supercomputer is the kind of 'infinity' that consists of the unexplored combination of the finished 'Given' within a 'finished' paradigm or algorithm.[250]

In the case of Living Thinking, as clearly demonstrated in the works of Steiner and other spiritual scientists, the human being accesses real innovations. This Living Thinking or deep creativity of real humans has the power to learn from the future.[251] Sophisticated AI cannot do this. It is the power that enables humans to make really new beginnings in freedom and love. In AI, on the other hand, the human being is trapped in the infinity of the 'Given' and the finished 'thought', the algorithm.

With Ahriman, the substitution and distortion of Truth comes in the form of technological substitution like artificial intelligence.

Why is humanity resorting to artificial intelligence? It is because the capacity to access higher realities and wisdom through cognitive intuition, Imagination, Inspiration, and spiritual Intuition, the higher evolutionary stages of human cognition[252] in the stage of conscious participation, has dried up in the mass of humanity who are now drowning in the ocean of materialistic culture that has engulfed them.

Chapter 7

The Two Milestones of the Global Anthroposophical Movement

Based on Steiner's remarks on the nature and mission of Evil in the previous chapter, it is clear that the gods, who are rooting for humanity, have a framework for preparing humanity to address the gigantic forces of Evil massing to destroy humanity. For it would not make sense for the gods to just leave us at the mercy of powerful demonic forces when we are not prepared and thus do not have the time to deal with them with our own inner power. It is like having a baby deal with complex computer issues even before that baby had the necessary preparation to fix these technological issues.

Thus, the fiercest believer in and champion for humanity, the Archangel Micha-el prepared in a very far-ranging way for his ascent to the rank of Archai and thus became the Time Spirit of the present age of humanity.[253] So Micha-el gathered together all spiritual and human allies that had been involved with his work since long periods of time and set up a spiritual school in the Heavens. And Micha-el himself taught directly in this school. Steiner called this the Micha-elic School.[254]

He had a 'plan' if we can use that prosaic term to describe these intense spiritual realities. *This 'plan' had two significant milestones.*

The First Milestone. The Birth and Cultivation of Spiritual Science

Steiner came and expressed the content of the School in a spiritual activity he called spiritual science and the first manifestations of wisdom from this science, he called anthroposophy.

That was the first 'planned' milestone of the Micha-elic School. And early on, shortly after Micha-el became the Time Spirit in 1879, his pupil, known to us as Rudolf Steiner, achieved an early victory of untold significance over Ahriman and over the future course of human evolution. In one of his notebooks, Steiner looked at the rhythm of his own biography, and then he noted '*1888: Ahriman is wrecked.*'[255] [Emphasis added.]

Steiner did this through his epistemological writings especially the *Philosophy of Spiritual Activity*, also called *The Philosophy of Freedom* and crowned it with the Foundation Stone Meditation during the Christmas Meeting of 1923 that established the global Anthroposophical Society.[256]

The significance of this victory can also be seen in the epistemological stance of artificial intelligence. As discussed above, one can say that this epistemology of artificial intelligence has this structure: big data + algorithms = the analytic 'truth' of artificial intelligence. (See previous chapter.) Big data analytics using artificial intelligence is now running many complex systems in the world. Steiner answered early on: percept + concept = truth or knowledge. (See his *Philosophy of Spiritual Activity*.)

The Second Milestone: The Culmination of Anthroposophy as Micha-elic Prophecy

When one thinks through it, Micha-el, through Steiner, had a reason for wanting spiritual science to be established on earth. For knowledge, that remains as knowledge, would not amount to anything. It would immediately turn egotistic and be useless to the world.

Steiner most clearly stated this second milestone in a lecture before priests of the Christian Community.

> Dear Friends, *everything we are able to do now in our time* by way of taking in the spirituality of these teachings [anthroposophy] is of great significance ... It *is a preparation for what is to take place at the end of the century*, initially in the form of great, all-embracing, intense deeds of the spirit, *after a great deal will have happened that is inimical to a spiritualization of modern civilizations.*[257] [Emphases added.]

Steiner speaks of 'great, all-embracing, intense deeds' that have the power to revolutionize the civilization of humanity and move it towards the spirit. This 'culmination' of anthroposophy, Steiner called the Micha-el Prophecy.

The Second Milestone: An Urgent Addendum

A few months later, just a little less than two days before he died on March 30, 1925, Steiner penned his last Leading Thoughts to members of the General Anthroposophical Society.[258] Even if he 'wrecked' Ahriman in the sphere of ideas, Steiner had to warn anthroposophists and humanity in general that we have to deal with Ahriman in the societal realm. And here the ahrimanic challenge is identified to be in the realm of sub-nature and the world of technology.

In his previous lectures, notably in the lecture on the 'Etherization of the Blood', Steiner specified sub-nature as the world of electricity, magnetism, and a still to emerge 'third force'.[259] This very sub-nature is what we see arising now and into the future of humanity as extreme technology including artificial intelligence. Present-day computers operate on electricity and magnetism for power, data storage and algorithms.[260] This is the basis of our present industrial technical civilization and threatens humanity with extinction. This is the 'abyss' of civilization Steiner repeatedly speaks about in his wide-ranging karma lectures of 1924.[261]

This danger of sub-nature is also found in technological singularity which is building a technological shadow, a counter image of a human being. Nanotechnology will mechanize the physical body of human beings. Biotechnology will mechanize the life or etheric body of humans. Information technologies will mechanize the body of consciousness (astral body) of humans. Cognitive technologies will mechanize human thoughts, destroying the bridge between the soul and spirit.

AI is the dark intelligence that will facilitate the mechanization of the entire human persona. Anything that is persona (body and soul) will be mechanized. Only those who are active in the realm of spirit (beginning with the spiritual activity of Living Thinking), and through that are able to maintain the life and integrity of their soul (psyche) and physical body, will be able to survive the age of technological singularity including Artificial Super Intelligence (ASI).

Tragically anthroposophy did not achieve the second milestone. It did not experience a culmination as a realization of the Micha-elic intention and prophecy. If it did then there would be no looming threat of technological extinction via Artificial Super Intelligence (ASI) which stares at humanity today.

Anthroposophists have a lot of catching up to do. For this non-culmination in large part was due to their shortcomings and mistakes. This is not the time to go into this now. We will return to this question near the end of this book in Chapter 19.

Hope: An Awesome and Remarkable Partnership

Steiner did not only warn us about 'sub-nature'. He also showed the way out.

The only force that can deal with sub-nature is the force that arises in us when we develop in ourselves the capacity to rise into higher forms of thinking and ultimately the spiritual realms. This is the other thought that is contained in Steiner's last message to humanity less than two days before he died. Again, here are his words that show us the way out.

> This makes it urgent for man to find in conscious experience a knowledge of the Spirit, wherein he will rise as high above Nature as in his sub-natural technical activities he sinks beneath her. He will thus create within him the inner strength *not to go under*.[262] [Italics in the original.]

Here again we can see the 'Ahriman-is-wrecked' theme that will prevent humanity from going under. The rising 'as high above Nature' as his 'sub-natural technical activities' sinks us is basically a statement, a challenge for humanity to consciously access the non-local etheric realm, whether through inspiration or in actuality, if humans are to solve the challenge of artificial intelligence.

Electricity is fallen light ether and magnetism is fallen chemical or sound ether. And the first step in this direction is nothing other than 'living thinking' that Steiner developed in full force in his *Philosophy of Spiritual Activity*. And this Living Thinking is etheric thinking. Once intensified, Living Thinking gives us access to etheric realities. And with this access giving humans ideas on how to transform ASI, plus the coming together of humans in collective problem solving and mobilization, Ahriman is wrecked in the societal sphere!

It is an awesome partnership. There on yonder side, in the spiritual realm (etheric realm) near the earth realm, is Micha-el, sweeping the etheric world clean of demonic influences to ensure that humans are able to access this world without distortion and, especially, to behold Christ in the Etheric.[263] And here on our side is Micha-el's greatest pupil, Rudolf Steiner, demonstrating and teaching humanity to access this purified etheric realm with Living Thinking. This is truly an amazing picture to behold. There is hope. For there is a societal equivalent of this process that we will see in Parts III, IV, and V that follow.

Part III

SELF AND COLLECTIVE MASTERY TO SERVE THE WORLD

Peter Senge, world renowned business thought leader, quoted a CEO of a large corporation, Bill O'Brien, 'The results of an intervention depends on the interior condition of the intervener.'[264] In other words, we want to transform AI to serve humanity. That is the 'intervention' that we want. But the outcome will depend on our 'interior condition', how we are when we are trying to achieve this goal.

We need to seriously prepare ourselves inwardly for what we have to do in the world. Chapter 8 details essential aspects of this preparation. But we cannot do this alone. The time is too short and the forces of destruction are massive and accelerating. We need to access the support and help of the Keepers of Humanity who have been nurturing the truly human for billions of years. Chapter 9 will show how we can do this.

Finally when we are inwardly and spiritually ready, we need to actively search for our colleagues in the world. These are those who are also prepared and ready to take on the gargantuan task of making Artificial Super Intelligence (ASI) beneficial for humanity.

If AI will have super intelligence, humanity needs to mobilize Collective Human Intelligence (CHI). This will be the task of Chapter 10. It will give an idea of the nature of Collective Human Intelligence and how humans can use it to solve the challenge of ASI.

This world we want to transform is already organized from the global down to the local, in all major institutions, whether it be the media, political structures, or the agreements being made at the World Trade Organization, the European Union, or the United Nations. We have to have sensing organs and action capabilities at all levels: the group, local, regional, national, and global levels. Our CHI efforts also need to be equally pervasive.

Steiner has a beautiful reminder to and challenge for all of us. After the disaster of World War I and the ensuing societal chaos in Germany, he gave a lecture with the title: 'Necessity of Finding the Spirit Again' (February 27, 1921). There he challenged members:

> Would it have been honest and straightforward to continue preaching
> that spiritual science can help mankind, and yet advance no social ideas

at a time when social requirements became as urgent as they are today? Would human love not have progressed in the direction of a social knowledge? Shall we content ourselves with declamations on human love? Or should we not rather progress to real social impulses?

Taking on this spiritual challenge, we permeate ourselves with the orientating knowledge we gathered in all the chapters of Part II. With Part III, we prepare ourselves for acting out of this knowledge. We prepare ourselves from the inside, and together with spiritual and human allies, we collectively engage in the attempt to save the planet for humanity.

As we have seen before, we only have one chance to make this work. We have to prepare to be our best and we have to prepare like we never did before. Our planetary and cosmic future depends on it.

Chapter 8

Self Mastery—Preparing Our Self for Spiritual Battle

The title of this chapter is the mood and essence of this chapter. We are engaging in self-mastery to engage in a spiritual battle, the survival of humanity in the age of extreme technologies including artificial intelligence. For in the process we begin to realize that the most powerful instrument in the spiritual battle is how truly we can be full human beings.

This chapter is the heart of the answer to the challenge of artificial intelligence in the world. Imagine what would happen to the world if even only a few thousand seriously understand, undertake and achieve the task of self-mastery. Steiner envisioned an even smaller number of such individuals to change the world: forty-eight (48)![265]

The first step in self-mastery is to learn to know the thoughts of the Gods. One achieves this through a meditative study of the content of spiritual science, for the contents of the latter are the thoughts of the Gods, not the least of which is the Cosmic Christ.[266] Then we will receive their inspiration on how to deal with extreme technologies. We become more spontaneously creative most of the time. It took a lot of sacrifice on Steiner's part to make this possible.[267] Let us honour it!

In this study phase, we can include an intense study and meditation on the *Philosophy of Spiritual Activity*. To repeat, this is the book that 'wrecked' Ahriman in the sphere of thinking and ideas. We need proficiency in this book to tame him in the sphere of societal life to serve humanity.

Working intensely with this book will activate living thinking and give one access to inspiration from the Etheric world. This access in turn will bring one closer to Christ and to other Etheric realities important in addressing the challenge of artificial intelligence that works with the forces of the fallen ethers.

The second step is to purify one's soul from disturbing influences. This is essential if we are to receive the thoughts of the Gods through our own efforts. If our consciousness is too shackled with the problems of day-to-day existence, we will be inwardly too 'noisy' to receive their inspiring thoughts.

A strong relationship here to the Mysteries of the Grail will be important and can be of tremendous help. It contains the 'method' of freeing one from the traps and allures of the sense world. It also links one up with Parsifal, the last known reincarnation of Mani.[268] When this link is established we get greater knowledge of how to transform Evil to serve humanity, in this case, to transform extreme technologies for truly human ends.

Success in this effort requires the knowledge that, in our present condition, we are not a unity. We can verify this for ourselves phenomenologically.[269] We have two selves: the constructed self (our persona) and our Real Self. Our constructed self holds our belief systems, our ideologies, our programming—all stemming from our socialization into the world. We did not give it to ourselves. The world constructed it into our selves. It is the 'Given' in our lives.

Our Real Self is our free and creative spirit. It has the power to transform the constructed self. It has the power to handle all the fluctuations in our life, our vacillations between doing the good for humanity and doing the good only for our self, as our persona would have it.

We have to learn to see all the automatic programs in our self before we can even dream and dare to change the programming of the world and transforming the algorithms of artificial intelligence. This is a painful process. It requires a lot of sacrifice. But we have to do it.

We will receive inspiration and resolve when we truly meditate on the sacrifices that Christ, Micha-el, Anthroposophia, Master Jesus, Mani, Christian Rosenkreutz, Rudolf Steiner, the Templars and many others did for the sake of awakening, nurturing and defending the truly human so that the latter can evolve into the fully human.

In all these stages, we should really FEEL the import of what we are studying, how we are doing our meditations and how we are purifying ourselves.

Anthroposophists often miss out this feeling aspect because Steiner purposely clothed anthroposophy in cognitive form especially in his *Philosophy of Spiritual Activity*. However, in the chapter 'The Human Individuality' of this book, Steiner shows the proper way that feelings in our soul can be elevated to accompany and warm up our cognitive relationship to the world and to the spirit. Then it prevents us from falling into the trap of cold intellectualism that lames us in life as well as pure sentimentality which mistakes strength of subjective feelings for reality.[270]

In addition, the second, recent and more spiritual scientific revolutions have affirmed the important role of feelings in achieving both inner and outer mastery. Interesting books in this regard are the books of Dr Joe Dispenza and Gregg Braden. They try to connect modern science including but not limited to quantum physics, psychoneuroimmunology, epigenetic biology, and neuroscience, with the spiritual practices of ancient traditions.[271]

A significant amount of their work converges with spiritual science but not in all aspects. But the similarities are significant and the potential for mutual learning and cross-fertilization is promising. (See also Chapter 16.)

Steiner took his own suggestions seriously. In his esoteric classes, he included ritual work as part of the path of development. Steiner made a comment of extreme importance: 'We should not forget that forming a conviction [which can be facilitated by rituals] is one of the holiest human concerns.'[272] Ritual triggers the feeling life, one that enhances the depth and connection with higher spiritual realities. It also makes one more confident and strong in life because the future is experienced in the present as doable.[273]

If one still feels weak, incapable, not knowing what to do, one can at least make a 'report' to the Keepers of Humanity, the highly evolved spiritual and human beings responsible for awakening, nurturing and defending humans. One does this by familiarizing ourselves with all the current news on artificial intelligence and mentally 'reporting' these developments to the Gods and the Masters.[274]

The Keepers of Humanity do not have direct perception of the physical world. They receive the necessary information about current developments in the earth plane when they mentally receive the 'report'. They can then respond by spiritually inspiring not only the person who reported but also others who are open to their inspiration.[275] 'Other' here means any individual anywhere in the world. Even modern science, in its discovery of non-local effects, is beginning to get a glimpse of this process[276] if they pursue this approach to its logical conclusion.

In short the impact of an individual 'report' goes way beyond the individual and potentially to all human beings who are open, consciously or unconsciously, to the substance of the 'report'.

I would like to end with a thought that comes from the very first chapter of Steiner's book on self-mastery, *Knowledge of the Higher Worlds: How is it Achieved?* 'Every idea that does not become your ideal kills a power in your soul; every idea that becomes an ideal engenders life-forces within you.'[277]

It is a very radical statement. If you do not do anything with the spiritual scientific knowledge you take in and transform this knowledge into deeds in the world, you are actually becoming a weaker and weaker person. Even though in your mind you have a lot of knowledge, you are actually laming yourself.

One can observe this in oneself. If we do not do what we are inspired to do, then slowly but surely, we are telling ourselves and becoming convinced that we do not have the inner power to pursue what inspires us. The inspiring idea sits dead and 'stillborn' in our inner life. This is one 'laming' process depicted in the *Knowledge of the Higher Worlds*.

Spiritual science is a map to change the world by activating your True and Essential Self, your Eternal self. Thus, if you say to yourself, 'I have all this wonderful knowledge but in the end, I am really powerless', you are really saying that spiritual scientific knowledge has no power to change the world, and therefore you are telling yourself you are worthless faced with these large challenges confronting humanity.

That is something we surely do not want to happen to us. The world deserves better of us. We must mobilize all that is honourable and worthy in us to take the ideas of anthroposophy and other convergent ideas from any other source, mainstream or not, and turn these ideas into enduring ideals to make technology serve humanity, not destroy it.

These are only initial insights and suggestions. There are many other facets of meditation and self-development that can only be covered in another book devoted to the topic of self-mastery.

Chapter 9

Accessing the Support of the Keepers of Humanity

When we have inwardly prepared, when we have purified ourselves from all egotistic self-serving motives, then this inner purity and clarity makes us ready to access the current wisdom of the Keepers of Humanity. As we have seen in Chapter 5, the Keepers of Humanity are the progressive spiritual beings and highly advanced human beings who have nurtured humanity since time immemorial.

We need their current insights, ideas and plans on how to deal with the existential challenge of extreme technologies. And, as we shall see shortly, they will respond when we consciously and spiritually ask for their guidance and help.

Furthermore, this is not only our spiritual battle. It is also theirs. Whatever happens in the near future, within the next 10 to 20 years, will determine the fate of worlds, ours and theirs. Thus, they are keenly wanting to help us while respecting our freedom and self-initiative in the process.

To do this we need to start rethinking our lives and initiatives as entry points for the entry of the spiritual into our earth world. For after all that is the essence of anthroposophy.

This reframing can happen during meditation. If one's meditation goes deep enough, the spiritual presence of these helpers of humanity will manifest themselves in all kinds of ways. And if we further develop the capacity for spiritual perception, this would be a blessing to humanity. If not, we just have to be conscious and open. And then the inspirations come in. We can test these inspired ideas in real life and, if the ideas are truly inspired, then we will find them accurate and effective.

The support of the spiritual world can also come from the external events of our day-to- day life. One does not have to be clairvoyant to experience the spiritual reality of the Keepers of Humanity. How does it manifest concretely? Here we take a statement from William Murray (who borrowed his last two sentences from Goethe) that has proven its Truth time and time again in the experience of many people who have tried it conscientiously.

Until one is committed, there is hesitancy, the chance to draw back, always ineffectiveness. Concerning all acts of initiative (and creation), there is one elementary truth, the ignorance of which kills countless ideas and splendid plans: that the moment one definitely commits oneself, that providence moves too. A whole stream of events issues from the decision, raising in one's favour all manner of unforeseen incidents, meetings and material assistance, which no man could have dreamt would have come his way.... Whatever you can do or dream you can, begin it. Boldness has genius, power and magic in it![278]

We need to understand the term 'commitment' here in the sense of Steiner's *Philosophy of Spiritual Activity*. In Part I of Steiner's book, one gets to know the thoughts of the Gods. (See Chapter 8 above.) Then, out of freedom, one has to decide whether to align oneself with these thoughts that concern themselves with cosmic processes and the future of humanity.

If one is committed, then Part II of the book shows us how to effectively execute that commitment that has now transformed itself, the language of the *Philosophy of Spiritual Activity*, from a moral intuition to moral imagination and finally to moral technique. Part II also shows us how to be faithful to this commitment no matter what blows and sufferings in life one receives. This is our 'love for the deed' that is highlighted in Part II of this book. Because of this real and unrelenting love and commitment to the higher ideals of humanity, then Divine Providence, the Keepers of Humanity, will respond.

If one keeps a daily journal, one can see the manifestation of Divine Providence in one's life. It can come in a crucial meeting; it can appear in a newspaper article that answers long-standing questions that one has; it can happen during a heart-felt or even ordinary conversation; it can appear in email messages; it can manifest in spiritual dreams; it can come in the central messages of movies; it can come in countless ways.

The key is to focus on your intention, your initiative, what you want to happen in the world as a result of your commitment and service to humanity. Then, inner and outer events will clearly reveal themselves as connected with your intention. The new science, the second and more spiritual scientific revolution, documents the reality of this personal experience.[279]

I need to emphasize a key temptation in this process. Knowing the power of this approach, one may start using it for personal gain, devoid of any sense of service to the world or even if externally this altruistic service seems to be the case. From everything that has been articulated, this egotistic motivation will attract a different set of spiritual beings to help achieve the personal goals.

These will not be the Keepers of Humanity that we have discussed in this book. In reality, the spiritual energies and beings of the universe that promote egotism will be the ones that will endeavour to make one's egotistic and self-serving intentions manifest.

In actuality, these are the spiritual beings that are in opposition to Micha-el, the spiritual being most active in ensuring the purity of human motive and execution, in service to the entire evolutionary future of humanity. Thus one may unwittingly lend support to the Spiritual Powers behind Artificial Intelligence due to one's selfish and self-serving intentions.

This is the reason why, in the Gospel of St Matthew 7:15–20, Christ warned:

> Beware of false prophets, which come to you in sheep's clothing, but inwardly they are ravening wolves. Ye shall know them by their fruits. Do men gather grapes of thorns, or figs of thistles? Even so every good tree bringeth forth good fruit; but a corrupt tree bringeth forth evil fruit. A good tree cannot bring forth evil fruit neither can a corrupt tree bring forth good fruit. Every tree that bringeth not forth good fruit is hewn down, and cast into the fire. 7:20 *Wherefore by their fruits ye shall know them.* [Emphasis added.]

And then in Matthew 7:21–23, the warning of Christ intensifies:

> Not every one that saith unto me, Lord, Lord, shall enter into the kingdom of heaven; *but he that doeth the will of my Father which is in heaven.* Many will say to me in that day, Lord, Lord, have we not prophesied in thy name? and in thy name have cast out devils? and in thy name done many wonderful works? And then will I profess unto them, I never knew you: depart from me, ye that work iniquity. [In short, egotistic desires and intentions are the opposite of genuine service to the cosmic order.] [Emphasis and commentary added.]

Clearly, Christ, having created humans, understands perfectly how the human mind rationalizes self-serving motives. The human being can claim to do things for the world but, in reality, deep within, this work (which seems outwardly good) is only for himself/herself.

That is why the key to real support from the Keepers of Humanity is to align one's purpose and intentions with the 'Will of the Father', the Divine Source of All Existence. In this way, our motives and intentions will be good if we align them with the evolutionary thoughts of the Father.

This is not a belief. We can draw out this kind of thinking from the current findings of astrophysics, if we are brave enough to do so. The scientific study of the nature and evolution of the physical universe as brought to light by current astrophysics[280] lends qualified support for the thoughts expressed above. The majority of professional astrophysicists prefer the 'deistic design' in place of the multiverse hypothesis to explain the 'anthropic principle' or the incredible fine-tuning of over a hundred parameters in the evolution of the universe.[281]

Incidentally, this highly significant development lends further support to the discussions in Part II above regarding the reality of spiritual beings. Chapter 16 below will give a fuller treatment of the 'anthropic principle' in astrophysics.

Before, we took things in faith. Now, both modern astrophysics and spiritual science are giving us the knowledge to align our intentions and actions, out of love, for the highest possibilities of humanity, which, in effect, is the 'Will of the Father'.

Steiner, using epistemological language, speaks about this in his book, *The Philosophy of Spiritual Activity*.

> My action will be 'good' if my intuition, immersed in love, exists in the right way *within* the relationship between things; this can be experienced intuitively; the action will be 'bad' if this is not the case.[282] [Emphasis added.]

These words may look vague and unclear or even gobbledygook if one has not read and worked with the entire book. So here is another quote to put the above statement in context of the spirit of the entire book.

> For an insight which recognizes how ideas are intuitively *experienced* as a self-sustaining reality [aka the rather vague 'relationship between things'], it is clear that in the sphere of the world of ideas man penetrates in *cognition* into something which is universal for all men, but when he derives from that same idea world the intuitions for his acts of will, then he individualizes a member of this idea world by means of *the same activity* which, as a general human one, he unfolds in the spiritual-ideal process of cognition.[283] (195–196)

What Steiner is saying is that the ideas that we have come from a unified 'idea-world',[284] the 'relationship between things'. We can phenomenologically experience the reality of this statement by seeing that this 'idea-world' has an inner coherence of its own. Thus they are 'universal' for all human beings. When we are really active in our thinking, we can inwardly experience gaps in our own thinking process and logic, resulting in doubts and uncertainty. On the other hand, we get excited when we are beginning to experience the true inner relationships of many empirical experiences that we may have had.

The late Sergei Prokofieff, the most lucid and encompassing scholar of Steiner's spiritual science, captures the discussions above with a different translation of the quote on what constitutes 'good' or 'bad' from the perspective of *The Philosophy of Spiritual Activity*.

> I do not work out mentally whether my action is good or bad; I carry it out because I *love* it. My action will be 'good' if my intuition, steeped in love, finds the right place within the *intuitively experienceable world continuum*. It will be 'bad' if this is not the case.[285] [Italics in the original.] [Emphasis added.]

Note how the phrase 'relationship between things' gets properly translated as 'world continuum'.

In short the 'world continuum' is the reality that the universe is one integral whole. It is a 'world continuum' in terms of space, time and Being. In the beginning, we access the space and time reality of this 'world continuum' through 'intuitive thinking'. This is not an abstract or nominal access. It is empirical access and is experienced as such.

This intuitive thinking is a spiritual faculty in humans that can have a direct *experience* of the inside of this 'world continuum' in the form of Ideas. These ideas constitute the Reality of this 'world continuum'. So our deed is 'good' if we align it to this dynamic, evolving 'world continuum'.

In the higher stages of knowledge as described by spiritual science and attained by Rudolf Steiner, the next higher stage of consciousness accesses the spiritual Beings that stand behind the Ideas of this 'world continuum'. This higher cognition can be in the form of images of Being (Imaginative Cognition), then 'words' of Being (Inspirative Cognition) until finally oneness and communion with Being itself is achieved (Intuitive Cognition).[286]

But the beauty is that the reality of these higher stages can be experienced like a holon in Ideas produced through intuitive thinking, the overlapping boundary between the current stage of human consciousness and the higher stages of consciousness where there is a direct experience of the spiritual, not one mediated by living Ideas. In other words, intuitive Ideas are accurate depiction of higher realities even without the necessary spiritual organs of cognition to achieve these higher realities.[287]

The search for a 'theory of everything' in modern science is a more technical expression of the belief of most, if not all scientists, regarding the underlying unity of all existence. Otherwise, the notion of universal laws in science could not exist. While mainstream scientists refer to the 'theory of everything' in a physical sense, epistemologically there is no barrier in including the spiritual in an all-pervasive monist view of the world.

Einstein went even further and remarked: 'The harmony of natural law reveals an Intelligence of such superiority that, compared with it, all the systematic thinking and acting of human beings is an utterly insignificant reflection.'[288]

We access the ideas from this idea-world through intuitive thinking or cognition. But this idea-world is nothing but the inner coherence of the entire fabric of reality, including, for the non-materialist, spiritual realities. And for those who have the capacity to see this from the other side, this 'idea-world' or 'world-all' is nothing but the coherence of the Logos.

And spiritually understood, as in this book, this Logos is the Cosmic Christ, the source of all existence. And as St John tells us in his very first verses, the Logos, the Word, was with God, the Father, and the Word was God.

So, to sum up, in our intuitive thinking, we have the capacity to access the World All, including the intentions and activities of Spiritual Beings. This is the 'providence' of Murray. And, if we freely, and in love, align ourselves with intentions of 'providence', then 'providence' moves too. Providence responds to this genuinely altruistic motivation and provides all kinds of amazing support.

There is another hurdle to be aware of in terms of aligning with 'providence'. To flow with the world process, one needs to be able to distinguish between two different kinds of Karma. There is Karma from the past which is the usual conception of Karma. What we have done in the past affects us today. But there is also a Karma of the Future which one creates as a result of accessing future intentions in the act of free and creative spiritual activity and puts this vision into action.[289] In this situation, the future we envision affects our present reality.

The mainstream world calls this capacity of humans as learning from the future. This learning is, at the same time, accessing the possibilities of the future that show themselves in the process of 'presencing'. The academic and professional equivalent of this learning from the future is the Theory U process of Otto Scharmer from the Massachusetts Institute of Technology.[290]

The Murray-Goethe 'quote' above deals with Karma from the Future. Your intentions have to be very clear when you activate them. For whatever events come to meet you, are deeply connected with your intentions.

You cannot interpret everything that happens to come your way spontaneously as Divine Providence. It may be past Karma masquerading as future Karma. Depending on the context and timing of its appearance, an unexpected event may be a temptation from powers opposing humanity, to divert you from what you really have to do in life. Your intention, arrived at through intuitive thinking as discussed above, is your key to discerning the essential from the non-essential that meets you in life.

Steiner also gives a systematic and deeper account of how to align oneself with the spiritual powers that guide humanity, or Divine Providence in this context. He gave the details in a series of lectures that are now collected in book form entitled, *Background to the Gospel of St. Mark*.[291]

One who has tried Steiner's suggestions knows it works. It can actually reveal the ideas of the Gods without one having to be clairvoyant or clairaudient to receive these Divine ideas.

Similar to what happens with the Murray-Goethe quote, the spiritual can speak to one in many different ways. And these ideas are living ones. They even suggest refinements on what you are intending to do. Their help can come in the form of new and innovative strategies. It is like being guided by the spiritual Keepers of Humanity on a daily basis.

This reality can also happen on a collective scale. And this happened in the 'How We Will' forum in Los Angeles, USA, in 2017.[292] Because of the proceedings of the previous days of intense conversations and spiritual insights and a collective mobilization of the will to do the good, the gateway to the spiritual world opened. Those who could sense or perceive it felt the reality.

There was an incredible amount of inspirations that flowed into the sacred space that the participants had created. The spiritual world communicated amazing insights and possibilities that, if participants cared and nurtured them, could enlighten them on what to do in the age of the fallen spiritual machine.

In Matthew 7:9–1 Christ gives this rebuttal to those who do not believe that providence (the 'Father') will respond to calls for help.

> Or what [kind] of man [is he], if his son asks him for bread, will give him a stone? Or if he asks for a fish, will give him a serpent? If you then, who are evil, know how to give good gifts to your children, how much more will your Father who is in heaven give good things to those who ask him!

In other words, what kind of Providence is it if an individual, consciously knowing the direction of the evolution of the world and putting his whole life in its service, is only given a 'stone', basically nothing, by the spiritual world? That will not happen. And knowing this makes us even more determined to be what the spiritual powers have nurtured us to be, that is to be fully human, and enable the spiritual Keepers of Humanity not only to journey with us, but to help us in our greatest of trials, the unprecedented possibility of human extinction through Artificial Super Intelligence.

The awesome allies and friends of moral humanity are there. The Keepers of Humanity are there, ready and willing to help us. But, respecting our freedom, they need us to make the first move. Let us all, in our own ways, ask for their Presence and help. They will respond. They, together with humans who consciously partner with them, will help transform Artificial Intelligence from a threat to a blessing for humanity.

Chapter 10

Collective Human Intelligence (CHI)

We have seen the actual face of the opposing powers that would doom us. We now understand the nature and mission of Evil. We have taken a closer look at our spiritual allies that can overpower these demonic forces and how to be in touch and in collaboration with them. We have taken a closer look at the two milestones of the School of Micha-el, the incredible defender and fighter for human freedom. We have seen the significance of Steiner's statement that 'Ahriman is wrecked'. We have taken a look at how we can inwardly purify ourselves for the spiritual battle ahead.

Now, for our final preparation, we need to appreciate the key strategic importance of *Collective Human Intelligence (CHI)* in our struggle to create a better world. There are eight aspects connected with its strategic importance. We will now go briefly through them one by one.

First, and most obvious, we cannot solve the AI challenge alone

Extreme technology is a collective challenge. Thousands of brilliant minds, with billions of dollars of resources backing them up are creating the machines that have the potential to wipe out humanity. We need to respond to it collectively. We have to gather all those who are awake and committed, give it everything we have collectively: resources, time, talents, networks, structures and all the rest.

Second, the spiritual task of AI/AGI/ASI is to awaken all human beings to their true and awesome spiritual nature

If only one or a few human beings will wake up and solve the 'alignment challenge' of ASI, if they could, then other human beings will be left behind in lower stages of human evolution. They will become the 'laggards' of humanity's evolutionary possibilities.

We are now moving past beyond the stage of the individual hero who solves challenges for others. That would not be proper in a spiritual age where all humans have the task to develop that spiritual wakefulness that comes from consciously facing the darkness that threatens to engulf humanity.

We are entering the stage of the 'collective hero'. But this is not a 'collective' that suppresses one's unique individuality and freedom at the bidding of the 'collective'. Rather this is the coming together of free and creative individuals who will work together for the larger goal of creating a better humanity. Out of this working, a free-flowing creative space results where unique solutions to seemingly impossible challenges emerge due to the proper associative creativity of human beings.

Third, collective action triggers what Steiner calls the Saturn path

Bernard Lievegoed clearly articulates this in his book, *Forming Curative Communities*. The Saturn Path is a totally different spiritual process that enables ordinary human beings, who breathe and work together, in service of the world process, to be as gifted as an Initiate or a highly advanced human being! It allows us to obtain capacities that we do not normally have as struggling individuals.[293]

Christ also referred to this. In Matthew 18:20, He said: 'For where two or three are gathered together in my name, there am I in the midst of them.'

And this gives a new angle to the last letter of Steiner to members of the Society on how to overcome sub-nature or ahrimanic technologies. First, we have to be united in our commitment to advance the intentions of Christ for humanity. Not our separate 'Is' but 'Christ in Us'. Then we access the Etheric Christ.

So now we can rise above to the Etheric world to the same extent that our technologies have plunged humanity downward into the abyss. This is a collective implementation of Steiner's challenge on dealing with sub-nature or AI in modern terms. It opens the possibility for the deployment of 'moral technology' or etheric-based technologies that act in the physical world. Paul Emberson has explained 'moral technology' clearly in his book, *The Human Spirit and Machines*.[294]

Fourth, Collective Human Intelligence (CHI) returns Cosmic Intelligence to Micha-el

Ahriman has used the technique of divide-and-conquer to capture significant aspects of Cosmic Intelligence. And with this, Ahriman has inspired millions of humans to do his bidding and create technologies that would ultimately degrade and exterminate true humans.

However, if human beings truly collaborate together in conscious service to the two milestones of Micha-el and his School, then that schooling would not have been in vain. Then Micha-el himself would be very active in further elaborating the free deeds that would arise from humans out of collective endeavours.

Spiritual science defines 'cosmic intelligence' to mean the appropriate relationships between the spiritual beings of the cosmos. Only if human beings mirror this on earth in the way they work together, will this earthly form of 'cosmic intelligence' become the appropriate basis for giving back to cosmic intelligence to Micha-el.

Fifth, Collective Human Intelligence (CHI) allows us to leverage the daughter and other movements in anthroposophy

Michaela Glöckler, MD once shared that a total of five million individuals are involved with or benefit from the daughter movements of anthroposophy.[295] The permutation of interactions contained in that number practically reaches infinity. There are infinite ways of making these individuals effective in the service of humanity.

Michaela tried to mobilize these individuals into a European-wide alliance called ELIANT.[296] The intent was to make the European Commission and Parliament, when they make policies, hear the perspectives of those involved in anthroposophic medicine, Steiner education, and bio-dynamic agriculture. It has achieved some form of success. But a lot more can be done and should be done.

From the karma lectures we know that anthroposophists have civilization-creating powers in their will. Unfortunately, many were or are afraid unconsciously of what Steiner calls 'the sting' that hits back on the anthroposophist whenever he or she wants to do something significant in the world. But we can decide not to grow with that fear, now that we know that our fear and lack of courage is starting to plunge humanity into the abyss. We have to forge ahead despite our past failures. We will deal more with the transformation of failure in Chapter 19.

But if we have the courage, we will acknowledge that we are embedded in a very rich network of relationships (karmic or not) that, if we are conscious about it, will enable us to achieve the task of turning the tide in favour of humanity. We need to take stock of our friends and network. Who among our friends are strategically poised to do something about the AI challenge?

Sixth, the need for Collective Human Intelligence allows us to appreciate other movements who are sincerely striving for a better world

Three things stare at us that are shaking us to remove our own worst attitude: the anthroposophical sense of privilege and exceptionality.

The first 'antidote' is to recognize that this egotistic sense of privilege has been and continues to be a stranglehold on the movement. This has held the global Anthroposophical Society back for so long, has made our daughter movements suffer, and ultimately became one of the major causes for the lack of 'culmination', the second milestone of the Micha-elic School and the ultimate mission of anthroposophy in our time.

Epistemologically, in *The Philosophy of Spiritual Activity*, we know the power of living thinking to access the thoughts of the World-All. Therefore, all human beings have the potential to uniquely enter into World-All from their own specific situation and place in life. And from that entry point, they can elaborate the 'organism of thought' to arrive at fuller and fuller understanding and appreciation of the World-All and then act out of love for it.

Others may not be anthroposophists but they may have more powers of intuitive thinking than anthroposophists who know a lot about the faculty of intuitive thinking but do little to activate it.

As we shall see in Chapters 16 and 18, there are a significant number of people in the world who have intuitive thinking and they have come up with some of the most amazing discoveries and initiatives in all walks of life. It would be much better to form alliances with them than to unconsciously think anthroposophists are far more advanced than these outstanding individuals. Anthroposophists have more knowledge of anthroposophy, but this knowledge mostly remains head knowledge and remains un-internalized, abstract, non-living, and not implemented.

The second antidote for 'anthroposophical exceptionality' which hinders Collective Human Intelligence, is the statement of Christ quoted earlier: when two or more are gathered in His name, then Christ is in the midst of them. Obviously, this statement did not just refer to two or more anthroposophists but two or more human beings.

Finally, the third 'antidote' is the nature of Micha-el's regency itself. Micha-el is the Time Spirit of the entire earth, for humanity (Chapter 5). He thus inspires all human beings. And this inspiration enters all humans through the manner of intuitive thinking described above. One can infer, when problems arose with humans (anthroposophists), who should have been more conscious carriers of His task here on earth, Micha-el further intensified His work with other humans who had the unconscious gift for truly free and loving deeds for the world.

Micha-el has a special relationship with the anthroposophical move-ment because most of the individuals who, in their true karma, found themselves there, participated in the School of Micha-el as preparation for their incarnation in the present time. But these were the very individuals who, for some weakness in their life, betrayed Him when they betrayed Steiner, then and now.

But Micha-el is not judgemental in the human sense. He does not nourish hurts or wounds. He objectively assesses the deeds of humans. If it is truly an altruistic deed, for the Cosmic Good, and, even if it comes from one who unconsciously betrayed Him in the past, then Micha-el will accept this deed and work out its ramifications into the Cosmos for times to come.[297] He is beyond the sympathy and antipathy of everyday human life. He is like Christ, in His Sun-like nature. The Sun shines on good and evil humans alike, including those that had previously betrayed Him. So, if we failed Him in the past, we have to learn to forgive ourselves and move on to do the deeds that Micha-el has awaited from us for so long. What better time to do this than the urgent now when human existence itself is in danger.

Let us start the joy of meeting others who are not within the anthroposophical movement. It is really possible to do this.

Seventh, understanding the urgent need for Collective Human Intelligence (CHI) heals our past and excites us to re-engage the future with fresh enthusiasm to do the task we should have done a long time ago

We touched aspects of this in the connection with Micha-el above in this chapter. Additionally, we need to move beyond the individual 'bubbles' of our own initiatives. This can take the form of consciously linking with the creative possibilities inherent in each individual initiative and skill as well as entire movements. Part IV and Chapter 11 below elaborate more on this.

Eighth, it allows us to prepare for the next stage of human evolution[298]

We need to prototype now the formation of true spiritual community that is the task of the next cultural stage of humanity, if it survives the genocide of humanity in the current age of artificial intelligence.

These communities will support all in striving to be fully human as well as enable the community to be the collective sheath of spiritual beings. The latter will then inspire these communities to do deeds that will lift us out of the abyss we are sliding into rapidly.

To bring into further focus all eight aspects above regarding the importance and necessity of Collective Human Intelligence (CHI), this passage from Steiner is more than highly relevant for the theme of this chapter.

The further effects of prayer . . . cannot yet be discussed today, however unbiased the discussion might be. Thus, to understand that a community [or collective] prayer in which the forces rising from a praying community flow together has an enhanced spiritual force and therefore an intensified effect on reality, cannot be easily accepted by the ordinary consciousness today.[299] [Emphasis added.]

This tongue-in-cheek statement by Steiner gives us a hint of the importance of collective prayer and action. He is speaking of an 'intensified effect on reality' that is hard to envision by ordinary human consciousness.

One small indication of what Steiner might have hinted at is the results of the research of the Global Consciousness Project, once based out of Princeton University. This scientific programme has convincingly demonstrated that collective human consciousness, even if coming from different parts of the world, can impact and affect the dynamics of matter itself.[300]

A second and more spiritual scientific revolution is also demonstrating in such diverse fields as astrophysics, neuroscience, quantum physics, and epigenetic biology the reality that consciousness affects the dynamics of matter. In Chapter 16, we shall see that some scientists go even further and are showing that consciousness itself is the 'matrix' of matter, that is, matter originates from consciousness. These point to the truth of Steiner's spiritual monist view of the world as articulated in his *Philosophy of Spiritual Activity*.

Never before has humanity been asked to act in a massively collective way to secure its future. We may all do our individual initiatives but if we do not start connecting the dots, those dots are going to be connected for us in a very different way by spiritual Powers opposed to the unfolding of the fully human. And if we do not form alliances for the Good, it is very clear who will win the day. Humanity will continue plunging into the abyss.

The time has come to go beyond the 'Islands of Light' strategy. That was appropriate in the initial phases of anthroposophy. But that is now totally inappropriate today. If we want to save humanity, we have to be braver and bolder. We have to advance Collective Human Intelligence at all levels of society and in every appropriate aspect of our life. Nothing else will do. Nothing less is expected of us.

Only by acting with unified purpose, that is, out of an awareness of the processes, direction and needs of 'World Cosmic Process' will we have a fighting chance. We cannot sit and ponder too long. We do not have much time before Armageddon finally arrives if we fail to find an answer to the 'alignment challenge' of artificial intelligence.

Part IV

ACTIVATING THE DAUGHTER MOVEMENTS

Cultivate spiritual science first of all as a concern of the heart, in the way in which it should be cultivated individually, so that we may progress. Cultivate what you have thus taken in, and then bring it out to humanity in every sphere of life, bring out what you have thus taken in! You will then gradually find the path enabling you, in the present difficult and earnest time of probation, to do the right thing for humanity, according to your place in life.[301]

This suggestion from Steiner is a good place to start in terms of getting an overview of how to develop Collective Human Intelligence (CHI) on the ground and then develop it further, starting from where we are.

Anthroposophists may already know this. During Steiner's time, there were 12,000 members and five initiatives. In 2017 there are 44,000 members and 40,000 initiatives.[302] As mentioned in Chapter 10, these initiatives attract the support of five million individuals. That is amazing and hopeful! But as we said, this is not enough when compared with the millions of initiatives of civil society around the planet.[303]

This is not the place to take a closer look at the quality of these anthroposophical initiatives. But it does reveal a desire among members to do something constructive in the world. There are two burning questions, though.

First, are these initiatives providing answers at the level where the burning questions of the world are being asked? Second, does the 'moral technique', in the sense of Steiner's *Philosophy of Spiritual Activity*, for social and societal engagement prevail in these initiatives?

The answer to the first question, with some outstanding exceptions, is a clear 'No'. If it were a 'Yes', then anthroposophy would have culminated. But as we saw earlier, and in more detail later (Chapter 19), the culmination did not happen.

The answer to the second question is also most likely a 'No' for most of these initiatives. This conclusion follows from the answer to the first question. If the moral technique did exist, it is most likely that there would be a positive answer to the first question because then the culmination would have happened.

There is no attempt here at fault-finding. This is a statement of an objective fact. As Socrates said, 'Awareness of ignorance is the beginning of wisdom'. As Plato more accurately sums it up: 'The wisest of you men is he who has realized, like Socrates, that in respect of wisdom he is really worthless.'[304]

At least we know where we are. Now if we have the Micha-elic Will (Chapter 21), we will try again. We will learn from our shortcomings and mistakes, and do things better the next time. This is the whole intent of this part of the book. We have to develop this goodwill and intent for the future of humanity because the cries for solutions are getting louder.

How will a complex and sophisticated movement like the global anthroposophical movement coordinate its efforts?

The organizing force for our present situation is the understanding of intentions of Christ, the Micha-el Mysteries and its mission in our time. This will act as the organizing force.

Just like the spiritual thought organism, that is the Logos, all the different efforts in service of the Logos and Micha-el are unified in the spiritual sphere. It also allows our spiritual allies to move and act in ways to integrate all the existing efforts. And those here on earth will get an inkling of this spiritual integration and respond accordingly.

While the AI scientists are trying to figure out the AI 'alignment' issue, we have our own 'alignment' issue to work out. We have to find a way to align with each other's work and initiative as well as align with the overall mission of the Micha-elic School, which is deeply connected with the future of humanity. We have to work in alliances so we can transform AI from a force of potential massive disaster and extinction to a powerful aide for the good of humanity.

Let us begin with some considerations of 'moral techniques', if you like, that we can take with us as we work with the daughter movements of anthroposophy. These principles apply across the board for all daughter movements. And they also apply when we build alliances with other social, spiritual and scientific movements of our time. (See Chapter 18.)

Chapter 11

Conditions for Decisive Action

We will flesh out two kinds of considerations in this chapter. One moves us through space and time in the sense that we start with the smallest possible source of change, ourselves, and then from there move on through time to greater and greater alliances with others. The other concerns itself with the substance that must permeate all the different efforts at the different levels of intensity and scale.

From Self to the World: Considerations in Activation

Here is an idealized picture of how one can start acting out of Anthroposophy from the individual up to the global level.[305] However, things may unfold in a different sequence depending on who is involved and what opportunities emerge.[306]

Self-Empowerment

We cannot begin the transformative work if we believe that we are too small compared with the AI challenges we are facing. Sure, it is a kind of David versus Super Goliath kind of challenge. But with self-mastery and the collective will of humanity, it can be done!

It cannot be over-emphasized enough that, if we think we cannot do it, then we will not be able to do it. This is known in social science as the Pygmalion Effect.[307] It is a self-fulfilling prophecy. If we think we cannot do it, then we will not be able to do it. We have to avoid this negative mindset at all cost!

Research

We all have to do a lot of research whether we are students, professionals, businessmen, scientists, teachers, and civil society activists. AI is invading and radically transforming all areas of human existence and it is important to be aware of these fast-paced changes. We cannot constructively engage in the AI transformation work if we do not have our facts straight.

There is a systematic way of doing research. We will be more than happy to help you out with it. Just contact us using the contact information provided at the end of this book.

Collaboration

We have to link with each other. When we inform each other and enrich each other's knowledge, we will enable Collective Human Intelligence (CHI) to emerge. When we help each other see patterns, then we can trigger the process of creatively transforming AI from a destructive force to a constructive one.

We cannot foretell what the strategies will be. They will only emerge when we collaborate. A greater intelligence will be born in the groups that collaborate, the greater wisdom of an intentional group or movement, that can generate unexpectedly effective solutions to the challenge of artificial intelligence.

Study and Action Groups

One manifestation of collaboration is to start forming study and action groups wherever you are. You can start organizing seminars and workshops. Doing research and developing a creative response strategy is much easier when you are doing it with others. As famous social scientist Margaret Mead once said: 'Never doubt that a small group of thoughtful, committed citizens can change the world. Indeed, it is the only thing that ever did.'[308]

Networking and Advocacy in Society

Once we have enough minimum preparation, we can then engage in advocacy in all spheres of life: in civil society, including and especially quad media, business and government. Government can begin the process of hearings in aid of legislation on the future of the country in the era of artificial intelligence. Those in business can work on ethical and empowering forms of technologies.

Convergence

When we have done all the necessary homework at the individual, group, local and national levels, we can all come together and project our efforts at the global level. There are all kinds of platforms in the Internet to scale up our local or national advocacies to the global level.[309]

The Mood and Substance We Must Carry from Self to the World

Entry Points

Daughter movements are Entry Points to the larger systemic issue, not ends in themselves. We need to find ways for daughter movements to move from having simple local concerns to be aware of the tremendous issues at stake.

For example, how can each daughter movement transform the AI temptations based on super health, super strength, super intelligence, and physical immortality? In case of the latter, AI scientists are seeking physical immortality because anthroposophy has not succeeded in making the scientific understanding of reincarnation a factor in global civilization. If it had, mainstream scientist would not spend time on their AI fiction because we are already immortal through our eternal spirit.

The Steiner Education movement, for another example, can create strong resistance and advocacies around the already existing issue of the digitalization of the education system at all levels. In fact, ELIANT, an anthroposophical initiative, is already doing this at the European policy level.

Celebrate and Respect Our Diversity

Some of us can act at the global and national levels. Others can only act at the local level. But all these are entry points to the larger whole, to the Logos that encompasses us all. Because we are diverse, we can activate different parts of the Logos 'organism'.

We have many entry points, many points that can flourish into something significant. At the same time, taken all together this will then truly begin the creation of a Micha-elic civilization which after all was the intent of all who participated in the Micha-el School and who have subsequently taken up anthroposophy as their life's path. Our diversity makes the Micha-elic civilization real.

Inspiring Movement Narratives

We need to develop inspiring narratives for our movement. Positive narratives give hope and help prevent burnout.[310]

For example, we can highlight amazing initiatives in the anthro-posophical movement that is really attuned to the challenge of the time. The anthroposophical 'emergency pedagogy' of Bernd Ruf is one such initiative. This pedagogy is now one of the world's most effective responses to natural disasters and is working mostly with non-anthro-posophists. Or another is the work of Ute Cramer, transforming a slum area into an international haven for inter-cultural exchange.[311]

Or these narratives can highlight stories about how to understand the darkness of our times. It can highlight that darkness is not merely the absence of Light, but the absence of hope that Light will return and it did return in this one particular initiative. There are many stories of this nature in the different anthroposophical initiatives around the world.

Or there may still be other narratives about never giving up and taking risks when things seem really hopeless and as a result amazing things started to happen.

Importance of Situating Even the Smallest Alliance In the Cosmic Context

All these different examples, and they are not complete, due to the limitations of number of pages in this book, show that there are infinite ways to live anthroposophically in the Age of Artificial Intelligence. The key is to have the larger context and framing of the Micha-el School as well as the whole spiritual scientific framework on universal evolution, and the cosmic challenges facing us, and then do the work in this context.

We need to think big, act small or in appropriate scales. This will create a large impact because the framing at the level of the School of Micha-el means that our initiative and alliance now have the inner spiritual force that can move them from the initial states of an Entry Point to being a strategic Point at the global and cosmic levels, which in this case, is a unique and powerful response to the challenge of artificial intelligence.

According to Lynne McTaggart in her book, *The Intention Experiment* cited above, intention creates a spiritual Field for its realization in the scale with which it is being envisioned. This totally converges with what anthroposophy considers Micha-elic Action as described in various places above.

There is a little-known fact about Steiner that has a lot to say about placing our actions in a larger cosmic context.

There was an article in *Das Goetheanum* which showed that during World War I Steiner was open to leaving Dornach and his construction project to become a news correspondent for one of the international news networks. He wanted to put forward a more truthful perspective about World War 1.[312] Had it materialized, that small initiative would have had a huge global and cosmic impact.

Steiner thought cosmically and therefore he saw the daughter movements as embedded in a larger context and they could only find their meaning in that larger context. If that larger context is cut off, then the daughter movements will start experiencing all kinds of problems.

One can see this very clearly when Steiner allegedly made this statement. 'Without the [societal] threefolding movement as context, Waldorf education is "cat's food".' In other words, without this larger framing, the impact of anthroposophical education would be limited.[313]

With these minimalist guidelines, we are now ready to take a closer look at the daughter movements of anthroposophy and then, later, at how we form alliances with global civil society and the rapidly emerging second more spiritual scientific revolution.

Chapter 12

The Strategic Role of the Bio-Dynamic Agriculture Movement

When considering how to activate the daughter movements of anthroposophy, we will begin with the bio-dynamic agriculture movement. This movement will have an unusual role to play in the age of artificial intelligence. Fortunately, the bio-dynamic leadership in the world, based in the Goetheanum in Dornach, Switzerland, is totally open to alliance building and networking and has organized pioneering conferences to this end. (See below, this chapter.)

In the Preface, we read about the exceptional strategic role that organic and bio-dynamic agriculture will play in the era of artificial intelligence. In the South, it will provide badly needed jobs for workers who will be displaced by the massive global automation using AI. In these countries, bio-dynamic and organic agriculture will also simultaneously eradicate poverty.[314] In the industrialized North, organic agriculture and bio-dynamic agriculture will also absorb labour rendered redundant by automation.

There are four reasons why organic agriculture will play an important and key role in the rapidly arising world of artificial intelligence. Starting here, to avoid confusion, the phrase 'organic agriculture' will also include bio-dynamic farming. And if bio-dynamic agriculture is meant, the term itself will be used.

First, there is huge demand for organic food, not just any kind of food, as we shall see below. Spain has over two million hectares of land under organic cultivation and they cannot keep up with the demand for organic food. In the 2016 Biofach Trade show in Germany, the largest supermarket of Germany wanted to stock a third of its shelf space with bio-dynamic products. That demand, from just one source alone, could not be met by all the existing bio-dynamic farms of Germany.[315]

A former executive of a global supermarket chain also revealed that the sales of conventional food have reached a plateau but the sales of organic foods are skyrocketing.[316]

Second, and connected with the first, there is also a huge search for holistic health products and services. According to Derek Gehl, an early pioneer in Internet-marketing and a global guru on digital marketing, the largest search category in Google is Health. He further mentioned that, when people get sick, they go to 'Dr Google', the search engine.[317]

People are getting fed up with the claims of the pharmaceutical industry as they get to learn about the dangerous side effects of medical pills and pesticides found in conventional food.[318] Furthermore, they are also starting to learn about the low nutritional value of conventional foods in addition to the toxic residues of pesticides found in these foods. This global search for better and more genuine health is spurring the demand for organic foods.

Third, people are getting more sophisticated in discerning the difference between organic foods and genetically engineered products. The rejection of these genetically engineered products is starting to snowball as can be seen in the global campaign against biotech giants like Monsanto.[319] They know the big difference between dangerous synthetic foods and organic foods.

And even if AI produces synthetic food from cellulose-based plants using nanotechnology and biotechnology, even if AI promises to produce meat by sophisticated 3D printing methods,[320] these foods will not find a market in a world that is well educated on the profound health benefits of organic food.

Fourth and one of its most important strategic roles, organic agriculture can help all daughter and social movements of the world. It can demonstrate how advocates can mainstream a more ecological and/or spiritual culture because organic agriculture has done it amidst all resistances.

If the awareness and culture is there, AI will not make headway in the lives of billions if there is no appreciation for or no demand for the AI product in question. It shows that, if citizens are truly awake and can distinguish between fake and real products and services, then they will go for the real thing. AI has been slowed down in the area of organic agriculture and AI can ultimately be transformed in other areas of life. Organic agriculture shows us how.

It is interesting to observe how anthroposophy played a key role in this whole process of the global mainstreaming of organic agriculture. First, because it was established earlier, bio-dynamic agriculture inspired many practices in organic farming. Many pioneers of organic farming were influenced by bio-dynamic agriculture.[321]

Second, the entire environmental movement began as a campaign against pesticide spraying. Rachel Carson wrote her famous book, *Silent Spring*, in the early 1960s. Previous to writing her book, Carson, together with M.C. Richards, an anthroposophist, had filed a legal case against pesticide spraying.[322]

Carson's book became a global bestseller, intensified interest in organic farming, and launched the largest social movement in history: the environmental movement. This movement is still very active today and is most visible in the global climate change debate. The environmental movement is also behind the massive interest in organic food and farming today.

We need to note though that it took more than 80 years to mainstream bio-dynamic agriculture together with organic farming. And we need to mainstream anthroposophy and all the daughter movements in less than two decades. If we think of the approach, as strategic homeopathic involvement, leveraging key existing movements, plus the appropriate use of the Internet, then it can be done.

It would seem ironic for some that we would use the Internet to transform AI to serve human needs. But this is actually what is required of us today. We should not be running away from technology. Instead we should be using it to bring about the global change that would enable us all to be fully human.

As mentioned above, we can learn from the lessons of the organic and bio-dynamic movement how they arose from being a marginal, heavily maligned movement to one of the most inspiring and dynamic movements today. We can then use the lessons learned in this movement to start transforming the other areas of life, from medicine, to education, to science, to art, and to all the other daughter movements of Anthroposophy as well as the social movements of the world.

Ultimately, if the big tech companies will not listen to customer demand and instead try to manipulate it through advertising and manipulative neuroscience, including the use of CCTV cameras in supermarkets that feed big data for AI to analyze,[323] and if consumers become awake, the big IT companies themselves are in danger of losing their market and plunging their own bottom lines. No matter how powerful they are, if there is no collective demand for their product, these corporations will perish. Consumers will boycott their products and services and create a huge demand for IT products that can truly serve human beings.

When I wrote this paragraph three months ago, I based it mostly on my past experience in global campaigns for integral sustainable development. The issues then involved nuclear power, genetic engineering, pesticides, and one-side economic globalization.

Now, as I write the final draft of this book, the global media is exploding with the Cambridge Analytica scandal involving Facebook.[324] In one week, due to the scandal, Facebook lost $10 billion at the stock market.[325] Two weeks after the scandal erupted, Facebook lost $100 billion in capitalization.[326] Powerful investors were threatening to pull out of Facebook if they do not find a social mission.[327] Governments, in response to citizen and investor outrage all over the world, are now taking a tough look at how to downsize and regulate Facebook.[328]

This development highlights the accuracy of the paragraph immediately above as well as the power for change in an awakened citizenry whether they are in business, government, or civil society.

That is why I am happy to observe how the bio-dynamic movement, for example, is now standing with dignity in the world with a series of global conferences that send the message that the leaders of this movement purposefully want to engage the world. This is very healthy.

Ueli Hurter and Jean-Michel Florin, the current leadership of the Agriculture Section in the Goetheanum at Dornach, have been opening the doors of the Goetheanum to world leaders in agriculture, coming from different streams. These include Vandana Shiva and Rajagopal (Rajaji).[329]

Vandana is one of the world's most articulate opponents of genetic engineering in agriculture, an inspiration to millions of farmers in India, an eco-feminist of world stature, and key mobilizer of activists around the world against the World Trade Organization (WTO).

From my perspective, I consider Rajaji to be carrying the mantle of Gandhi's non-violent resistance movement in India today. He has been tirelessly mobilizing tens of thousands of poor peasant farmers all over India for decades. He also has a global support base in partnership with activists around the world, including anthroposophists.[330]

The Agriculture Section of the Goetheanum has also invited Hans Herren, who wrote a massively popular analysis of world agriculture and the prospects of organic farming[331] and Patrick Holden,[332] a very close colleague of Prince Charles and a leader of the British organic farming movement.

And there are others. They were all invited to Dornach for exchanges with the bio-dynamic movement.

These conversations with the world are starting to enliven the bio-dynamic movement because it returns this movement to its true origins. The task of bio-dynamic agriculture is not just about farming a piece of land bio-dynamically. The task of the movement is to transform and re-sanctify the earth. And if we carry this kind of global mission in our consciousness and it is really alive in us, then all kinds of providential support will start happening. (See Chapter 9.) We will start attracting experiences that will allow such intended transformations to manifest more and more, because we are carrying that awareness in our Higher Nature and thus together with the spiritual world.

This kind of global-shaping conscious action can happen too in the other daughter movements of anthroposophy if the intention and intensity are there.

But if we do not really believe in ourselves and what can happen in partnership with others and the spiritual worlds; if we carry a kind of self-defeating attitude; if we want to remain small; then all these amazing possibilities for humanity will NOT happen.

We will continue doubting ourselves. We will remain small and inconsequential, and we will betray who we really are as anthroposophists and why we incarnated at this time in the world. Our irrelevance to the world process will happen because that is what we want to happen for ourselves as revealed by our conscious or unconscious negative thoughts. We then get cut off and we become inconsequential to the world.

The Bio-Dynamic movement is an exemplar of how we can be faithful to and return the Cosmic Intelligence back to Micha-el. This happens when we build alliances and networks for humanity and harness Collective Human Intelligence (CHI) in the process, a now earthly manifestation of Micha-elic intelligence essential to placing a counterweight to artificial intelligence.

Chapter 13

The Truth-Force of the Youth Movement

The underlying mood, substance and inspiration of the bio-dynamic movement is strategically important as these can have fruitful ramifications for the other daughter movements of anthroposophy. To build upon these, let us consider the anthroposophical youth movement because, as we shall see, what happened to the agriculture movement to a certain extent had a spiritual, if not, a direct connection to what happened and is happening with the youth movement.

And the potential good to humanity is large if we understand this connection. The millennials are the largest cohort group in human history with 92 million individuals in the US alone.[333] And they also have values and technological savvy that make them an ideal group to critically engage in the issue of technological singularity and artificial intelligence.

There is a global survey of millennials. When asked what is the purpose of business, around 72% of them said that the goal of business should not be profits, but service to others and humanity.[334] This is the reason why the emergence of the social entrepreneurship movement around the world is fuelled by millennials.

The Youth Movement

Even during his time, Steiner himself had to deal with the Youth movement. They came in loud and clear and disturbed the quiet studying mood of the older generation of anthroposophists. They wanted action. They had fire for the good in their will. And not surprisingly they generated a lot of misunderstanding with the older generation of anthroposophists. This misunderstanding turned into conflict and Steiner had to create a separate and independent movement from the existing anthroposophical society.[335]

This development led Steiner to clarify the difference between the wisdom path and the action path to advance spiritual science. The Wisdom Path (or Moon Path) went from Imagination, to Inspiration to Intuition. The Action Path (or Saturn Path) went from Intuition, Inspiration, to Imagination.[336]

The Wisdom path began with study and, from this point, proceeded slowly but surely, to action in the world. That was the ideal and, during

Steiner's time, this ideal did not manifest too strongly in the Anthro-posophical Society despite continuous encouragement from Steiner.

Out of an esoteric law, an Initiate cannot be both a spiritual researcher and an administrator of an earthly organization. Thus, Steiner was not a member of the Anthroposophical Society but more the latter's teacher and mentor. He did not make decisions that affected the Society. He simply gave guidance and sometimes his advice was not followed.

Later on, due to circumstances that are familiar with most anthro-posophists, including the failure to take appropriate action, he took on both the leadership of the Society and the esoteric leadership of the movement and united the two in his person. That came about during the Christmas Foundation Meeting of 1923.

The Action Path started with deeds that gradually matured to a deeper understanding of one's field of action. Here, one is more in touch with a future that wants to happen. Of course, there had to be some level of understanding of spiritual science but, on the whole, it could not compare with the level of understanding brought by those who journeyed via the Wisdom Path.

Because of the lack of complete conscious understanding, mistakes will be made and they were made. But it did not stop the initiative takers from learning from these mistakes and then moving on to a higher level of sophistication in implementing their initiative.

It is interesting to note that this approach is quite visible today in such movements as action research and the innovation approach of Silicon Valley. In the latter, they call it Principle 0.7 also known as rapid prototyping. Begin with some basic idea of what you want to do and then do a rapid prototype. Be open to making mistakes but learn quickly from them and then go to the next level of prototyping until finally your innovation is ready for the mainstream.[337]

Concretely, first do a 'beta' version and call it 0.7 or something like that. Try it out. There will be some kinks, some imperfections. Learn from it and do a 0.8 version This too will have limitations, but not as many as before. Learn from it and then go for a 0.9 version and finally a 1.0 version. When it reaches this stage, it can now be released to the general public. But even then, the 1.0 becomes Version 2.0, then 3.0 and so on. This was the path that the Apple iPhone took. Now the Apple iPhone has surpassed Version 6 and has released its iPhone 10.0 or iPhone X.[338]

Probably the most systematic map of the Action Path today is Otto Scharmer's Theory U where learning takes place not from the past but from a future that wants to be born. Scharmer did not create Theory U so he can verify the Action Path of spiritual science using today's science. He discovered Theory U phenomenologically by doing over 150 interviews around the world with thought leaders from all walks of life.[339]

His Theory U has now mainstreamed and it is being used in such diverse institutions as large corporations, governments and the United Nations.[340]

We will note that the Action Path is intimately connected with the creation of Collective Human Intelligence. In the Wisdom Path the group is often beholden to one who knows a lot. Knowledge is important but it cannot be the basis of group life. In the Action Path, one assiduously cultivates a mood where all different points of views are able to arise and out of this the possibility of a new insight, a new Intuition, can arise from anybody in the group. And that intuition is connected with the future and is the answer to what individuals in the group are striving for.

Those who took the path of Wisdom often criticized those who took the path of Action for not knowing enough. But Steiner pointed out that, for the spiritual world, enthusiasm makes up for the lack of fuller knowledge or wisdom. Lievegoed opens a lid on the deeper reason for this reality. Individuals who often have this enthusiasm may have already encountered their intentions and ideals when preparing for a new incarnation. Some of them may even have participated in a process of spiritual training in the Micha-el School so they are excited about realizing these visions and intentions in their incoming earth life. Hence these individuals have enthusiasm for action because they already have the knowledge, albeit unconscious. And as they do rapid prototypes, the innate wisdom they have brought with them starts surfacing and emerging.[341]

One could add that with enthusiasm one would have the staying power to keep an initiative moving and improving until it gets more and more perfect. To do this also needs courage, a very important trait of the ancient Northern European people as they pursued their version of the Action Path.[342]

But as we pointed out earlier, one important principle in engaging with others is deep respect for diversity. We all can value the importance of both paths. Lievegoed points out beautifully the harmonization and integration of both the Wisdom and Action Paths in the fourth cluster of verses in the Foundation Stone Mediation:

Christ Sun, Light Divine, Warm Thou our hearts (the enthusiasm of the Action Path), Enlighten Thou our heads (the clarity of the Wisdom Path), so that Good may become what we from our hearts would found, what we from our heads would direct, in Conscious Willing (synthesis).

The Youth Section at the beginning of the twenty-first century had this Action Path gesture. What they also had was a real interest in the world.

I want to express my gratitude to the Youth Section of the School of Spiritual Science in Dornach, Switzerland, for being a pioneer in the twenty-first century in reaching out to the world and awakening and nurturing the young to craft their own understanding and initiative in this perilous age of artificial intelligence.

The Youth Section understood much earlier than the Agriculture Section the need to reach out to the world, to care for the world and to love the world. It did this at a time when the leadership of the global Anthroposophical Society was stuck in relative insignificance to the world. The leadership then of the Society was bedevilled with 'mission drift'. It was not assiduously pursuing its chief task of realizing the Prophecy of Micha-el. It also had a self-imposed negative and limiting framing that it was under 'occult imprisonment'.[343]

This 'crack' in the crust of the Goetheanum was a very important beginning. It has led to a serious questing for new social forms in the leadership of the global Society. And it is an inspiring sign, even if for some too slow, that the leadership is finally awakening to a greater sense of their social responsibility for the world. It is true there are still old habits of doubt and unconscious obstruction. But there is clearly a new wind blowing in that part of the world.

The work of the Youth Section may be invisible to many but that work is alive and well in the dozens of initiatives that young people have started for themselves as a result of the inspiration that came from the Youth Section.

The global Youth Initiative Program (YIP) is one of them and one of the most visible of such initiatives.[344] In 2018, they celebrated their tenth anniversary after training more than 300 people in over 40 countries.[345]

These young individuals are amazing to observe as many have abandoned a totally traditional lifestyle in search of and in furtherance of a totally different world; one more loving, caring, and more harmoniously interacting with the different identities of the world, and one more consciously aware of the challenge of artificial intelligence.

They also bring new capacities. They can feel the pain of the world as their own pain. They cannot stand it when people do not walk their talk. They are bored with constant lecturing. They want to work with their hands. They volunteer in some of the most difficult places to be in today's world.[346]

In short, they live, breath, and sleep the equivalent of unconscious anthroposophy and the global Anthroposophical Society needs to meaningfully engage them using their own language, and, if there is openness to esoteric reality, then introducing them to the cosmic vision of spiritual science and its methodologies.

The upcoming young leaders of the new generation will reinforce the voice of the periphery so essential in the total harmony of the entire global anthroposophical movement. While the centre was stuck for some time, this resulted in the birth of initiatives in the periphery.

There are many, what I call, second-generation daughter movements, that have sprung up in the periphery. (See the next chapter.) These are not as well known as the first wave of daughter movements in the fields of agriculture, education, medicine, curative education, and other areas. However, the recent revitalization of the Global Social Initiative Forum, under the leadership of Ute Cramer and Joan Sleigh of the Executive Leadership of the global Anthroposophical Society, will make these diverse non-traditional initiatives more visible not only in the global anthroposophical movement but, in the world itself. The World Social Initiative Forum, held in Japan last March 2018, demonstrates both possibilities.

In the Era of Artificial Intelligence, it will be important for the centre and periphery to understand each other and to harmonize their efforts together.

The Foundation Stone Meditation[347] could help in this regard. It says:

For the Christ Will in the encircling Round holds sway.
In Rhythms of Worlds bestowing Grace on the Soul.

It is indeed graceful to see the rhythmic exchange of focus between centre and periphery depending on what is needed by the times. In some issues, the centre would take the lead. In others, the periphery would take the lead. Christ works in this weaving of the Centre and the Periphery.

Global civil society understands this principle, albeit unconsciously, and this accounts for its effectiveness in changing the course of certain aspects of world history.[348]

For example, it successfully changed the direction of the World Trade Organization, which wanted to be the new organizing force of the world after the end of the Cold War. Global civil society groups that had been the centre in other issues including the Jubilee 2000 campaign for debt forgiveness, had no problems becoming the periphery on the WTO issue.

But when global civil society focused on the Jubilee 2000 campaign then the global civil society groups that were the centre of the WTO campaign gradually 'moved' to the periphery and from there supported those groups who had more competence, expertise and experience on Jubilee 2000 issue.[349]

It is this give and take between Centre and Periphery that was so crucial in a number of successful campaigns of global civil society.

This innate understanding in the Youth movement, which gravitates towards expertise, passion, and action without any ego issues, will help considerably when the anthroposophical movement reaches out to other spiritual, scientific, and social movements in its quest for unified action on the AI challenge.

Chapter 14

The Original Daughter Movements: Dynamos to Awaken, Nurture and Defend the Truly Human

The strong growing points of anthroposophy into the world are the original daughter movements of anthroposophy. Like bio-dynamic agriculture, Steiner himself had a hand in establishing them. In addition, they have the numbers. They have the name recognition. They have the networks. And relatively speaking, they have the resources. Some of them are fairly widespread in many parts of the world, especially Steiner education, anthroposophical medicine, and bio-dynamic farming.

Anthroposophists are familiar with all of these daughter movements including those beyond the big three. If they have internalized the introduction of mobilizing daughter movements in Part IV above, and they have the inner fire to do something about the urgent situation of the world, they will have the talent of knowing what to do to make their movement relevant to the world.

Steiner Education

I purposely use the term Steiner education instead of 'Waldorf' education to stress a specific point connected with the task of this particular daughter movement to prepare itself to truly engage the all-encompassing challenge of artificial intelligence.

One of the first things that anthroposophic teachers and parents have to do to really engage in the challenge of artificial intelligence is to drop their habit of distancing and dissociating themselves from Steiner. Not all teachers do this and many others are not aware that they may be doing this.

But significant numbers of other teachers, for whatever reason, are alienating themselves and the general public from Steiner himself including the school movement's place of origin, in Germany. There are some schools that have given specific instructions to their teachers not to mention Steiner even in their orientation before parents.[350] Preference for the name, Waldorf education, over Steiner education, is one form of this alienation.

Times have changed. Labelling anthroposophical schools as 'Waldorf' schools was appropriate during Steiner's times. It would have been too self-serving for Steiner himself to call it a 'Steiner' school.

Furthermore, during the time that the Nazis considered Steiner as their public enemy, with Hitler himself writing an article against Steiner,[351] one can understand why proponents of anthroposophical education would call it, 'Waldorf' education. One can understand why advocates at that time did not want to attract the attention of the violent Hitler dictatorships that started World War II.

But to retain this practice in today's time is anachronistic. It is normal to speak about Montessori schools, Piaget education, and Gardner multiple intelligent schools. Why not abandon the cover of a 'Waldorf' label and directly use the name of the founder himself? Then the general public can have direct access to the man himself. They would then straightforwardly ask: Who was Rudolf Steiner?

Is there fear of losing public funding in countries that are antagonistic to spiritual science and to Steiner? Is there an attachment to the 'branding' advantage of the name, 'Waldorf'? No matter what the reasons may be, are these trade-offs still appropriate in the current time when there is an urgent need for the world to know about spiritual science and its greatest exponent, Rudolf Steiner?

The Blessedness of Persecution due to Integrity and Steadfastness on a Principle

Since the core of Spiritual Science is Christology, the science or 'Logos' or Wisdom of the Cosmic Christ, then it would be appropriate to quote this statement of Christ from the Gospel of St Matthew. The implications are self-explanatory.

> 5:10 Blessed are they which are persecuted for righteousness' sake: for theirs is the kingdom of heaven. 5:11 Blessed are ye, when men shall revile you, and persecute you, and shall say all manner of evil against you falsely, for my sake. 5:12 Rejoice, and be exceeding glad: for great is your reward in heaven: for so persecuted they the prophets which were before you. 5:13 Ye are the salt of the earth: but if the salt have lost its savour, wherewith shall it be salted? It is thenceforth good for nothing, but to be cast out, and to be trodden underfoot of men.[352]

As Sergei Prokofieff has shown very clearly in his book with Peter Selg,[353] isolating Steiner's name from the very movement that he helped to start and inspired, will enable the ahrimanic takeover of that daughter movement.

And that would be a real tragedy because Ahriman is behind the current onslaught together with Sorath to destroy humanity. This is tragic given the huge contribution that Steiner has made to dealing with the challenge of artificial intelligence that we are all facing now.

The Timing for Mainstreaming Steiner Education is Perfect

Interestingly enough, however, the opposite trend is happening in the US. Because of the rapid rise of digital education in that country, more and more mainstream authors, who have no connection with Anthroposophy, are referring to Steiner education as a major antidote to the digitalization of the education system.[354]

Unfortunately, because of force of habit due to the use of this term by Steiner educators themselves in the United States, these authors are still calling it 'Waldorf Education'. This delays the time for the general public to know the potential significant and urgent contributions that spiritual science can make in the Age of Artificial Intelligence.

If Steiner's name were referred to directly as in 'Steiner Education', then this would rapidly mainstream the recognition of the spiritual science associated with Steiner's name. The resistance of parents to the digitalization of their children would fuel that global recognition of Rudolf Steiner to this urgent topic.

I know the thoughts above are controversial and we do not need a division in our own ranks especially at this time. I offer the above thoughts here for reflection, not for judgement and separation. The intent of this reflection is to surface one's motive in being in a daughter movement of anthroposophy and not to demean the efforts of parents and teachers to provide good and healthy education.

Most initiative-takers in Steiner education start from narrower concerns, that is, finding a good school for their children. That is very important. But in the age of rapid takeover of the schools by artificial intelligence, such initial motives will no longer be good enough. Higher aspirations, like the survival of humanity, have to come in.

So in this context, the framing of a school initiative will no longer be simply about a good education for children. The new and larger framing will be: how can the school itself be a bulwark against the illicit advance of artificial intelligence in education and how can the truly spiritual human become the standard of present-day society? This will mean appropriate involvement of the school in extending its goals towards a more sustainable society.

A key aspect in this regard is to realize, as seen above,[355] that Steiner himself characterized anthroposophical education as cat's food (that is, of minimal relevance) unless it placed itself within the larger context of societal threefolding. If we take heed of his warning, we would make the school community realize that they are strategically located in society's cultural ecosystem that is responsible for drawing out the truly human so students and everyone else can be fully human. A more holistically educated individual has more inner resources to deal with artificial intelligence in whatever area they may later on end up in life.

If the courage to do this internal individual and institutional purification is present, the Steiner education movement can play an amazing role in making the Micha-el Prophecy come true and in putting artificial intelligence in its proper place, and that is to serve humanity.

Steiner schools have an amazing network of parents that they can mobilize. These parents are already inwardly attuned to a more holistic image of the human being and the education of the child.

This reframing of the task of education, especially shifting it to a cosmic context, prepares the movement to deal with the larger possibilities that exist in colleges and universities around them. For example, they can encourage the shifting of the curriculum to increase more the teaching of goetheanistic science to balance materialistic science in conventional schools.

Within the societal threefolding context, Steiner schools have to form alliances within themselves and other schools to prevent the increasing commodification of education.

The Invasion of AI in Schools: Opportunity to Mainstream The Image of the Truly Human

There are already policies in some countries around the world that require the use of IT devices in kindergarten. Some schools use academic software programs in order to meet the stringent educational policies of their countries. In some schools, four-year old children are exposed to technology.[356]

They have also imposed educational policies that require students to learn programming in grade school.[357] Discussions are starting in the United States to digitalize the entire education system: no buildings, no teachers, only digital classrooms and instructors.[358]

Those who know the deleterious impact of these policies on children should now step up to prevent their wider adoption and even the repeal of existing such laws and policies. Failure to do this, would make children fodder for ahrimanic intentions.

These are just some pointers. Steiner teachers, administrators, parents and students themselves can come up with more ideas and initiatives once they are convinced that the education of the truly human is endangered by the growing digitalization of education.

Anthroposophic Medicine

Anthroposophic Medicine can be the source of a real strength of the global anthroposophical movement in a number of significant ways.

First of all, its practitioners know what it means to be truly human. That is their special field of focused study. They can therefore be in the forefront of defending the true image of the human being when it is under attack. And they can heal on the basis of that knowledge and practice.

In this context, Peter Heusser's book, *Anthroposophy and Science*, has tremendous significance in the world to rescue the truly human.[359] He goes on to demonstrate in some detail the serious flaws in the epistemology and methods of one-sided materialism and locates the proper sphere for and usefulness of materialistic science. It also gives spiritual science the necessary epistemological and ontological grounding in the hyper-scientific age of the twenty-first century.

We discussed Heusser's book in some detail earlier in Part II and we will see more of his ideas in Chapter 16 below. If his book is widely read in present-day society, it will make people realize the false promises being peddled by creators of radical technologies, including artificial intelligence.

Secondly, an anthroposophic physician undergoes an incredible amount of scientific training to be a medical doctor. They are in touch with the latest scientific developments in the field of neuroscience, physiology, biochemistry, epigenetic biology and a host of other fields.

These skills enhance their capacity not only to diagnose and heal a human being; but if they do not master these disciplines, Watson, IBM's AI 'medical doctor' will replace them. Watson uses big data analytics to analyze presence of cancer and other diseases.[360] But Watson can never replace the intuitive capacity of a committed anthroposophical physician. They may or may not work with Watson depending on the level of their intuitive and spiritual development.

As with educators, we can be certain that when anthroposophical medical doctors awaken to their Micha-elic mission, they will both know and be innovative in how they would defend the truly human. They could be a real source of spiritual answers to such burning questions about the nature of consciousness and the scientific reality of reincarnation, among others. Both these topics are ground zero in terms of ahrimanic takeover through artificial intelligence and the search for digital immortality.

Because of the increasing demand to defend the truly human, anthroposophic physicians can hold appropriate public seminars and invite, collectively, their tens of thousand of patients to attend these seminars so that the public may know what their options are in the age of artificial intelligence.

In this regard, it is heartening and important to know that an international training of physicians has taken and is taking place in dozens of countries. It is called the International Post-Graduate Medical Training. It has been going on for many years and it continues to take place, year after year.[361]

Physicians can also leverage their scientific training to interface with the leading individualities in a powerful new movement in mainstream science: the second and more spiritual scientific revolution. Many of these scientists are not happy with materialism. And a number of them, some of whom have won the Nobel Prize in Medicine, unexpectedly attained more spiritual results while they were trying to prove the reality of materialism.[362] The whole thing backfired on them in a way that is beneficial to humanity.

So anthroposophic physicians can easily open lines of communications with these individuals who are more well-known and regarded in public. Chapter 16 deals more with these exciting scientific developments.

Thirdly, as already mentioned in the section above on bio-dynamic agriculture, there is a global thirst and search for holistic health. More and more people will seek out anthroposophic physicians among others. This in turn will make the whole daughter movement visible. All these are imminent possibilities in the age of a global search for real health.

In the context of these different ways anthroposophic physicians are strategically positioned in the world to defend the truly human in the age of artificial intelligence, there is the interesting case of Dr Thomas Cowan. He is a well-educated medical doctor who authored the book, *Human Heart, Cosmic Heart*. It is about a spiritual and medical way to cure cardiovascular diseases. He is up to date on the latest heart science but at the same time he brings in spiritual scientific aspects connected to the heart with inspiring clarity.[363]

So here is someone who has the courage to publicly acknowledge his debt and gratitude to Rudolf Steiner, communicates his topic with knowledge and competence, and is now known by millions of people around the world because his very public work is widespread.[364]

The latter happened when Internet natural health guru, Dr Joe Mercola, favourably featured the work of Cowan.[365] Note that the Mercola's site receives over 10 million visits every month[366] and has over a million email subscribers.[367] These subscribers are very conscious and discerning regarding their health alternatives.

In addition, Cowan has also set up his own website that operates as neatly and effectively as the mainstream websites. He is a harbinger of what the future of anthroposophical medicine can be when it courageously engages the significant battles of the time to rescue the true image of the human being.

Other Original Daughter Movements

Because of the limited space and time available for this book, the other original daughter movements will only receive brief aphoristic mention. It does not mean to say that they are less important. All of them significantly advance different facets of what it means to be truly human.

Steiner architecture originated with Steiner himself in Dornach. Although its style and content are unique on their own, architects often consider them a part of the global movement on organic and green architecture. Anthroposophical architecture, once it is part of a rural or a city landscape, is almost an eternal, non-stop message about the deeper potentials of the truly human. In this sense, it is a potent antidote to the massive rectangular rigid shapes of most buildings in the world, buildings mostly created on the basis of money considerations.[368]

Curative (special needs) education teaches us all to move beyond the utility tendency of modern existence. It demonstrates the power of love in healing an incarnation full of challenges. There are and will be increasing numbers of differently-abled human beings who will incarnate in this earth. Curative educators can help a lot with these individuals and with the current situation by reframing what a 'handicap' can mean. Humans cannot be categorized according to a set of parameters determined by a materialistic understanding of the human being. Reframing curative education into a larger context would really contribute to the humanization of the world.[369]

Steiner considered *true art* as a powerful antidote to the ahrimanic attack on civilization. And this is the reason why he spent seven years of his work birthing new forms and understanding of art.

The different arts work to strengthen the different sheaths (bodies) of the human being. Music, for example, can strengthen the presence of the 'I' in humans and can provide a source for moral inspiration in the world. Painting can enliven the working of the body of consciousness (astral body) of the human being, enabling the latter to be more creative. Drama that results in catharsis in the audience can help purify the soul of the latter. Eurythmy can help us visualize the inner dynamics of the soul and the human body of formative life forces as well as the inner speech of the human being, awakening similar latent capacities in the audience. And it is the same with the other arts. Each one of them has a critical contribution in making us fully human.[370]

But all the arts have a major obstacle. They belong to the cultural sphere of life. They are a not-for-profit activity. They need financial support and generous amounts of it. We will address the challenge immediately below.

The Cosmic Context is Everything

Meanwhile, all the original daughter movements have to do *one urgent thing* in common. They have to *reframe what they are doing in the largest context* appropriate to them.

For in its degraded way, this is what artificial intelligence is doing. It is infusing all its creation with the cosmic context and intentions of Ahriman. The thinking of the advocates of artificial super intelligence is galactic in perspective.[371]

Only when anthroposophists infuse their work in these areas above and beyond (initiatives still to come) with the 'cosmic context' of the Michaelic School can all their efforts start aligning to make anthroposophy not only relevant, but a shaping force in the Age of Artificial Intelligence. We then begin to answer the questions of humanity at the level these questions are being asked.

AI asks questions about the evolutionary future of humanity. For AI, this evolutionary future is about the advent of the purely mechanical and digital human being, a shadow of the true nature of the human being. They embody their answer to this question in their philosophy of transhumanism and the technologies of transhumanism.

If the challenge of AI is at the cosmic level encompassing thousands of years into the future, we obviously CANNOT be satisfied with a response from the level of the very local group or community.

The local initiative is an important beginning. But it is not enough nor should it be the end goal of the initiative. Individuals have to see their initiatives as ENTRY POINTS so that ultimately they can place their initiatives in a field of spiritual possibilities so that their humble beginnings can then evolve towards and take on cosmic dimensions.

An analogy may help. Einstein as a baby is an example of an entry point. Einstein as the greatest scientist in the twentieth century is an example of his evolution to cosmic dimensions with his General Theory of Relativity and other scientific works. If Einstein remained as a baby, he would then become totally irrelevant to the world.

Thus, if one's initiative has the potential of being significant to the world, we should not hold it back by framing it as just any ordinary initiative. Then it will ultimately remain stuck to its point of irrelevance. But if the initiative is seen as an entry point to a much larger vision of what it can be, then we allow the initiative to evolve the way it needs to evolve so that it can provide meaningful answers and examples of what it means to be truly human. In this way the initiative will surely provide an answer at the level where the questions of AI are being generated.

Here is one of my favourite stickers in Metro Manila: 'Christ is the answer. But what is the question?!' I am sure that this has more meaning now given what we have already discussed.

The works of Rudolf Steiner are filled with the importance of finding the necessary relationship between these two poles of human existence: Self and World.

One's personal self is focused mostly on one's personal interests and needs. That is a normal starting point for a human being. It is essential if one is to find one's place in the world. However, if it gets stuck in its own personal agenda, then that personal self becomes irrelevant to the world process.

As this point, our spiritual True Self has to become active in one's personal life. With its origin in the wider world context, the True Self can assist in creating enabling conditions in the world so the transitory self can evolve towards the eternal True Self. And the primary means for this to happen is when the personal self, guided by its True Self, undertakes meaningful social action in and for the world.

It is extremely instructive that Steiner gives the following brief but profound remarks in the lecture cycle, *Spiritual Science as a Foundation for Social Forms.*[372] First he emphasizes that spiritual science should ultimately lead to social action. '... what matters today is that spiritual deeds are accomplished and carried into social life as well'.

And it was not just any kind of social action. He wanted spiritual knowledge to shape ALL life. 'Spiritual science should not merely reassure our souls, so to speak, concerning the narrowly confined affairs of our individual personality; it is supposed to produce impulses for shaping *all of life.*'[373] [Emphasis added.]

To shape all life was not enough. Steiner expected us to do this, including inner work, from the CONTEXT of the entire universe itself. 'In spiritual science, knowledge must turn into action, action in the whole cosmic world context.'[374]

In his book, *The Christian Mystery*, Steiner emphasizes the same point from another perspective: 'The movement for spiritual science is not something that came into our age through the arbitrary initiative of a single individual or this or that society. It is connected with the entire evolution of humanity . . .'.[375]

Therefore, if one may add, to act out a true understanding of spiritual science, means to act in the context of the 'entire evolution of humanity'.

He warns us all if we fail to place our efforts in self-mastery and world service in a *'grand' context*:

'. . . if one is not in a position to handle the major questions on a grand scale, one will never reach the summit of this age, which is a time of hard trials for [hu]mankind'.[376]

Let us remember this warning also in connection with the 'Culmination' question in Chapter 19 below.

Anthroposophy came into the world in order to serve the world. Thus, to be a real citizen of the world today means to awaken to our true spiritual nature in the context of the evolution of the world and the entire universe. On this basis, one can then truly serve the world.

Anthroposophy can contribute tremendously to this understanding and activation. But this can happen only if we want to, and only if we want to with spiritual passion and dedication.

Chapter 15

The Second-Generation Daughter Movements: Widening the Horizon of Impact

The second-generation daughter movements of anthroposophy are those that engage in issues different from the original well-known focus areas of anthroposophy on farms, schools, health, curative communities, architecture, art. These are the clusters of initiatives and small movements that are moving into such areas as disaster relief and trauma healing work, social outreach with the poor, anti-poverty work, organizational development and social work, alternative currencies, banking and finance, social enterprise, and societal threefolding.

Even though most of them are small, with some notable exceptions, they have the strength of working in situations where most of the people they are working with are not anthroposophists. Especially important in this regard, is that they have the social intelligence to be able to speak with other identities using the language of these other people. They flourish in situations of cultural diversity. They will be important in the outreach to other non-anthroposophical movements and the general public.

Because of the many diverse initiatives under this heading, we will just have very brief comments for most of these initiatives just to highlight what special role they may play in achieving the Micha-elic Prophecy and stemming the urgent and dangerous tide of artificial intelligence. The same qualifying remarks regarding limited elaboration apply even more to the second-generation movements.

Anthroposophical Banking, Businesses, Foundations and Gift Money

Anthroposophical economic initiatives in the area of banking, finance and businesses have two main tasks like all the other daughter movements plus a special third task.

First, they have to renew the area of banking and finance and bring spiritual perspectives to the whole task. The Knights of the Temple of Solomon (Knights Templar) have shown that this is possible.[377] Anthroposophical bankers and businesses of today need to build upon the foundations laid by the Templars. It is understood that this is a different age and time so they will need to build differently for our time.

Second, they need to find a way to mainstream these innovations in banking, finance and business into mainstream society. This is a difficult and daunting task. But it needs to be done and it can be done. One has to be adept in navigating the regulatory waters of the State as banking and finance is one of the most tightly controlled institutions in the world. One has to have the savvy to expand within the constraints of the regulations while, at the same time, retain the spiritual substance of the initiative.

And the third task is to wholeheartedly and reasonably support cultural life like the arts that are very important for the human spirit to flourish. And in this task, anthroposophical foundations and anthroposophists with considerable surplus wealth, will join the bankers and businessmen in empowering cultural life to awaken, nurture and defend the truly human.

They should also focus part of the gift money or grants on computer-related innovations. One huge area waiting for support are for programmers who can create websites, web browsers, email services, and social media applications that are immune to security breaches and vendors monitoring and/or stealing their data.

In Chapters 1 and 2 we have seen that we are in the midst of constant global surveillance and we need to have the proper technology to protect ourselves. And if the programmer is really gifted, then banks, businessmen and rich anthroposophists need to devote resources to enable these programmers to create different types of artificial intelligence that would truly benefit humanity.

Anthroposophical resources also need to support those individuals and groups that have decided to devote their time, connections and talents to find creative solutions to the urgent challenge of artificial intelligence. Their work could be in the form of research, organizing and/or advocacy. The need for support is obvious in this case as said activities are not-for-profit but for the benefit of the whole of humanity.

Gift money should also flow to enhance the capacity of any individual or daughter movement, or even the School of Spiritual Science itself, to truly embark on initiatives that would help the daughter movement or the entire global anthroposophical movement embark on efforts to bring the Micha-lic Prophecy into fruition and with it the proper transformation of AI from a massive threat to a helper of humanity.

There is a huge potential for mutually supportive relationships between foundations, gift or grant money and the diverse cultural initiatives. The urgency of the times calls for Collective Human Intelligence (CHI), something that needs to happen more and more frequently and intensely within the global anthroposophical movement. All the daughter movements, whether first or second generation, have to find ways to synergize their efforts and activities with each other. This increases the feasibility and possibility of creating a global force for a new civilization, one that could address the huge challenge of extreme technologies.

Direct Democracy and Good Governance

It is true that the Anthroposophical Society is not a political organization and is not into politics. It is first and foremost a cultural-spiritual movement and society. However, it does not mean that such a provision in the statutes of the Society prevents a member in the global anthroposophical society from becoming involved in politics.[378]

For if some people with high moral integrity and strong sense of justice and protection of human right do not enter into the political arena, then we will get the kind of political leaders we have today: visionless, spineless, abusive, and corrupt. And if they do have a vision, it is usually so highly egotistic that is destructive of the fibre of society.

Gerald Häfner is one such anthroposophist. He became an activist at age 12 when he strongly felt the pain of people around the world who spent their lives in poverty. Häfner realized that the rules of political and legal life were made and rigged by those who wield economic and political power. He emphasized the importance of citizens being able to change the rules of political life or forever be marginalized by the unjust decisions of the rich.

And he spent the better part of more than 40 years of his life establishing an institutional arrangement in Germany for people to make their own rules. This is done through direct initiative voting, also known as Citizens' Referendum. Häfner, together with many friends, organized the Direct Democracy Movement, a national then later on an international movement, to make this possible. All regions of Germany have this referendum arrangement. While involved in this process, Häfner cofounded the Green Party in Germany and became a member of the German Bundestag and the European Parliament as a representative of the Green Party.[379]

There is another movement in Germany, this time from the sphere of civil society but actively engaging the state by advocating its own version of governance. This movement is the Omnibus, which drew inspiration from the work of anthroposophist Joseph Beuys, considered the most important post-war artist in Germany. The current leader of this active movement is Johannes Stuttgen, also another anthroposophist.[380] The movement is also a movement for direct democracy but with a different focus. Among others, the Omnibus emphasizes the importance of inner spiritual change in the attempt at societal transformation. And they take their inspiration from the creative process of art.

This is very important because, properly organized, and with the support of all daughter movements and allies, anthroposophists and other concerned citizens can put up the question of artificial intelligence in a public referendum. In this way, since a mandatory period of information and debate is required, millions of people will become aware of the AI issue and will start thinking what to do with it. It is a kind of giant Collective Human Intelligence (CHI) at work and will have very powerful results.

A similar possibility for citizens exists in Switzerland, which is the world pioneer in referenda. Some anthroposophists are already involved in this movement. Germany and Switzerland are poised to take a lead in this regard.

These individuals and their movements demonstrate what one person or a few people with persistence, compassion, and social intelligence can do in a large public way.

Societal Threefolding and Civil Society

Such considerations on democracy and governance above naturally lead to discussions on civil society and societal threefolding. Both areas of work are quite difficult as witnessed from the paucity of anthroposophical activists involved in civil society at large or individuals involved in societal threefolding work.

Societal threefolding is an attempt to move from a state-centred governance system to a society-centred governance system where government (representing the political sphere), business (the economic sphere) and civil society (the culture realm) are in a participatory process of decision-making to ensure the integral sustainable development of a society.[381]

Many in the global anthroposophical movement think that efforts at large societal threefolding work died a long time ago. This is not the case.

At least in the Philippines it is alive in relatively large areas, the size of cities and towns involving hundreds of thousands of people. One prominent example is Bayawan City in central Philippines where the City passed a P1billion budget using a threefolding consultative process.[382]

In these areas, anthroposophists and non-anthroposophists are mobilizing civil society, government, and businesses to be involved in sustainable area planning and implementation. And there are an increasing number of mayors of cities and towns, dozens of them, interested in implementing threefolding together with organic farming. They are all part of a national association called the League of Organic Agriculture Municipalities and Cities—Philippines.[383]

At the national level, the Cabinet-level National Economic Development Authority (NEDA) of the Philippine government laid out the policy context for the pursuit of threefolding in its medium-term development plan of the Philippines from 2017–2022. The national government's Department of Environment and National Resources (DENR) has also adopted threefolding as the process for achieving Sustainable Integrated Area Development (SIAD).[384]

None of the people involved there know about anthroposophy but they resonate with anthroposophical substance if one says it in another language. This is the key to working in the world of different identities. We have to find what the language is in that specific setting and be comfortable with that language, even if we cannot keep on using our familiar anthroposophical terminology. We just have to be comfortable with the language that's there. It requires skills in societal phenomenology in this case threefolding. One can see invisible social forms emerging from the different situations.

No, threefolding is not dead. Instead the highest levels of world governance are beginning to understand the power of societal threefolding and are starting to hijack it for their own ends.

For example, Bill Gates speaks about it in a certain way. He calls it creative capitalism, and he speaks about business, government and civil society cooperating, with civil society there to support the goals of business.[385] But this emasculates civil society because the function of civil society is not to be an adjunct of business but to be the conscience of society and the exponent of ways to create new societal forms.

The US State Department is very interested in what it calls 'impact investment', and this is significant also because it is trying to bring cultural institutions of civil society together with business and government, all with the objective of eradicating poverty.[386] It is a noble goal but the execution is another story. One working in these contexts has to be very awake to ensure that authentic threefolding holds in the process and that civil society is not a mere instrument of the state or business.

Societal threefolding is essential in the age of globalization and artificial intelligence. In Chapter 18, we will see global civil society advancing other forms of threefolding. It enables all in society to be actively involved in the pursuit of policies and societal arrangements that prepare society to achieve integral sustainable development despite the massive challenges of artificial intelligence.

Without free and independent civil society operative in a society, it is difficult to achieve systemic, radical, and visionary change in the political governance of society, especially one that can stand up to the challenge of artificial intelligence.[387]

From the perspective of the sociology, the global anthroposophical movement (GAM) is a civil society movement. From there, some individuals, but not institutions, get involved in political and economic initiatives spinning off and creating their own movements from their initial embeddedness in culture. I have already discussed the intricacies of this approach in my book, *Shaping Globalization: Civil Society, Cultural Power, and Threefolding* cited several times in this section.

Enabling the Work of the 'Masters'[388] Through Threefolding

Societal threefolding also holds the key to something that Steiner rarely spoke about but instead shared with close associates. Ehrenfried Pfeiffer was a close pupil of Steiner. He once asked Steiner about the possibility of creating new kinds of technologies to serve humanity, new technologies that would be powered more by living etheric (life) forces.

Steiner gave Pfeiffer some indications as to how he may do this. Pfeiffer made some initial promising discoveries but Steiner requested him to discontinue the experiments. Steiner said that the spiritual worlds said it was not yet time to develop such technologies. Improper access to and use of these energies can bring devastation to humanity as did happen in Atlantis.

Instead Steiner said that these technologies can arise if anthroposophical education AND societal threefolding were active in shaping the culture and societal dynamics of the area *at the same time*. Furthermore, Steiner told Pfeiffer that Mani, humanity's highest initiate who has the task and the power to transform Evil, would need such social conditions to incarnate towards the end of the century, that is in our time.[389]

Steiner education is necessary to defend and nurture what is truly human in us. Threefolding complements this effort by providing the societal structure where the truly human can become fully human and thus be able to bring the necessary spiritual impulses into society. The inner and outer situation has to be there for these kinds of profound esoteric knowledge, experience, and energy to be made available to society.

In this context, one can also surmise why threefolding is the societal sheath of Christ. Initially Christ enters into earth life through individuals. He imbues individuals with the Truth in their thinking, with Love in their feeling, and with the Way in their willing. When this truly happens, we can say: Not I but Christ in me.[390]

But that is only true at the individual human level. Now if we want to make the non-dogmatic Truth, Love, and Way of Christ effective in society, then we need to shape society in such a way that these spiritual realities, forces and capacities can live in society. This societal structure imbued with the Christ in turn works back on the individual and further nurtures and strengthens his/her latent and/or emerging capacity for Truth, Love, and the Way. This is to be understood, in the context of Christ, as connected with the future evolution of the planet and the Cosmos.

And this is where the spiritual significance of societal threefolding comes in. There are different ways of looking at this and what follows is one of those ways.

In a functioning threefold society, freedom is the guiding principle in the cultural realm. Individuals in that society can now pursue the Truth without hindrance and fear of being strange or censored.

In the political realm, equality is the operative principle. Objective non-egotistic Love enhances the capacity for empathy and compassion. Out of these emerges the sense of equality and fairness because we all begin to inwardly experience the true humanity of each other. True democracy prevails, not out of a mere concept of rights, which is the Western concept, but out of a sense of what others truly need because one can truly feel the needs and striving of that person.[391]

In the economic realm, solidarity (brotherhood/sisterhood) is the pervasive ideal. Business people can now pursue economic initiatives that are not based on the egotistic principle of competition but out of a sense of community for the whole. And the macro-economy works in harmony with the planet, leading both its people and Nature towards a prosperous and vibrant future that fully nurtures and empowers the fully human. The Way of the all-inclusive Christ is effective in that society.

The French Revolution understood this unconsciously in their cry for *liberté* (liberty or freedom), *égalité* (equality) and *fraternité* (solidarity). But the activists of the French Revolution failed to realize that these ideals could not be collapsed into the state alone and that these ideals have their own realms out of which they have to work harmoniously with each other.[392]

If one overpowers the other, or if one is missing in the society, then that society cannot function in a healthy way. It will implode, like the French Revolution, where the state became totalitarian and it ate up the sense of freedom and solidarity of its citizens, and eventually violated its own innate strivings, imposing another form of hierarchy with the one it destroyed. They had the hierarchy, not of the king they deposed, but the hierarchy of a totalitarian state that dominated everything and trampled on the true freedom, equality, and solidarity of its citizens.

Now we begin to understand why Mani and the other Initiates need a supportive societal structure to incarnate so that they can awaken the latent powers that they are bringing with them for the good of humanity.

The Tragedy of Plato

In this context, the tragedy of Plato's incarnation in the nineteenth century gives a stark reminder of what is ahead of us in terms of creating societies that do not suppress the karmic tasks of humans but allow them to flourish. This is especially important in the on-going crisis with extreme and often times immoral technologies. We need all the help we can from gifted and committed individualities, not the least of which are the Initiates of humanity.

In his very last karma lecture of dozens of lectures contained in eight volumes, Steiner started speaking about the incarnation of Plato, the famous Greek philosopher. Plato is not only famous among anthroposophists. He is a giant in Western philosophy and has influenced human civilization for over 2000 years. Alfred North Whitehead, the father of Process Philosophy, said that the 'safest general characterization of the European philosophical tradition is that it consists of a series of footnotes to Plato'.[393]

That is a very powerful characterization of the impact of Plato. One has this powerful individuality, an Initiate, and he incarnates again in the nineteenth century as Karl Julius Schröer. It was the task of the reincarnated Schröer to introduce anthroposophy to humanity, not Steiner's task. According to him, Steiner's task was to build upon Plato and give a spiritual scientific account of reincarnation and karma. The reincarnated Plato failed.[394]

I have continuously reflected on this shocking revelation and really tried to understand what happened and what were and are the consequences for the future of humanity. Three things clearly stand out in my mind.

Here is this individuality we know as Plato. All of Western philosophy is but a series of footnotes to what he taught. But in his Schröer incarnation, he was not able to bring out what he was supposed to bring. He could not fulfil his mission because the education of his time lamed the highly evolved gifts that he was bringing due to his status as an Initiate in his previous life.

Here is a clear case of the strategic importance of societal threefolding. We have to have educational freedom, and the societal structure of the country should be such that it allows gifted humans to awaken to their true potential and then place these awakened capacities for the benefit of society.

We do not know how many other initiates and spiritually-developed human beings are also being lamed or are having difficulty finding out about and making their mission a reality. We do not know how many of the thousands of young people are similarly afflicted. And, if they chose to incarnate at this time, their mission obviously has a lot to do with helping deal with humanity's current entanglement with Artificial Intelligence. That is the first clear lesson.

And this laming of gifts of humans will rapidly worsen when AI advocates succeed in digitalizing the entire educational system, starting at the level of the womb and early kindergarten.[395]

The second lesson is that we should never rest on our laurels. We may have a very high level of spiritual development but it amounts to nothing if we do not continuously try to nurture it in whatever circumstances we find ourselves.

Third, Plato's failure had the added effect that Steiner was only able to partially fulfil his mission in connection with karma and reincarnation. From everything that I know of anthroposophy and Artificial Intelligence, a scientific articulation of karma and reincarnation would have totally destroyed the intentions of Ahriman in the social sphere and diffused global interest in illicit kinds of Artificial Intelligence. If people are already spiritually immortal due to the process of incarnation, why would they need to toy around with childish concepts like physical digital immortality?

Here is an image. Steiner is one of the leading individualities in the Micha-el School. There, he hones his instruments of battle. He has two of them. He incarnates and writes his epistemological works, especially the *Philosophy of Spiritual Activity*. 'Ahriman is wrecked.' His first instrument is spiritualized thinking. And he is successful while at the same time rescuing Plato's mission.

His second instrument was to be his own mission: karma and reincarnation.[396] But, due to all kinds of challenges and hindrances, especially those coming from members of the Anthroposophical Society and movement then, he could only start in earnest with this Micha-elic task very late in life. One year later, he dies. He only partially fulfils his task. Ahriman breathes a sigh of relief.

Steiner would have 'wrecked' Ahriman in two strategic places. First was the successful use of his epistemological thinking. He stops Ahriman *inside* the human being. Second, with his second battle instrument, the teaching of reincarnation and karma, and its subsequent widespread dissemination, Steiner would have stopped Ahriman *outside*. It is now up to all of us to carry on this part of his mission as best we can.

The current trajectory of Artificial Intelligence would have stopped dead in its tracks if global culture had a scientific understanding of karma and reincarnation. People will not be toying around with digital physical immortality and related ideas unless they are desperate materialists who are subconsciously dreading the prospect of disappearing into nothingness as posited by their own belief system.

Moral Technologies

Given the alarming situation with Artificial Intelligence and faced with very limited possibilities of action, some anthroposophists today are starting to research more deeply into new forms of technology that can serve humanity better. They call these new ways of creating human-activated machines, 'moral technology'.

A moral technology initiative has emerged in Australia around a group of young people initiated by Rose Nekvapil.[397] In the USA, the Centre for Anthroposophical Endeavors has also started a new project, called MysTech.[398] It also deals with intensifying the research efforts on moral technology. The key person behind MysTech is Andrew Linnell.[399]

Both of these groups and individuals build upon the work of AnthroTech and the late Paul Emberson, who wrote books about this whole area of Artificial Intelligence from the perspective of anthroposophy. Among other works, Emberson has written a two-volume work on Artificial Intelligence and anthroposophy called, *From Gondhishapur to Silicon Valley.*[400] Not much is known about the late Emberson because he consciously stayed away from all aspects of the Internet.

The work of these individuals and groups is courageous, far-sighted, and strategically important even if inadequate in some areas. But these initiatives are initial ones and have the possibility and capability of evolving and improving through time.

The work of critiquing AI is important but it is not enough in the long term. Some parts of the anthroposophical movement have to develop moral forms of technologies that can safely be used by humans to advance their evolutionary development on earth. This is the contextual importance of moving into the area of 'moral technologies'.

Emerging Movements in Anthroposophy: Philosophers, Psychologists, Scientists, and Others

There are a significant number of anthroposophists who are scientists, philosophers, psychologists and sociologists. Now is the time to hone their skills and place them in the frontlines of the struggle connected with transforming extreme technologies to serve humanity, rather than to destroy the human species.

Burning areas of research include the reality of consciousness outside the brain and how it interacts with the physical brain; a clearer elaboration of intelligence and what cosmic intelligence would look like in this context for the general public; what aspects of the true human beings are being trapped in digital versions of themselves; a clearer understanding of the spiritual nature of memory; how to make the scientific community and the general public understand the nature of the Etheric; reincarnation and karma understood scientifically and spiritually and its implications for the search in AI for digital immortality; the spiritual answer to super health, super strength, and super intelligence. These are only initial research questions.

Once the answers are found, deepened and clarified, the professionals in all fields of scientific endeavour can widely share their findings. They can come up with articles and books on said topics. They can write long scientific reviews or even books in response to a plethora of AI books out there, including the *Virtual Human*, *Life 3.0*, and *Homo Deus*, discussed above.

These AI books all view consciousness as basically material or ultimately just an algorithm that is randomly generated by matter in the form of our genes. Of course, this is grossly inaccurate and has to be refuted clearly.

The second milestone of anthroposophy is for it to be a force that shapes planetary civilization. Therefore, these professionals should find ways and means to make their thoughts and writings available to the general public. In this regard, the anthroposophical movement has all the necessary publishing and distribution infrastructure to make this possible. There are also publishing outlets in the mainstream that will publish publicly-oriented books of this nature. And for those who are not averse, they can judiciously use social media to spread the word.

The publishing and distribution infrastructure of the anthroposophical movement would *include ALL the in-house publications of all the daughter movements*. Together, and in unison, the reach of the publications of all the daughter movements would reach millions. And when these are further leveraged with the publications of the alternative movements in the mainstream, then we are speaking of tens of millions. When this becomes effective, we are seriously honouring our mission, promises and commitments to Micha-el, Rudolf Steiner, all the Keepers of Humanity, and most of all to Christ, whose second crucifixion was caused by the spiritual darkness of materialism.[401]

Part V

FORMING ALLIANCES WITH OTHER SPIRITUAL MOVEMENTS

This Part of the book and the chapters that constitute it are so crucial not only for the fulfilment of the Micha-el Prophecy but are also deeply connected with Micha-el's intentions, the ability for humanity, in a massive global alliance, to effectively respond to the threat of Artificial Super Intelligence and human extinction. It is so important that I want to emphasize again a point regarding alliances that I made earlier in the introduction of Part IV.

I am going to touch upon something that is particularly sensitive, but I really have to say this with a sense of historical conscience.

In terms of how we view our connection to the world, anthroposophists often have the unconscious sense of privilege that they have a special and direct connection with Micha-el, the Time Spirit. While this is true, it can lead to an unhealthy inner and effective outer disconnection with the world. This special connection often slips to an unconscious egotistic version that Micha-el is working only in the anthroposophical movement.

This is not a theoretical consideration. It is a fact. We can see this in how a significant number of anthroposophists conceived of creating movements that rarely substantially involve the potentially allied movements and the general public.

Of course, it is a huge lie and deeply arrogant if one has the shortsighted belief that Michael is a Time Spirit only for the anthroposophic movement. It also betrays a lack of understanding of who Micha-el really is. What about the rest of the world?

Spiritual science is about allowing the sacrifice of the Christ to continue to make evolution work for everyone, for the entire human species including Jews, Hindus, Muslims, atheists, and other human identities. The Christ Deed, understood spiritually, also works in Nature as a force, for the Christ Force is the Logos Force.

What Christ did is not a belief. The Deed of Christ works as an objective force in the universe in much the same way that gravity works in the world no matter what one's belief system is. Micha-el works with individualities that can take up this impulse, even if they do so unconsciously. Christ is Love and His Love knows no bounds.

And by 'unconsciously', I mean it in terms of lack of awareness of the wider context of spiritual science, not 'unconsciously' in terms of the sub-conscious. Many of these non-anthroposophic individuals and their movements are active in the world today, more or less aligned with Micha-elic intentions. And from my experience of some of these global civil society leaders, they also have access to higher cognitive states, especially intuitive thinking, understood in the spirit of Steiner's *Philosophy of Spiritual Activity*.

Many leaders of global civil society are out there shaping the world. They are not anthroposophists, in the literal sense of what it means, and yet they are creatively thinking and engaging with the world fearlessly—through their own thinking processes, which are not born out of fear. They too have access to aspects of the world process, to the inherent directionality in the evolution of the universe, and they engage and serve the world with real courage and great force. That is why we find these people all over the world, people that we can really relate to. The young especially are deeply attracted to these kinds of individuals.

This latter point is also striking. *We may have the legacy of the Micha-elic Prophecy but many anthroposophists behave as if there is nothing urgent about it.* We are not attractive to the younger generation as reflected in the number of members and the ageing population of the Anthroposophical Society because, with outstanding exceptions, we do not appear in the world with passion and courage.

This is indeed ironic because those who are not anthroposophists attract a lot of young people because the civil society activists and some business leaders have what we call Micha-elic Will. Many card-carrying members of the global Anthroposophical Society, with outstanding exceptions, do not have it. This may be too harsh a judgement, but the objective conditions of the world bear this out.

This was true in the past and in the present time. We need not persist in this attitude. We can have a very different attitude if we want to. We can have the fire and the courage it needs to turn around the current crisis of humanity no matter where we are in life. This can happen if we understand what we are truly being called to be and to do at this unprecedented moment in human history.

This has massive strategic and practical implications on how we are in the world, because in one sense, our anthroposophical brothers and sisters are out there, but in a much larger sense, we need to realize that our brothers and sisters are potentially the whole of humanity. Each individual has a spiritual form, a spiritual essence, that has to be nurtured and nourished. Every human being has the ability to play a role in the future of humanity through the unfolding of his/her intuitive thinking and selfless, loving action.

The most important spiritual movement outside the anthroposophical movement that all anthroposophists should consciously connect with, started surfacing in the 1980s. It is the movement of the new science. And it is happening in many fields of mainstream sciences today.

I have been calling this exciting development, the 'second scientific revolution' and now, the 'second and more spiritual scientific revolution'. It is a potentially powerful ally of anthroposophy in addressing Artificial Intelligence. It gives scientific support to many of the central tenets of anthroposophy and contributes new insights from which Anthroposophy can learn as well. We shall see this shortly in the next chapter that immediately follows below.

And even more importantly, with the proper integration of these new sciences, one can more easily transform its tendencies into pure spiritual science in much the same way that Rudolf Steiner transformed the materialistic evolutionary theories of Ernst Haeckel into his book, *Outline of Esoteric Science*.

But the second and more spiritual scientific revolution is not perfect. Sometimes the similarity is in the thought structure and not actually the actual thought substance. A good example is the nature of non-duality as it is understood in quantum physics. This is quite different from the non-duality of the field of etheric formative forces as understood in spiritual science.

Nonetheless, quantum physics makes it easier to understand some of the ideas of spiritual science (including non-locality itself) that were far too advanced when Steiner introduced these ideas, especially in their mathematical form, in the twentieth century.

This second and more spiritual scientific revolution is happening in so many different fields and, in some areas, including epigenetic biology, has become the mainstream framework of the discipline. The developments in the new sciences are so extensive and substantive that I have decided to devote a whole chapter below to this new science.

There it becomes clear how these new scientific developments significantly reinforce what spiritual science, in its first form as Anthroposophy, has given to the world. Furthermore, spiritual science itself can learn significantly from their new discoveries.

Chapter 16

The Second and More Spiritual Scientific Revolution

The world is burning down fuelled by materialistic science. Ironically many of its major assumptions are questioned on scientific and philosophy grounds.[402] It is simply technology ran amok unmindful of whether or not its search for truth is accurate or not. Rather it has taken Francis Bacon's dictum literally that knowledge is power and control. Thus, torture Nature so she will reveal her secret knowledge.[403]

And while they are doing this, the scientific world is being swept by a second and more spiritual scientific revolution. This is happening in areas as diverse as astrophysics, biology, neuroscience, quantum physics, psychology, philosophy, linguistic and other scientific fields of study. The basis insight emerging from these new sciences is that the human being is not a machine and that our consciousness is not a mere by-product of material and mechanical processes. On the contrary, consciousness is the 'matrix' out of which matter itself arises.

These new discoveries in mainstream science have the potential to provide a powerful counterweight to the assumptions and intentions of technological singularity and Artificial Intelligence. Many of the modern scientific frameworks that created these radical technologies—their scientific foundations—are either collapsing and/or being radically supplemented with a more accurate understanding of reality.

For example, Newtonian mechanics and Einstein's relativity are now subsets of the more comprehensive science of quantum physics. The science of quantum physics is changing our understanding of the kinds of energy that exist as well as our causal relationship to the universe.[404] It has altered our notions of space, time, and causality.

We are now being liberated from the mechanical vision of the nineteenth century. The frontiers of science are now saying not all things are material and mechanical and that there may be aspects of reality that have not been accounted for within the framework of technological singularity and Artificial Intelligence. For example, as we shall see below, biotechnology, which is based on Darwin's theory of evolution, has now also been radically challenged and the deconstruction of Darwinism is happening at a speed that was unthinkable just ten years ago.[405]

Before taking an overview of some of these scientific developments, we need to note the importance of the new science to the task of defending and nurturing the truly human in the age of Artificial Intelligence. This topic can contribute in five ways to our deliberations:

- First, the new science has made radical discoveries that tame materialism, move mainstream science towards the spiritual, and give greater understanding of what it means to be truly human in a technological world.
- Second, the new scientific revolution reinforces what Anthroposophy has discovered some 100 years ago.
- Third, these new scientific discoveries themselves advance, in new and unexpected ways, the Science of the Spirit introduced over 100 years ago.
- Fourth, the second scientific revolution helps answer the four major temptations of technological singularity and Artificial Intelligence and much else besides.
- Fifth, it has the stature, with its millions of adherents and practitioners plus its networks and resources, to create major transformations in many areas of life, not the least in the area of extreme technologies.

These may seem like exaggerated statements. But let us take a closer look at what is going on.

Quantum Physics

One of the most radical discoveries, experimentally verified in 1982[406] and substantiated through the years, is the non-local nature of the universe. Non-locality means the radical instantaneous interconnectedness of everything in the universe.[407]

Take a particle that has been connected with another particle from the beginning and then separate the two particles millions of miles from each other. When activating a property of the first particle, this activation will simultaneously affect the dynamics of the second particle even though the latter is trillions of miles away.[408]

Many scientists are starting to realize that since the whole universe started, interestingly, from a singularity event that they call the 'Big Bang', then all particles in the universe have a non-local relationship with each other.[409] The human being is in a deep relationship with the fabric of the universe and all reality within it.[410]

Here's a quote that exemplifies the strategic importance of spirituality in science and how we do science, and ultimately, technology in the world.

> I regard consciousness as fundamental. I regard matter as derivative from consciousness. We cannot get behind consciousness. Everything that we talk about [and] . . . regard as existing, postulates consciousness.
> Max Planck (1859–1947) co-founder, Quantum Physics[411]

We can immediately see from this quote that the AI project of downloading human consciousness into the machine will ultimately not work. What they will capture, though, are snippets of the past consciousness of a person that have been artificially uploaded into the machine. The project of transferring human consciousness totally into a machine is doomed to failure because consciousness is a much larger reality than plain matter. What will succeed is that one has imprisoned human consciousness in a robot that now begins to have a life of its own. But it is not the same full you.

And here is another quote, this time from another eminent scientist, George Wald, world famous physiologist and Nobel Prize winner:

> . . . mind, rather then emerging as a late outgrowth in the evolution of life, has existed always as the matrix, the source and condition of physical reality—that the stuff of which physical reality is constructed of is mind stuff. It is mind that has composed a physical universe that breeds life, and so eventually evolves creatures that know and create: science-, art-, and technology-making creatures.[412]

Now, if more scientists really knew about this and agreed with Wald, we would have a very different attitude towards developing AI and convergent technologies.

Astrophysics

Astrophysicists are beginning to realize that the structure of the universe is such that the values of its structuring forces are very exact. They are such that only a slight deviation from the original value would make the universe uninhabitable for human life on earth. They call this the 'fine tuning' of the universe or more technically, the anthropic principle.

Let us take the case of gravity. A slightly stronger gravitational force would crush the whole universe into a black hole within a million years. But a slightly weaker gravitational force will not enable the universe to form galaxies. Without galaxies, there would be no solar systems. And without solar systems, we will not be around.[413]

And what is the slight deviation or fine-tuning involved? The deviation should not be greater than a trillionth of a trillionth of a trillionth of one percent or one in one followed by 59 zeroes.[414] What is interesting here is that statisticians consider as 'impossible' values beyond one in one followed by 50 zeroes.[415] In short, the deviation of the gravitational force is not due to chance. Clearly, some other factors are involved.

And the 'fine tuning' is much more precise in the case of dark energy that constitutes around 70% of the physical universe.[416] It is even more improbable or statistically impossible, than the value for gravity. The value for 'dark energy' cannot deviate beyond 1 in 1 followed by 120 zeroes. If it does, then humans will not be around in the physical universe.

These two examples give a good idea of the 'fine tuning' that astrophysicists talk about. And there are dozens more of the same.[417] And no one really questions them. Dr Ed Harrison, former NASA cosmologist and one of the world's top astrophysicists, draws out the obvious conclusion.

> Here is the cosmological proof of the existence of God. . . . The fine tuning of the universe provides prima facie evidence for deistic design. Take your choice: blind chance that requires multitudes of universes or design which requires only one. Many scientists . . . incline toward the teleological or design argument.[418]

Robert Jastrow, Head of the Goddard Institute for Space Studies, shares Harrison's assessment. Jastrow refers to this phenomenon as:

> . . . the most powerful evidence for the existence of God ever to come out from science.[419]

The materialist alternative of 'multitudes of universes' has been deconstructed by the work of astrophysicist Dr Jeff Miller and his two-part article entitled '7 Reasons the Multiverse is not a Valid Alternative to God'.[420] One cannot get into this now because of the overview nature of this chapter.

Neuroscience

While classical physics and astrophysics are undergoing profound universe-shaking changes, another field of science is undergoing revolutionary paradigmatic change. This is the field of neuroscience.

This will be a longer section as findings here and in the related sciences of consciousness are central to the refutation of the dogma of materialism which powers Artificial Intelligence. Here, in this scientific field, it is clear that the AI project is based on a very profound distortion of truth.

Basically, AI has a very inaccurate, almost a completely false picture, of the nature of the human being. It works on the basis of very different considerations, including wealth, power, and control. Truth is not the primary motive even if many AI scientists believe in the truth of their premises.

Of the many amazing discoveries, we will discuss only one and postpone the discussion of another major discovery to the next chapter. Here we begin to see the fallacy of the simple model of AI regarding the human brain. It is much more complex and sophisticated than they ever imagined.

The central finding of current brain science is neuroplasticity. This is the way by which consciousness etches its presence in physical matter,[421] not the other way around as believed by materialist and reductionist scientists. The full development of our brain awaits our own inner activity, especially the prefrontal cortex.[422]

Synapses, the connection between the neurons or brain cells, are not hardwired. They can be modified. Hence, the technical term for neuroplasticity is synaptic plasticity.[423]

The brain changes its synapses when you learn or remember something new. This is why neuroscientists developed the saying: 'Cells that fire together, wire together.' And they also advised: 'Use it or lose it.' The 'it' they are referring to are the new neural connections that become the physical basis of new behaviour and habits.[424]

We can rewire our brain in two ways: action or active imagination. It is extremely important to note that the brain does not distinguish between the two. This is the scientific basis of mental rehearsal, the 'secret' of high performing individuals, especially Olympic champions.[425]

In mental rehearsal, one envisions the desired outcome of an activity. That visualization starts to rewire our brain so as to enable us to carry out or perform that action. And if we keep on doing this mental rehearsal consistently, especially with feelings, then our imaginations become a kind of self-fulfilling prophecy. It will happen![426]

Clearly brain science is useful on so many levels. It can help us break habits, understand the profound practical value of meditation, concentration, skill development and so on.

In another support for neuroplasticity and also psychoneuroimmunology, neuroscientists have demonstrated that the brain changes through Mindfulness Based Stress Reduction training within eight weeks. There is a lengthening of the telomeres that are associated with slowing the ageing process. The practice also leads to the thinning of the amygdala part of the limbic systems thereby reducing emotional reactivity in humans. And the mindfulness training also thickens parts of the brain that promote calm and clarity and which positively affect gene expression in the body as well as the creation of new neural pathways.[427]

The health consequence of chronic stress is another example, albeit a negative one.[428] This condition of chronic stress results in a:

- weakened immune system;
- reduced, dysregulated reproductive hormones;
- increased vulnerabilities in cardiovascular system;
- disturbed nervous system; and
- hastening of the ageing process.

Discussions of neuroplasticity are interestingly hard to find in the literature of Artificial Intelligence. It seems that AI engineers are subconsciously aware that neuroplasticity can totally destroy the assumptions behind the machines that they are making. Instead they are focusing on the software, not the hardware of AI. Machine learning, deep learning and evolutionary or genetic algorithms are substitute versions of the human mind to shape its own brain. It is indeed a poor substitute.

Neuroscience is contributing something even more profound especially in this age of Artificial Intelligence. Neuroscience is providing us the empirical evidence for the reality of the human spirit. The anatomy and physiology of the brain are the 'footprints' of the spiritual in the physical world.

Interesting in this regard is that Rudolf Steiner pointed out several times about the impact of consciousness on the brain.[429] This was many decades before the discovery of neuroplasticity. And the neuroscience of today did not exist in his time. Thus, neuroplasticity could not be demonstrated then even if Steiner could perceive through his developed powers of seeing, supersensible processes. Today scientists have affirmed that consciousness etches itself on the human brain.

Neuroscience has also discovered that the human brain has a four-fold anatomy. Brain science has revealed that we have four major parts of the brain: brain stem (reptilian brain), limbic (emotional or mouse brain), neocortex (monkey brain), and prefrontal cortex (the executive brain).[430]

The interesting phenomenological lesson here is that these four parts of the human brain are showing the evolutionary sequence of functions of the human brain and its connection to human, social, identity, and spiritual processes in humans. The reptilian brain is devoted to physical survival, the limbic or emotional brain to social connectedness (community), the neocortex to the development of a sense of identity connected with the processing of thoughts, memories, and mental images, and the executive brain to the activity of the human spirit.

It is also interesting to see the connection of the four parts with Maslow's famous and widely used hierarchy of needs.[431]

Most importantly, there is a message here regarding human evolution that is very different from what the transhumanists would like us to believe.

If you recall, the transhumanists are the cheering squad behind: 'Go ASI even if humans become extinct.' The transhumanists do not worry about human extinction. Sergey Brin, co-founder of Google, for example, is longing for the day that he will achieve physical immortality by transferring his consciousness into a machine, more accurately, an Artificial Super Intelligent machine.[432] He had this to say about developing an artificially super intelligent machine: 'if you had all the world's information directly attached to your brain, or an artificial brain that was smarter than your brain, you'd be better off'.[433]

They see human beings as imperfect. Humans are sickly, weak, not too intelligent, and they are prone to die. They propose the creation of Artificial Super Intelligence (ASI) as the next stage of natural evolution, a more perfect species from the framework of the materialistic worldview. Along the way, they aspire to give humans super health, super strength, super intelligence and physical immortality. This is why transhumanists are rushing the advent of ASI.

They make their claims on the basis of neo-Darwinian evolutionary theory. Unfortunately, this theory is now facing a major crisis with the rapid and totally unexpected emergence of epigenetic biology. Just like the revolutionary developments in physics that made Newtonian physics a subset of quantum physics, the neo-Darwinian worldview is rapidly becoming just a subset of the more comprehensive, spiritual and extraordinary breathtaking theory of epigenetic biology. (See below, this chapter.)

In this sense, the transhumanist paradigm, driving ASI, is like the emperor with no clothes. Its version of human reality is nothing but a caricature of what it means to be truly human. It is a product of one-sided materialism. Yet many are getting attracted to its dangerous and ultimately fatal illusion. Transhumanism is the siren call to human extinction.

The evolution of our brain is about the development of the capacity of the human spirit, through the power of its thoughts and behaviour, to modify not only the hardwiring of our brain, but also, as we shall see below, to alter the functioning of our genetic structure.

In effect neuroscience is providing us with powerful empirical evidence of the footprints of the spirit in the very way our physical body and our brain are structured and how they function.

To cap this discussion about neuroscience, I would like to cite a statement by Sir John C. Eccles, Neurophysiologist, 1963 Nobel Prize

Awardee. Eccles spent 30 years of his scientific career trying to prove that brain secretes consciousness, that consciousness is nothing but the arrangements and interaction of matter in the brain. Instead he came to the opposite conclusion.

> I maintain that the human mystery is incredibly demeaned by scientific reductionism, with its claim in promissory materialism to account for all the spiritual world in terms of patterns of neuronal activity. This belief must be classed as a superstition . . . we have to recognize that we are spiritual beings with souls existing in a spiritual world as well as material beings with bodies and brains existing in a material world.[434]

John Eccles demonstrated empirically that it is not the neurons in our brain that give us our intentions. It is the other way around. Our intentions set off the chains of firing neurons that eventually lead to free human action. He identifies this reality in the supplementary motor area (SMA) of the human brain. The human intention came 200 milliseconds before the firing of the neurons of the brain.[435]

Thus, if this is the case, then human consciousness does not emanate from the brain. But human consciousness uses the brain as an instrument to function in the physical world.

Materialists tend to counter the findings of Eccles by citing the research of Benjamin Libet of the so-called 'readiness potential'.[436] Libet purported to show that neuronal events initiated the consciousness of doing the relevant movement. In short, it is not the human spirit responsible for consciousness. According to materialist scientist, Libet, it is the pattern of neuronal activity that triggers consciousness and the movements associated with consciousness.

Peter Heusser, in his book, *Anthroposophy and Science*, has given a powerful scientific refutation of Libet's findings and other scientists who further developed the findings of Libet. His refutation is detailed and complex and it is best to read the book itself.[437] But, in essence, he shows that Libet's discovery is of limited value as it refers to the 'unfree will' of humans.

Philosophers and scientists distinguish between the 'unfree will' and the 'free will'. Libet's research referred more to the 'unfree' instinctive will of humans. This is not the free will of humans who can know the motives of their actions and act according to these motives.

Heusser writes: 'Decisions and acts which we base on the conscious consideration of variables, in other words on the rational treatment of content which is capable of consciousness, we judge to be free' . . . In this sense Libet's urges which become conscious are in no way free.[438]

Referring to work of other scientists, Heusser writes:

Haggard and Eimer explicitly point out that the urges examined by them and Libet are not based on a conscious rational consideration of this kind: they are 'events pertaining to the implementation of a specific movement, rather than more abstract representations of action occurring at processing stages prior to selection of a specific movement'.[439]

Because of its central importance to this book, let us cite the more technical language in which the debate is articulated. In the words of Haggard and Eimer that Heusser cites:

While the LRP [lateral readiness potential] may bear a causal relation to W [will] judgement, the *LRP is a relatively late event in the physiological chain leading to action*. In our terminology, LRP onset represents *the stage at which representation of abstract action is translated into representation of specific movement*. Thus, *the LRP onset is not the starting point of the psychological processes that culminate in voluntary movement*, but it may be the starting point of conscious awareness of our motor performance. [Emphasis added.]

Heusser then goes on to develop a rigorous defence of human freedom and a kind of consciousness that is not based on the firing of neurons in the human brain. Readers are encouraged to see Chapter 5 of Heusser's book, especially the section on 'The Question of Freedom'. In effect, current science affirms the reality of Eccles' statement above on the 'superstition' of neuronal activity as the primary basis of our consciousness and actions.

Global Consciousness Project

The findings of neuroscience also apply outside the brain. In effect, consciousness can operate outside the brain, one of the points rigorously shown by Steiner in his book, *Philosophy of Spiritual Activity*.

One of the most radical scientific findings that consciousness affects the functioning of matter is the aggregated result of the Global Consciousness Project originally based in Princeton University. Scientists set up a network of Random Number Generators (RNGs) in 70 host sites in different parts of the world. RNGs, 'based on quantum tunneling, produce completely unpredictable sequences of zeroes and ones'.[440]

The Global Consciousness Project is showing that RNGs become 'subtly structured', that is, begin showing patterns beyond randomness when an important global event galvanizes the feelings of millions of people to focus and synchronize around the event. Think of the election of Barack Obama, for example.

The Global Consciousness Project estimates 'one in a trillion odds that the effect is due to chance'.[441] 'The evidence suggests an emerging noosphere or the unifying field of consciousness described by sages in all cultures.'[442] Such a finding is a violation of existing understanding of the nature of reality using materialistic lenses.

The Science of Near Death Experiences (NDE)

And to bring this deeper understanding of the nature of consciousness to a radical climax, the new scientific field of Near Death Experience (NDE) is providing evidence that human consciousness survives physical death, defined clinically. In his book, *Proof of Heaven*, medical doctor and neurosurgeon Dr. Eben Alexander, a non-believer in NDE, documents his own experience.

> To experience thinking outside the brain is to enter a world of instantaneous connections that make ordinary thinking (i.e. those aspects limited by the physical brain and the speed of light) seem like some hopelessly sleepy and plodding event.[443]

This is a very important quote because his experience is showing that humans are capable of having higher states of consciousness where their thinking can actually be faster than the fastest supercomputers. If humans consciously develop this capacity, then humanity will have a spiritual chance of taming the extinction path of sophisticated AI.

What is particularly important in Alexander's book is that, in Appendix B, he refutes nine alternative materialistic explanations of NDE. He clearly shows that none of these apply in his case and so NDEs are real. This has a certain weight to it because Dr Alexander is also a neuroscientist and he discussed his experiences with other neurosurgeons and scientists.

The field of NDE can have a lot of synergy with Steiner's spiritual research into life after death as well as Steiner's experiences of the spiritual world that form a significant basis for anthroposophy. But that altogether is another conversation.

Epigenetic Biology

As if all these were not enough for believers in materialism and the radical Artificial Intelligence it is creating, let us take a look at the field of biology and the amazing scientific revolution that is taking place in this area. Here too the footprints of the human spirit including human consciousness become visible in the very functioning of our DNA, of our genetic system.

Materialistic mechanical model in biology goes like this. We observe all kinds of traits in us. In the end, these traits are really nothing but expression of our genes. But genes are nothing but a sophisticated and ingenious combination of molecules. And molecules are nothing but combinations of atoms, and atoms, with their subatomic particles are the basic stuff of matter.

If I have a thought, the materialist will say that that thought comes from the brain. But the brain, for all its complexity, is nothing but a biological organ, an aggregation of specific kinds of tissues. But these tissues, in turn, are made up of cells and cells function according to the genetic code that is found within. So thought, in the end, is nothing but expressions of one's DNA, which is nothing but matter.

Typical among materialists is the widely read historian, Yuval Noah Harari. He writes, with supreme confidence:[444]

> ... as scientists opened up the Sapiens black box, they discovered there neither soul, nor free will, nor 'self'—but only genes, hormones and neurons that obey the same physical and chemical laws governing the rest of reality.

He elaborates further:

> To the best of our scientific understanding, determinism and randomness have divided the entire cake between them, leaving not even a crumb for 'freedom'. The sacred word 'freedom' turns out to be, just like 'soul', a hollow term empty of any discernible meaning. Free will exists only in the imaginary stories we humans have invented. ... The last nail in freedom's coffin is provided by the theory of [Darwinian] evolution. Just as evolution cannot be squared with eternal souls, neither can it swallow the idea of free will. ... According to the theory of evolution, all the choices animals make—whether of habitat, food or mates—reflect their genetic code. ... If by 'free will' we mean the ability to act according to our desires—then yes, humans have free will, and so do chimpanzees, dogs and parrots.

Extending this thought further, one would arrive at the following conclusion. If one voted Democrat instead of Republican during an election, it is not because of inner reasons of certain beliefs about the qualifications of the candidate. It is because we were predisposed by our genetic inheritance to vote for a democratic candidate!

Again, Harari is quick to support this kind of tempting speculation.

Why do I prefer voting for the Conservatives rather than the Labour Party? I don't choose any of these wishes. I feel a particular wish welling up within me because this is the feeling created by the biochemical processes in my brain. These processes might be deterministic or random, but not free.

I have selected this long quote because millions of people are reading this kind of outdated science. And people, like Harari, get well-known because of it. Obviously, Harari is not aware about the revolutionary developments going on in epigenetic biology and neuroscience.

The worst of the lot is biologist Richard Dawkin's polemic, *The Selfish Gene*. He firmly believed and argued that our notion that we are human beings is an illusion. He wrote that genes make us, the organism, survive from one generation to the next. The reality is the gene. The organism is nothing but a convenient carrier of the genes that are seeking their own survival. That is why he titled his book *The Selfish Gene*.[445]

The applications to AI are very clear. AI scientists try to imitate and improve upon human consciousness through digital means. If they are materialistic AI scientist, they believe that the human brain houses all human thought and memory. Consciousness is nothing but a secretion of the human brain. So, in principle, AI scientists believe that they can replicate the human being, and all the contents of its consciousness, in a sophisticated and powerful Artificial Intelligent machine.

There is a book out by Dr Martine Rothblatt called *The Virtually Human*. Ray Kurzweil, the famous guru of Singularity wrote the Forward of the book. Rothblatt describes the technological effort to create a digital equivalent of a person.[446] For all its sophistication, it is nothing but a variant of the above scenario.

Well if AI scientists and proponents take notice of developments in other scientific fields, like the present ones, they would not be so naïve and foolhardy in their intentions.

One of the foremost of these scientists of the second scientific revolution is Dr Bruce Lipton, one of the de facto founding fathers of the new paradigm in biology known as epigenetic biology. What this new biology is we will see shortly in what follows.

We have all heard of the massive multi-billion dollar project called the Human Genome Project (HGP). They wanted to sequence and map out the entire human genome. They believed, based on their materialistic framework, that they would then be able to identify the location of the specific genes that determined both phenotype or traits of the human being, like disease genes, behaviour genes, structural genes, and so on. More than 20 universities and research centres were involved.[447]

Scientists expected to discover and decode the postulated 50,000 to 140,000 genes to explain the manufacture and presence of 150,000 proteins in the human body. But what did the Human Genome Project find? Scientists only discovered 20,500 genes! That really puzzled them.[448]

But, what is worst is this nightmare of materialistic biologists and scientists in general. They made the mind-blowing discovery that one gene, using epigenetic control, can make 30,000 proteins! Epigenetic control is control coming from outside the nucleus and its DNA.[449]

Here comes the earth-shaking discovery of epigenetic biology. The signals can be anything from the environment, physical (like toxic compounds) and non-physical, *including thoughts, feelings, and trauma!*[450]

A person can have a good gene, and through epigenetic control, can create cancer, diabetes, heart disease and so on. And the reverse is true. One can have a bad gene that gives a predisposition to certain kinds of illnesses, like heart diseases. Yet, through epigenetic control, one can prevent this bad gene from expressing itself and thus producing the expected dreaded disease. Thus, scientists have discovered that only 5% of illnesses is due to mutant genes. That leaves 95% of illness affected by various epigenetic factors.[451]

We hear a lot about stem cell therapy. But, if we only know how, we do not need stem cell therapy from the outside. Our bodies are full of stem cells and they can repair and replace any tissue or organ in the body.[452]

Why are we ill? It is because we have not found a way to control cellular and genetic processes with our mind, with our consciousness. If we did, then we can mobilize our stem cells to repair the damaged tissues and organs of our body. And why do we age? It is because the belief systems in our mind control the cells and the genes and those belief systems may be negatively self-fulfilling.

One immediate field of application to healing is the placebo effect. Medical scientists have now discovered that more than 30% of all healing is not due to the drugs or the chemicals that doctors give their patients. Instead, it is the belief and the positive attitude of the patients that heal them from their illnesses![453]

This profound discovery of epigenetic control provides the death blow to the Central Dogma of Biology. The Dogma says that the DNA inside the nucleus is impermeable to any external influence outside the nucleus. Thus, there is a one-way deterministic causation (and not vice versa) from

DNA to RNA to the formation of amino acids and then finally to the protein compounds that give us our structure and determines our physiology.[454] In reality, the causal chain runs in the opposite direction: from our consciousness down to the DNA.

And if there is this death blow to neo-Darwinian biology, then it is epigenetic biology. This would unravel the transhumanists agenda, the mindset fuelling the engine of the AI revolution. As we have seen, the transhumanist believes that it is no problem to move from human evolution to natural evolution. The latter is the larger process. It is a natural law that evolution moves to higher and higher more intelligent forms of expression. The next stage of evolution is Artificial Super Intelligence.

Transhumanists are using natural law as their justification for not worrying about human extinction. Since that is the law of Nature, then there is no human moral guilt involved. There is nothing immoral about reducing humans into a machine. From their perspective, the human being is nothing but a complex biological machine. But as we have seen, this framework is totally baseless. The emperor has no clothes!

In the end, our destiny does not lie in our genes. We are more than our genes. We can control the way the genes express themselves. Epigenetic biology has given us very powerful evidence that our consciousness is not in the gene, nor its neural phenotype, the brain, contrary to what AI engineers believe.

It is indeed ironic, and is increasingly the gesture in the other scientific fields, that the results of the Human Genome Project (HGP), meant to prove the Central Dogma, instead destroyed this deterministic and materialistic image of life.[455] HGP also gave birth to the flourishing field of Epigenetic Biology. Sure, DNA has a role. But it is a very different role than one had ever imagined before.

I would like to stress one final point before looking at how all these impact on how we perceive and deal with Artificial Intelligence.

The promises of Artificial Intelligence are overblown. The creators of AI believe that they can reduce the real human from a complex intuitive, free, reflective, thinking, feeling, and living being to one that is ultimately a very much reduced version of itself, to a mere biological machine, and as such permeated with the forces of the non-living or ultimately death.

And so, if consciousness does not originate in the brain, but expresses itself in the brain, then we begin to see the full dimensions of the horror Artificial Intelligence is trying to impose on humanity. Because most AI scientists are materialists,[456] they will reduce the amazing and beautiful complexity of the human being to simple digital logic. Freedom will vanish as AI becomes pervasive in society. For freedom exists contrary to what AI scientists believe. It is at the core of our spiritual essence as true human beings.

Our spiritual consciousness co-evolved with our biological body. And one can argue that this innate intelligence in our consciousness, understood as a force that is causally effective in the physical world, as clearly demonstrated in epigenetic biology, helped shape our biology to its present level of sophistication.

But all these will be reduced and caricatured in the artificial human being most now adore as Artificial Intelligence. We have 50 trillion (50,000,000,000,000) living cells within us, with each gene within these cells capable of more than 30,000 different kinds of expression. We have a total of 10 to the 17th power of a vast possibility of potentials that reside in us, just waiting to be actualized by the power of our consciousness.[457]

Instead of this awesome possibility inherent in our spiritual nature, we will be forced with AI to inhabit a world where all of this will be reduced to a very limited amount of digital, mechanical expressions, which has nothing to do with our meaning and purpose as spiritual beings on this planet.

If people realize the unscientific nature behind the worldview of the transhumanism driving AI, they will fight against the extinction scenario.

The Science of Meditation

In recent years, neuroscience and Buddhist meditation joined together to create a special field in neuroscience known as the neuroscience of meditation.[458] There is no need to go to the specific scientific experiments. But the short of it is that this science has lifted meditation from an obscure practice to a much-sought practice in the world.

The implications for anthroposophy are huge, even if the Buddhist meditation is different from anthroposophical meditation. There are points of convergences as shown clearly by Arthur Zajonc, a quantum physicist, in his book, *Meditation As Contemplative Inquiry*.[459]

Zajonc is one of the scientific advisers to the Dalai Lama and the former Chairman of the Anthroposophical Society in America. Zajonc is the head of a network involving 800 universities that have mainstreamed meditation as part of its higher education.[460] He was also the Scientific Director of the Mind and Life Institute until June 2015. This Institute is closely linked with the Dalai Lama.[461] And so, standing publicly in the stream of spiritual science, Zajonc is in the middle of orchestrating many of these developments that have an affinity with Wisdom 2.0 (see immediately below).

All these researches in the neuroscience of Buddhism and other spiritual practices have resulted in the emergence of Wisdom 2.0. This movement is saying that the mainstream wisdom in the world that produced the Western world's high-tech society is not the only wisdom there is. The world needs to complement this high-tech world with a different kind of wisdom if we are going to survive the impact of technology.[462]

And the interesting, most bizarre thing is that high-level executives in the high-tech industries of Silicon Valley are actively promoting this Wisdom 2.0.[463] It is basically the first practical response to the question: How do you deal with all the stress experienced in the innovation centres of the world? It is a beginning answer and is leading to other directions.[464]

The interesting thing is that Wisdom 2.0 is now bringing into the picture some of the world's top meditation masters from different meditation streams. You have the Sufi stream, the Buddhist, the Hindu and so on, including the anthroposophical stream in the presence of Arthur Zajonc.

However, one can quickly add that this development is a mixed bag. Some of these corporations are involved in activities that are problematic in the area of private security—including allowing some of their data to be used by the intelligence agencies of the United States, third parties and changing our settings automatically without our permission.[465] Facebook employees are prominent attendees of Wisdom 2.0.[466] Yet Facebook is currently facing the crisis of its life due to its connection with the Cambridge Analytica scandal.[467]

Google employees and executives are also prominent attendees of Wisdom 2.0.[468] Yet Google has been engaged in systematic lying about its true intentions and also in manipulating the minds of other people.[469]

There is a disconnection between the meditative activity and the motives of corporate activity in many cases. The question of this disconnection was brought up in Wisdom 2.0, and there was no direct answer.[470] They found it a very difficult question, even though this inner work, this mainstreaming of meditation, is seen as a necessary part of existence in the twenty-first century.

Meditation is being explored and practised in some of the leading centres of world power including the World Economic Forum, the United Nations, the Heritage Foundation, the World Bank, financial centres in New York and some cities in Europe.[471]

Google has a university and a guru teaching mindfulness to all its employees—full-time.[472] Mindfulness has been informed by the work of Daniel Goleman, who wrote the book *Emotional Intelligence: Why It Can*

Matter More Than IQ, which has sold millions of copies around the world and is considered as one of the most influential books by *Time* magazine.[473]

Wired magazine, the premier high-tech geek magazine of the world, featured an article in respect to this titled 'In Silicon Valley, meditation is no fad. It could make your career'.[474] Meditation is now regularly mentioned in *The New York Times*, *The Wall Street Journal* and other mainstream newspapers.[475]

Thus, in today's world, it is no longer 'soft' to speak about meditation. For better or for worse, it has now entered into the hard power structures of the world. Maybe some of these executives are just doing this for stress reduction, for more creativity and productivity, for better health—there are various reasons—but whatever the reasons, the topic is now mainstream.

The dominant meditative form is Buddhism, because Buddhism is not a religion. It is seen as the highest form of a science of consciousness from the past, and that is why many neuroscientists around the world are starting to do neuro-scientific studies of the brain patterns of Buddhist meditators.

The rise of Buddhism would not surprise anthroposophists who are familiar with Steiner's lecture series called *Background to the Gospel of St Mark* given in 1910–1911, (GA 124). Steiner makes the very interesting comment that the increasing materialism of the world will be deflected by Buddhism, just as Islam deflected the early hardening of humanity through materialistic science that was going to be introduced around the seventh century AD.[476]

This is starting to happen. But aspects of Buddhism itself are also becoming more materialistic in the process. However, if spiritual scientists genuinely engage Buddhism, its promise as a haven against materialism may yet be fulfilled.

There are still other scientific developments, including scientific evidence for the evolution of human consciousness, a topic already discussed extensively in Part II above. But this is already a very long chapter. Let us end with this consideration.

We are not complex biological machines that can be simply replaced by a superior AI or even Artificial Super Intelligence. And we should spread this discovery far and wide. Pursuing the AI, AGI, and ASI dream one-sidedly, is tantamount to abandoning who we really are with massive spiritual consequences for ourselves, our future, our societies, and our planet.

Chapter 17

Answering the Four Grand Temptations of
Artificial Intelligence

Technological singularity, combining nanotechnology, genetic engineering, information technology, and Artificial Intelligence first gained prominence by promises connected with super health, super strength, super intelligence, and physical immortality.[477]

From their perspective, the transhumanists want to help human beings. They see that humans have certain natural challenges. They are often sick so why not give them super health? They are weak so why not give them super strength? Most humans are not too intelligent. So why not give them super intelligence? And, then, they want humanity to benefit from a very radical notion and technological intervention. Humans die. So why not give humanity physical immortality?

To do this, however, transhumanists want to transform natural humans to cyborgs, half human, half-machine. Many people are excited by this vision. But there are also a large number of individuals that are horrified with the prospect of turning humans into machines. What could the combined scientific acumen of spiritual science and the second more spiritual scientific revolution say to this?

On the Appropriate Coming Together of Humans and Machines

The first observation is that Steiner, too, speaks of the coming together of machines and humans. But he did not envision it in the form of a cyborg. Instead he thought of humans magnifying their inner capacities in resonance with machines. And at the more advanced stages, he envisioned humans would impart some of their formative forces of life (etheric forces) to machines making the latter alive in a certain sense. Some observers of Steiner's comments on machines and technology would call this the development of 'moral technology'. Paul Emberson, *Machines and the Human Spirit* gives a succinct summary of this process.[478]

Second, the spiritual scientist would say that the image of the human being that transhumanists have, is simply not accurate and is incomplete. Yes, there are mechanical aspects in humans but the human being is far richer than just being a machine. There are many facets of the human being that are not mechanical especially consciousness, love, compassion, thinking, moral intuition, the capacity to sacrifice for another and the reality of the existence of a Spiritual or Real Self beyond the day-to-day personality that we often confuse as our real self. What transhumanists are doing is forcing a very limited reality unto the world through their cyborg technology thereby going against billions of years of cosmic evolution.

Physical AI-Created Super Health or Fully Human Holistic Health

As to the temptation of super health, there can be two responses from the side of spiritual science and the new sciences. First, poor health is not just simply physical. Illness can be a blessing. We see that poor health gives us an opportunity to transform the distortions in our psyche, especially in our thinking and feeling life. Dr Mees explains the anthroposophical perspective on illness in his book, *Blessed by Illness*.[479] Illness helps us overcome our weaknesses as human beings so that we can have healthier relationships and more sustainable societies.

Second, a combination of the findings in epigenetic biology neuroscience, psychoneuroimmunology and neurocardiology or the science of the heart can help us attain super health in a more organic and natural way. The combined works of Bruce Lipton, *The Biology of Belief*, Joe Dispenza, *You are the Placebo*, Gregg Braden, *The Divine Matrix*, plus the amazing research findings on the heart by the scientists at HeartMath, can show us the way.[480]

Briefly the sequence goes like this, very roughly. We have certain belief systems in our brain. These thoughts, through neuroplasticity, imprint themselves in the structure of the brain. The imprinting is stronger if feelings are involved. These thoughts trigger the release of neuropeptides that then get sent to the cells in the heart and other organs. These neuropeptides then trigger specific biochemical processes inside the cells of the various organs. This is the second imprinting of our thoughts and feelings: in the biochemistry of our body.

Once inside the cell, these neuropeptides trigger still other processes inside the cell, including the release of specific compounds that now choose which sequence of DNA will be activated. This is the third level of imprinting of our thoughts and feelings in our body: at the level of our genetic system.

The DNA is then instructed to produce the necessary amino acids and proteins needed by our body. Millions of chemical reactions are taking place simultaneously.

If our thoughts and feelings are trained to harmonize with the wisdom of the body, then we achieve super health. The body is the most sophisticated pharmaceutical factory in the world.[481] It can manufacture virtually anything needed for your health. And our own body has millions of stem cells waiting to be activated so they can repair any damaged tissue or organ in the body. The wisdom of the physical body is awesome. And it can be activated by our intentions, thoughts and feelings.

We are only attracted to the illusory promises of transhumanism to the extent that we are ignorant of who we really are and what our bodies are capable of.

Finally, there is the spectre that the super health that nanotechnologists, biotechnologies, and AI scientists are promising is not based on an accurate picture of the workings of the physical human organism.

Take the case of the proposed development of precise delivery, aided by AI, by nanotech means of pharmaceutical chemicals at precise locations in the cell. This technology presumes a certain working of cellular processes, often in the image of biochemical processes. However, epigenetic biologists are pointing out that there are side effects caused by drugs that are delivered to the human body.[482] Precision delivery of drugs may be affected by epigenetic mechanisms triggered by the emotion and mental condition of the patient.[483] So even if precise delivery as envisioned works, it may not necessarily be beneficial to the human beings involved.[484]

AI Super Intelligence or Multiple and All-Pervasive Spiritual Intelligence

What would the spiritual response to the temptation of super intelligence be? The notion of super intelligence itself is a case of extreme reductionism. Harvard psychologist, Howard Gardner, demonstrated over 30 years ago that the human being has multiple intelligences, at least eight, and probably some more.[485] And this is different from the other scholars who are pointing out that the human being has twelve senses, not just five.[486]

By focusing on super intelligence simply understood as super IQ, the cyborg revolution will start eliminating all our other intelligences and senses by simply ignoring them or substituting them. And when they get substituted imperfectly, we lose them.

What will happen is that people will become less emotionally and socially intelligent, as one example. And the loss of these two intelligences will develop human beings who will be emotionally immature and will be incapable of interacting socially with others.

The net result will be the loss of empathy and the emergence of a more chaotic world where people will be quarrelling more often and powerful weapons of mass destruction will be in the hands of people who are moral dwarves and incapable of sound moral sentiments and judgements. We do not need one-sided super intelligence. Instead we need the full and harmonious development of our multiple intelligences as human beings.

One of the least understood is the super speed of intuitive thinking. Flashes of insight seem to come from out of nowhere suddenly synthesizing a whole constellation of ideas. In spiritual science when this capacity is developed more fully, it turns into higher states of consciousness (Imagination, Inspiration, and Intuition) that then impart massive amounts of knowledge of beings and forces that are responsible for the creation of the material world itself. If, in the highest state of anthroposophical Intuition[487] you experience the Christ, you are in total oneness with the Christ and therefore have Christ consciousness, that is, the intelligence of the entire universe. No supercomputer can claim that or overcome that.

Physical Super Strength or Inner Super Strength?

The temptation of super strength is another false panacea. How should we understand strength in this context? Is strength the be-all and end-all of human existence? Or is the search for super-strength a mere psychological projection of experiences of impotence in childhood? For example, one may be physically weak but also be a scientific genius. The late Stephen Hawking, the world-famous mathematician, is an example of this.

And what about the inner strength that gets developed because of a physical weakness? Would Helen Keller have been the way she was if she had had normal functioning eyes and ears?[488]

In saying all these, I do not mean to imply that it is good for people to be born blind, to have physical defects, and so on. Nor do I mean to criticize the promising efforts to give prosthetics to those who need them. But then to desire them when you do not need them is not only superfluous but also dangerous. It only bolsters egotistic and domineering behaviour.

The focus on physical super strength is also a displacement of our need to have super inner strength. Humanity has all this technology. But people are becoming spiritual and moral weaklings. Too much fascination with mechanical exoskeletons that can give one super strength may be useful in certain situations, but not all kinds of strength are physical. More often than not, the longing for physical substitutes is often just a symptom of an inner weakness for which one wants an external compensation.

Compensation for inner defects is a well-known psychological defence mechanism. 'Object relations' psychology, for example, has turned Freud upside down. Freud believed that human beings are basically driven by the sex and death instincts. 'Object relations' psychology, on the other hand, clearly demonstrates that humans often seek sexual intimacy because they had a limited or problematic bonding with another human being, usually their parent, during their baby stage.[489]

Given the psychological dynamics of compensation and/or psychological projection, the almost compulsive search for super strength, of the physical variety, will most likely be discovered to be a displacement in one's search for some kind of inner strength that one longs for but does not have. In this sense, the yearning for super strength is a can of worms!

Yes, one can hear the screams of objections to the above thoughts. But if we, as humans, continue to have pathological kinds of upbringing as children, then the search for super strength will always be present in the world. This is a world that is increasingly becoming violent because one set of people want to impose their belief systems and will on other groups of people who do not agree with them. And, compulsive imposition is nothing but a substitute for the lack of strength of inner character that one has inside.

Physical Immortality or the Existing Immortality of the Human Spirit?

All three temptations (super health, super intelligence, and super strength) are deeply connected with the fourth temptation: immortality. Transhumanists desire to live forever because they fear the void, the nothingness, which, based on their belief system, comes after death.[490] Otherwise they would not have an obsession to live forever.

But is this belief of a void after death really true? There are now thousands of recorded, medical cases of Near Death Experiences (NDE).[491] There is no void. There is fullness in what awaits us after death. The human spirit survives death.

The most dramatic example of this is the story of Dr Eben Alexander, whom we read about earlier. As a neurosurgeon, he is very familiar with the capacities and limits of the human brain. Dr Alexander thoroughly and scientifically debunks claims that NDEs are merely after-effects of a diseased or altered brain.

So NDE is real. And if one now brings this fact to its logical conclusion, then we would have to speak about the reality of reincarnation. For one thing, the evolution of consciousness of humanity, which is already the subject of study in hundreds of universities worldwide and which has already been clearly delineated by Ken Wilber in his book, *Integral Psychology* as discussed above,[492] would not make any sense. It would only make sense if the same spiritual individuality is the one experiencing these different stages in the evolution of consciousness and learning from them. Thus, when an individual is born, he or she is totally prepared from the previous context and suited in the present life context, to perform adequately in the current world.

The Human Spirit is already immortal through the process of reincarnation. And it is not a static immortality. It is an immortality that continues to co-evolve and deepen with the evolution of the universe itself.

It is important to remember that, while scientific studies are starting to be done in this area, reincarnation is already enshrined in the belief system of billions of people around the planet and many religious systems of the world.[493] One needs to point out, however, that some of these current beliefs in reincarnation, for example that a human being can revert back to an animal, are inaccurate. This is not the kind of reincarnation we are speaking about here.

There is a second way to understand physical immortality in spiritual science. It is at once both subtle and powerful. It is this. spiritual science confirms the traditional belief of the Catholic Church that we will all arise, in the long distant future, in our 'transfigured body' which is a physical body immortalized by the resurrection forces of Christ.[494]

Prokofieff ties together the various phases of the process. The journey begins with the use of the resurrection forces of the Christ to enliven our dead thoughts, to think livingly outside the brain. This process is preceded by human consciousness actually suppressing the workings of matter in the brain and, in this free space, instilling it with new thoughts and new arrangements of matter.

Going another step forward, with our moral intuition, we actually transcend existing mechanistic causality active in the brain and create the matter of a future world through the moral substance we are introducing into the world. Moral intuition is not just what is good or not good for the world. Out of it, humans create the substance of a new world. From there, the highly spiritual human being, working with the resurrection forces of the Risen Christ, eventually creates new worlds as well as immortalizing his own physical body.[495]

What would one prefer: a digital immortality where one's consciousness is imprisoned in a digital robot, if indeed transhumanist scientists are successful in achieving this? Or would you prefer human immortality where one's spirit is continually enriching itself through various earth lives that have been blessed by re-immersion in the fabric of the entire universe and in the process building up the substance of future worlds?

We now see that the temptations of the Four Horsemen of technological singularity including Artificial Intelligence, are hollow and can be replaced by the real capacities for health, intelligence, strength and eternity that truly humans already have within them as potential, except for immortality which we already have as spiritual beings. We should now be more prepared to engage in the spiritual struggle that lies ahead.

And for that we need to appreciate the role that global civil society can play in this struggle. Organized civil society is the leverage that ordinary citizens have against the gigantic economic, political and cultural forces and institutions that are arrayed against the human interest and future.

Chapter 18

The Sleeping Giant: Global Civil Society 2.0

We just saw the powerful discoveries of the new second and more spiritual scientific revolutions and how they can free us from the wild temptations of transhumanists. But for this to happen, we need to have the new science and its blessings reach as much of humanity as possible. And for this we need the genius and competence of global civil society especially its talent for mass mobilization.

Global Civil Society is a veteran in global mobilizations. Mainstream commentators have called it the 'third force' after governments and big business.[496] Joining forces with global civil society, as appropriate, can go a long way towards creatively addressing the challenges of Artificial Intelligence. But we need to understand better who they are and what they can do.[497]

What Global Society Has Done and Can Do

Global Civil Society (GCS) has been around since the nineteenth century even earlier than the birth of the anthroposophical movement.[498] Just think of the anti-slavery movement in the mid-nineteenth century. But GCS became visible in the global public eye starting in the early 1990s.

The UN Summits and the Mainstreaming of Threefolding at the Global Level

The GCS reality as a global 'third force' surfaced clearly when representatives of more than 10,000 organizations around the world showed up at the United Nations Conference on Environment and Development (UNCED), more popularly known as the Earth Summit in Rio de Janeiro in Brazil in June 1992. There they crafted their own global agreements and lobbied to have these agreements passed at the official sessions of UNCED. GCS followed up their initiative at Rio +5 Summit in Brazil in 1997.

As a testament to their success, the Philippines Cabinet Secretary for Socio-Economic Planning, Dr Cielito Habito, as Chair of the UN Commission on Sustainable Development (UNCSD), with the prominent assistance of Philippines activists, including a few anthroposophists, introduced societal threefolding as a process at the UNCSD. It was successful, so much so that the UN General Assembly itself introduced their version of threefolding as one principle of the UN Millennium Development Goals (UNMDGs). Their version, called tri-sector partnerships or public policy networks, spread to all countries in the world that adapted the UNMDGs.[499]

There is even a Masters Program on tri-sector partnerships at Singapore Management University to help develop the new skills required to make tri-sector partnerships work.[500] In 2015, the UN scaled up it development goals and renamed it the UN Sustainable Development Goals (UNSDGs). Tri-sectoral partnerships remained one of the 17 principles for implementation by all countries pursuing the UNSDGs. This global agreement involving more than 100 countries remains in effect until 2030.[501]

From the Earth Summit on, GCS became active in all the UN Summits in the 1990s including the Beijing Summit on Women, attended by over 40,000 civil society activists, and the Social Development Summit in Copenhagen. GCS influenced the outcomes of all these Summits.

World leaders started to take notice of GCS but it was not until the embarrassing defeat of the World Trade Organization (WTO) at the hands of Global Civil Society at the Battle of Seattle that they all realized that GCS was a global force to be reckoned with.[502]

To appreciate the scope and far-reaching consequences of that victory by GCS over the WTO, let us begin with some important details regarding global civil society's (GCS) successful struggle to diffuse the impending domination of the world by the World Trade Organization (WTO). When we understand how global civil society did this, then we can have hope that we can also diffuse the existential risks associated with the advent of Artificial Super Intelligence (ASI).

David and Goliath: The Historic Battle of Seattle and the Decline of the WTO

There was a time when the biggest struggle on the planet was not Artificial Intelligence, but destructive elite globalization. And the poster boy for this menacing globalization was the World Trade Organization (WTO). After the collapse of the Berlin Wall, political and economic elites carefully designed the WTO to replace the Cold War as the organizing force of the world.

The WTO Agreement was 26,000 pages. Its Executive Summary

alone was around 450 pages. In the Philippine Senate, most of the senators who approved the Agreement had not even read the Executive Summary, let alone the 26,000 pages of the entire Agreement.

The WTO pretended to be just an economic agreement, on how nations traded with each other. But in reality, it was a Trojan horse to control nation states, by starting to take control of the economic system. And in the guise of economic advantages, the governments of nation-states would slowly release their own control over their economic future.

WTO was going to be the de facto constitution of the world. As part of the Agreement, countries would allow the WTO to repeal existing laws of a country so that all remaining laws would be compliant with the WTO Agreements. The Philippines, for example, had to repeal, despite massive citizens opposition, 32 carefully crafted and debated laws that become illegal once the Philippines decided to join the WTO.[503]

Activists involved themselves with passion against the WTO because the Agreement would affect everything. The Agreement would erode what activists had achieved in the last 25 years. For example, civil society activists in the Philippines had just succeeded in banning 32 pesticide formulations that were poisoning millions of rice and other farmers, not to mention the collateral effect on the drinking water supply of communities and the wildlife of the environment.

But there was the Sanitary and Phyto-Sanitary Standards Agreement in the WTO that would prevent governments from banning the entry of hazardous pesticides into their country.[504] There would be certain acceptable or tolerable levels of pesticide residues in the imported food products under the WTO. A secretive and non-transparent body within the UN system called the Codex Alimentarius would craft many of these standards. And so, no one was surprised that the standards of Codex defended the unsafe levels of pesticide contamination as determined by other scientific studies.[505]

In short, over a decade-worth of efforts to ban hazardous pesticides would be wasted. The WTO would force the entry into the country of food with dangerous levels of pesticide contamination. And this would not only be true in the area of agriculture. This dynamic of reversing long-standing victories of civil society would operate in all areas of GCS advocacy: fair labour standards, human rights, genetic engineering, sustainable development, and so on.

The pervasiveness of the impact of the WTO was its own weakness. It made it easy to organize nationally and globally around the issue. One just demonstrated very clearly what the impact would be on one's advocacy, and then one can easily jumpstart a movement around any overarching issue like the WTO.

Here clearly, the same possibility will happen in the case of AI. Artificial Intelligence is affecting and will continue, with accelerated power, to affect all areas of human life, including the possible extinction of humanity. It would be relatively easy to awaken citizens and organize massive strategies and mobilization to temper the existence of AI in the world.

For example, take a look at the emergence of the 'Delete Facebook' movement. This is one result arising from the Facebook/Cambridge Analytica scandal.

In the beginning, there were only very few organizations around the world concerned with the WTO issue. And then as information about the destructive potential of the WTO spread, the number of civil society organizations opposing the WTO blossomed into a few hundred. Then activists from different parts of the world formed the International Forum on Globalization, a global coalition to harmonize the efforts of GCS organizations and make their collective efforts more strategic.[506]

As the WTO continued to leverage its influence, civil society continued to gather strength and become more sophisticated with its oppositional strategy. Four years after the WTO was approved worldwide, civil society movements defeated an even more dangerous version of the WTO called the Multilateral Agreement on Investments or MAI.[507]

Two years after that, there was the Battle of Seattle where the Ministers and Heads of States of the WTO were not even able to sign any agreement because they were totally surrounded and harassed by tens of thousands of activists not only near their venue in Seattle, but also around the world.

The Battle of Seattle shocked and awakened the world. Most of the major newspapers and TV stations headlined the Battle of Seattle event. David had just defeated Goliath. The world was informed about how activists had just shut down a global organization that many showed was more important and powerful than the United Nations itself.

The agreements of the UN Summits are all voluntary. In contrast, the Agreements in the WTO are all obligatory and punitive. There would be sanctions against countries that would violate the treaties.

Most shocked of all were the very elite powers that tried to hijack the democracies of the world. In almost every major meeting of the global elite, plenary and important speakers had to preface their talk with the Battle of Seattle.[508] They were traumatized. That event deconstructed their most carefully laid out plans.

The WTO advocates thought that the victory of civil society was just luck. They were mistaken. Every year thereafter, activists would organize and harass the WTO Ministers in meeting after meeting. Most people still remember the violent Battle of Genoa and the bloody Battle of Cancun. In the latter, a South Korean activist killed himself. His highly visible placard said: 'The WTO kills.' And that message, reported by quad-media around the world, reached tens of millions.[509]

The WTO never really recovered from all these setbacks.[510] Furthermore, the global elite had to deal with a serious crack in their own ranks as Europe and the US locked horns over the war in Iraq.[511] The WTO is no longer such a deadly economic force that it once was. This is the reason why bilateral and regional block trade agreements have started to blossom in recent years.[512]

Civil Society Activists: Who Are They?

To work with global civil society, the global anthroposophical movement has to know the nature of global civil society (GCS). First of all, many in GCS are activists. They walk their talk. They are annoyed if others do not walk their talk. They spend most of their time tackling some of the most urgent issues in the world. Name an issue and it is most likely that there is a civil society organization addressing this issue. In his bestselling and inspiring book, *Blessed Unrest*, Paul Hawken documents the work of the millions of civil society organizations around the world.[513]

They are also adept at organizing at any level: local, national, and global levels. We saw this above. Some are familiar including Greenpeace, Amnesty International, Caritas, the International Forum on Globalization and 350.org. Others, including the Civil Society Alliance of South Korea, World Parliamentarians for Nuclear Disarmament, and Civicus, the global alliance of civil society, are not as well known but they do very important work.

Many of these are so committed that they are willing to die for their cause, and indeed a number of them have been assassinated, because of their uncompromising spiritual ideas and values including justice and respect for human rights. Every year, the Right Livelihood Foundation, based in Sweden, recognizes their work, sometimes, posthumously, and gives them the prestigious Right Livelihood Award, also known as the Alternative Nobel Prize. The Right Livelihood Foundation took its inspiration from the Eight-Fold Path of the Buddha.[514] This information is offered here in light of the role of Buddhism in the twenty-first century as discussed above.

The individuals awarded come from all continents and dozens of countries indicating the kind of outstanding work done at the grassroots, national and global levels. Recently the Right Livelihood Foundation gave an honorary award to privacy activist Edward Snowden,[515] the whistle-blower from the CIA, causing the Swedish Parliament to withdraw its partnership with the Right Livelihood Awards.[516]

Instead of diminishing the reputation of the Right Livelihood Foundation, its global reputation soared.[517] The Foundation was not going to be politically correct and naïve in light of the massive global violation of the privacy of billions of citizens of the planet. It demonstrated the same kind of Micha-elic courage that Snowden displayed when he risked his life and career to expose the surveillance abuses of the most sophisticated intelligence agencies of the most powerful countries of the world including the United States of America.

If we want to have a short description of these global civil society activists in the language of spiritual science, we can aptly say that they display Micha-elic long-range thinking, courage and perseverance amidst their battles with the most powerful individuals and groups on the planet.

Four New Trials and Skills for Global Civil Society

Now the same organized resistance with the issue of technological singularity and Artificial Intelligence can well happen as in the case of the WTO and UNCSD. The issue is more urgent and pervasive than the WTO, which, at its relatively simpler level, already triggered resistance. But several things need to happen first to GCS. Despite their sophistication and abilities, significant parts of GCS are going to experience things that will be totally new for these activists, at whatever level they operate.

Critical Relationship with Technology
First, activists will need to learn to see that these technological behemoths not only threaten their advocacies, but their very lives. Many activists are in love with technology. But they have to discern which technologies are of real benefit to humanity and which are not.

Inner Spiritual Challenge
Second, activists have to take a serious look at their own humanity. Artificial Intelligence is forcing humans to ask the question: What really does it mean to be human? If an activist is a materialist, then he would find himself in inner conflict if he opposed the technology. He would himself be hand-tied by an inner contradiction.

AI simply accentuates our mechanical nature. And even when it replaces us, then that would not be a disaster from a materialistic perspective. That would be an advancement in natural evolution. This is the reason why transhumanists are not worried about the extinction of the human species. They have a kind of religious belief that their consciousness and sense of self will continue. But this time they will be in a silicon-based body with super health, super strength, super intelligence, and immortality!

A materialistic activist cannot have any objection, in principle, against this materialist worldview of Artificial Intelligence. How can he fight for human rights if humans are machines? Human rights come from a sacred interiority that machines do not have. However, if he is a spiritually-based activist, this would the height of human folly, the act of consciously making the human species extinct and replacing our species with a new digital-based overlord of evolution.

If the activist is agnostic, then there will be an inner struggle. He can no longer retain his/her agnostic stand. He/she will have to stand up either to affirm the transhumanist agenda or be active in the emerging new global movement that would challenge the emergence of Artificial Super Intelligence or ASI.

Technological and Scientific Literacy

Third, assuming that an activist will take up the task of challenging the current direction of AI, that activist would now need to be familiar with a totally new set of arguments to support his or her advocacy. The activist would have to be familiar with the technological jargon. The activist would have to know the various new kinds of more spiritual scientific findings that show the folly and peril of technological singularity and AI.

Total Focus on AI as a Framing Challenge

And finally, the activist needs to make this AI issue the overriding issue of his/her life. Nothing less would be required if we are all going to turn the extinction threat around.

The Emergence of Global Civil Society 2.0

This is the reason why I have been calling for the creation of a more sophisticated form of civil society. And I am calling this, Civil Society 2.0. This new kind of civil society will be animated by activists who have consciously undergone the inner process of self -transformation and self-mastery. They have therefore struggled with and encountered their true humanity. And this true humanity, at its core, is spiritual. They cannot defend what they do not have nor experienced.

And then out of this inner understanding, Civil Society 2.0 activists can then have more passion, enthusiasm, creativity, determination, perseverance and more effectiveness in what they are trying to do for the world in the era of Artificial Intelligence. And then they would be more internally consistent with their new spiritual worldview when they defend the rights of humans, rights that stem from the sacred nature of humanity itself.

As we have seen, spirituality has huge implications not only in how science research is done and how technologies are developed and deployed. Spiritual considerations will also be important in how civil society activists would strategically engage in the greatest issue humanity has faced since its emergence in the world tens of thousands of years ago.

The Strategic Importance of Millennials and Partnership Among Generations

Here again the young generation is super important. Gina Lopez, former Secretary of the Department of Environment and Natural Resources of the Philippine Government, did a survey among millennials in two very large universities in the Philippines. Ninety percent of them said that they are deeply concerned about the environment and would get engaged in efforts to protect the environment.[518]

As we have seen above in the discussion about the anthroposophical Youth movement, they are also allergic to authoritarian structures. The recent trend of voting for outrageous heads of states like Trump is fuelled by millennials. They are so sick and tired of the same old structures that perpetuate the misery of the world. Because of this feeling, they become adventurous in their political behaviour.[519]

Unfortunately, this often means change at any cost. They have no strategic vision yet of what really needs to be done in the world. But, inwardly, they are prepared, with all their energy, dedication, and innovativeness, to take on causes that they see would benefit the world.

This is the reason why small action groups on Artificial Intelligence are starting to form in different countries around the world. Millennials and even younger individuals are animating these new initiatives for a better world. It is very inspiring.

As with all demographic groups, there is also a dark side to the millennials. We have to know this if we want to engage with them. If they do not find themselves engaged with meaningful activities in the world, they turn inside and become totally selfish. *Time* magazine devoted a whole cover issue on millennials and called them the most selfish generation in human history.[520]

If they cannot find their meaning and purpose, millennials would then be perfect fodder for AI. The selfishness of millennials is perfect for some of the technologies that are starting to mainstream out there. This is ironic because millennials are driving the revolution in information technology and Artificial Intelligence.

Take Virtual Reality. One can be totally lost and self-absorbed in this make-believe world. And that would be just perfect for millennials who have not found anything meaningful to engage in and are just basically drifting their life away.

In any event, any technology that makes people self-absorbed or selfish prepares the inner condition to be accepting of technology, any technology. For after all, technology is a form of substitution for any internal capacity that we may have.[521] The more we rely on a specific technology to do things for us, the more we lose that inner capacity in us to be discerning because that capacity has now been removed and substituted by the technology.

The key is to focus the bubbling energy and passion of millennials on the great issues that face humanity. That is what they are longing to do. Anything less for them would not be satisfactory. In this context, their involvement in the whole issue of Artificial Intelligence would be perfect.

While I support consciousness raising and organizing with millennials, we should not forget the Baby Boom generation and Generation X. They also need to be involved. This is a collective threat involving all of humanity.

There is a very interesting movement afoot in the US called the Encore Movement. This movement is made up of the Baby Boom generation who are now senior citizens. The movement is called the 'Encore' movement because it refers to the possibility of the older generation getting involved again, a second time, in creating a better world.[522]

This generation has now gathered a wealth of experience, expertise, networks, independence (from any familial obligations) and resources, including financial, that could play a valuable and vital role in shaping the future of this planet.

Now that we have a better sense of what Global Civil Society is, we are now ready to form alliances and partnerships with them. But first, the global anthroposophical movement has to undertake its own process of purification.

Part VI

LEARNING FROM FAILURE:
THE LAST STAND

This is the final section of this book. And I would like to approach it with a certain frankness not to blame anybody but to hold a mirror to fire the will of all concerned to do better for the future of humanity. Steiner sometimes had to do this at certain periods in the birthing of the global anthroposophical movement. His memorable words: '... measured against love, the truth is cruel'.[523]

One can speak on and on about this subject. But there is a clear and simple reality. We have seen that ultimately AI is challenging humanity to come up with a clear articulation of what it means to be fully human. Furthermore, this image of the fully human needs to be so widespread that it will become a civilizational force, that is an idea that is powerful enough to shape global societies.

The terrifying reality of ASI scenarios powerfully mirrors the paucity and the erratic nature of the alternative articulation that should be coming from spiritual science. As Chapter 19 below shows, anthroposophy clearly did not culminate. If it did, then the world would presently understand what it means to be truly human and would find it inwardly nauseating to have a world organized around the needs of predatory AI. Artificial Intelligence is in the world because a spiritual scientific understanding of the human being is a niche, even queer perspective in the modern world.

And this failure to culminate has had a tragic effect on the global Anthroposophical Society (GAS) itself. There are young people in the world who eat, sleep and work anthroposophy but many of them do not want to have a connection with GAS. As a result, GAS faces the challenge of its ageing leadership as well as its declining number of members.[524]

Based on wide-ranging conversations with them, the young people see GAS as sclerotic and detached from the mainstream of the world. They do not see GAS as truly engaging the world process. Yes, there are many initiatives coming from the daughter movements but the quality of these initiatives is getting more and more diluted.

But then there is always the Micha-elic Will. We are free to learn from our shortcomings and do better. Chapter 19 reflects what this could mean for the global movement of anthroposophy and for humanity. For we need to take 'our last stand' and do it as if our very life depended on it! For unfortunately, this is no longer a figure of speech. Our very lives do depend on how we undertake our last stand!

Chapter 19

The Wisdom of Failure

There is a debate within the global anthroposophical movement (GAM) on whether GAM achieved the Micha-elic Prophecy, that is Culmination, or not. A few say it did. Most say it did not.

But others within the latter group say that culmination happened within the daughter movements. And still a larger majority would say: No, culmination did not happen even within the daughter movements.

And on this latter point, Sergei Prokofieff had been the de facto spokesperson that culmination did not happen, the general one and the more specific one within the daughter movements.[525]

One can ask this key question: What daughter movement has succeeded in changing the paradigm and practice of a specific area of life? Unfortunately, the answer is none, not even in the oldest and most widespread movements including the education, medical, and farming movements of anthroposophy.

If there are over a thousand Steiner schools around the world, what about the hundreds of thousands or even millions of schools in the mainstream in all countries, teaching materialism and a narrow focus on IQ?

There may be over two thousand anthroposophical physicians, but what about the millions of medical doctors all around the world treating patients with a disease-centred materialistic understanding of illness?

If organic and bio-dynamic farming together cover over 70 million hectares, what about the billions of hectares treated with toxic pesticides and artificial chemical fertilizers?

If there was such a culmination, why are we now all in danger of getting physically wiped out when the human species becomes extinct?

If we culminated in education, why is mainstream education still focused on IQ and intends to digitalize the entire education system in total disregard of the child's evolving consciousness? And we can make similar observations on all the daughter movements.

This opens the question of Culmination wide open. Maybe we did not understand the meaning or the method properly? Maybe we were trying to do it all on our own? Is not that the gesture of an egotistic (luciferic) temptation?[526] Maybe it really means more of a culmination with others who are headed in a similar direction?

Before continuing with what we can all learn, let me state one point very clearly. I am not the type to cry over spilled milk. If we failed, we failed. We now have to learn and lift ourselves up and try again, albeit in a new way. And, this new way means to learn fast from our mistakes and stop obsessing over whether anthroposophy culminated or not. Friendships need not be broken over this question. We all need to come together and redouble our efforts if we and humanity are to survive towards the next generation.

Part of our learning could be to realize that maybe our task is to be homeopathic. This means to stimulate much larger processes with only relatively small numbers. This appropriate and properly timed stimulation is enough to trigger the culmination event in the specific area where the daughter movement is active. And when a similar strategy and process becomes effective in other realms of life, then we can speak of a Culmination, of anthroposophy becoming a civilizational force.

We can see this approach more clearly in the case of bio-dynamic agriculture and the environmental movement.[527] The bio-dynamic movement is part of a larger movement with non-anthroposophists in what is called the sustainable agriculture movement. This movement includes organic farming, permaculture, ecological agriculture, biological agriculture, agro-ecosystems, indigenous farming systems, and of course bio-dynamic agriculture.[528] All these forms of alternative agriculture, except the last one, are non-anthroposophical and may not have the larger understanding of what agriculture is in the context of the cosmos, but they definitely have the passion to care and nurture the earth as well as human beings living off the earth.

If the sustainable agriculture movement did not culminate yet, it definitely is strongly on its way to get there. More and more countries are putting laws in place to target specific land areas to be in sustainable agriculture by a specific target date. Sweden is the leading example in this regard.

And in the chapter on Global Civil Society just discussed, we also see a similar thing happening in the area of sustainable development, societal threefolding, and alternative approaches to elite globalization.

And when one looks at the culmination this way, it is amazing to see that there are parallel efforts everywhere by people outside the global anthroposophical movement (GAM).

If we have bio-dynamic agriculture, the outside world has organic agriculture. If we have anthroposophic medicine, the outside world has a very large movement on holistic health. If we have anthroposophical banks, the outside world has Green banks. And so on. For me, this is a symptom of an unconscious Micha-elic movement because it is headed in a similar direction. By their fruits, you shall know them.

Ultimately it is not surprising to observe this in the phenomena of the world. As we have seen, Micha-el is the Time Spirit of this Age. He is the Spirit for Humanity as a whole. He is the Time Spirit even for atheists who do not believe in spirits like Micha-el but who may sometimes end up giving more support to Micha-el in surprising ways than anthroposophists. I refer to atheists, already cited above, who are deeply concerned and passionate about the possibility of human extinction through the coming of Artificial Super Intelligence (ASI). Elon Musk, Max Tegmark and Sam Harris are prominent examples.

A similar phenomenon is especially visible in the area of materialistic science where some such scientists end up becoming defenders of consciousness as the determinant of the behaviour of matter and not the other way around as reductionist science would have it.[529]

Eventually, as pointed out in the principle of diversity above, tens of millions of people are moving in the direction of Micha-el, consciously or not. If this were not happening, we would all be worse off than we are now. It would be a disaster for humanity.

If so, reframing our perspective of culmination towards a broader understanding of what it means, opens up huge possibilities for bringing about the Micha-elic Prophecy and providing a powerful answer to the challenge of Artificial Intelligence. We can consciously set up alliances with key individualities and movements around the world, outside and within the anthroposophic movement, and together start shifting the inertia of civilization away from an increasingly ahrimanic destiny.

In this regard, in a lecture to members in Dornach, Steiner specified the possibilities and condition of success in this endeavour:

> Only when a spirituality such as is seeking to flow through the anthroposophical movement on earth unites *with other spiritual streams* will Michael find the impulses which will unite him once more with the Intelligence that has grown earthly but in truth belongs to him.[530] [Emphasis added.]

Unfortunately, some anthroposophists interpreted and still interpret this in the narrow sense. Many only thought of the Platonic and Aristotelian spiritual streams within the global anthroposophical movement.

However, if one takes a closer look at the statement, it is clear that the 'spirituality ... seeking to flow through the Anthroposophical Movement' already contains the Platonic and Aristotelian streams because that was what he was speaking about in his lecture. The Platonic and Aristotelian souls, with their spirituality, are already 'seeking to flow through the anthroposophical movement'. So it is clear that Steiner was referring to much larger 'other spiritual streams'.

This broader interpretation is supported by Steiner's 'definition' of what a Micha-elic Age would look like:

> An Age of Michael is characterised by many different conditions, but especially this, that in such an age the most spiritual interests of humanity (*according to the particular disposition of the time*) become dominant. In such an age especially, a cosmopolitan, international character will permeate the world. National distinctions cease.... A common feature runs through all humanity—something of an all-human character, as against the special interests of single groups or nations.[531] [Emphasis added.]

This description of the Age of Micha-el could also have been a description of the work of global civil society itself already discussed immediately above! As one who has worked in this area for more than 50 years, this description describes many of the colleagues in global civil society that I work with.

This also becomes clear upon reflection. There are individuals, outside the anthroposophical movement, who unconsciously have access to Micha-elic inspiration because they have 'intuitive thinking' in the sense of the *Philosophy of Spiritual Activity* as discussed earlier. This accounts for the cosmopolitan Micha-elic character of their thinking and actions. And this fact fits well with Steiner's statement above.

In referring to the 'spiritual interests of humanity' comes the phrase, '(according to the particular disposition of the time)'. Modern materialistic civilization is the 'particular disposition' of our time, making it difficult for many to be consciously spiritual. But it does not mean that one cannot be unconsciously spiritual if one's intuitive thinking is still alive and therefore has access to Micha-elic thoughts because in this realm of living thinking, 'Ahriman is broken'.[532]

Clearly, the role of the global anthroposophical movement was to have been homeopathic and in unity with all the other identities of the world that authentically yearn for the realization in the world of the truly human. The failure to recognize this approach, among others, resulted in the failure to bring about the Micha-elic spiritual civilization that would have been the proper context of the increasing relationship between humans and machines including Artificial Intelligence.

Failure is failure if we accept it with finality. We cannot learn from our mistakes if we do not recognize our failures. And it will not help the future of the anthroposophic movement if it obsesses itself and dwells in debates regarding 'culmination'. That concern, whether it happened or not, is moot and academic. It is now so irrelevant and meaningless.

The world has moved on, and very rapidly at that. Now we need to focus all our energies to dealing with *what has indeed culminated in our time, Artificial Intelligence*, the mirror anti-image of the wished-for Micha-elic culmination.

This highly sophisticated, non-human Artificial Intelligence seeks to morph into Artificial Super Intelligence that can wipe out the human species in a few decades or less. This will happen unless all of humanity collectively figure out how to make it 'beneficial' in a relatively very short period of time.

Failure is wisdom if we learn the hard lessons it teaches us so we can do a better job next time. Socrates believed that Wisdom starts with ignorance. Failure is a kind of ignorance or not knowing how to do things right. Even the techno-materialists in Silicon Valley get this point. As we have seen earlier, they go about with the attitude that 'failure is success'.[533]

Wisdom begins when we accept that we failed and that, in a sense, we were 'ignorant' about the ways of the world so we could not culminate. How can we do better if we already think that we have succeeded?

So let us admit that we are all wounded as a movement, that we have a version of the wounded Amfortas in us, but that there is also a Parsifal in each one of us.[534] And ultimately this Parsifal in us will heal our wounded Amfortas and prepare us to re-engage the world with fresh understanding, fresh love and enthusiasm and fresh energy! Our very future depends on it!

Chapter 20

The Last Stand

The phrase, 'The Last Stand' may be over dramatic. But in truth it is appropriate to the gravity of the situation. This is indeed not only our last chance but also the last chance for humanity. Even Micha-el is deeply concerned.

In earlier statements about Micha-el, Steiner has glowing, fiery and inspiring words about the Archangel most devoted to Christ. In addition, Steiner often highlights that Micha-el, as compared with his peers, believes that most humans will use their freedom in a responsible manner. Present humanity's adoration of Artificial Intelligence clearly creates a challenge to Micha-el and his role among the other Archangels who are not so convinced that it was a good idea to give humans full freedom.[535]

Steiner captures the growing concern of Micha-el in a number of 'Leading Thoughts', which include the Leadings Thoughts connected to the 'Michael Mystery'. He sent these to the members of the Anthroposophical Society, as he lay in his sickbed in the final months of his life.

> And Michael sees too that the danger of mankind's falling into the snares of the Ahrimanic Powers [via Artificial Intelligence] is becoming ever greater. *For himself, he knows that he will always have Ahriman beneath his feet; but can he do the same for Man?*[536] [Emphasis added.]

And then, in another 'Michael Mystery' Leading Thought, Steiner becomes more explicit. It becomes clear that with our freedom, Micha-el cannot interfere. Thus Micha-el also has to rely on what we do on our side to stem the luciferic and ahrimanic attack on humanity.

And now come words from Steiner that all who truly feel a connection with the Micha-elic School and/or the future of the earth have to take strongly to heart. For it is a unique and rare description of the Being of Micha-el, the spiritual being of 'courage', 'fiery thought'. The following words, written near the end of Steiner's life, come with a powerful urgency.

> One can see *Michael, full of anxiety* as to whether, after all, he will be in a position to keep the Dragon permanently in check, when he perceives how men are engaged in the one field only, trying to obtain from the picture they have just obtained of Nature a similar picture of Man.

Michael sees the way in which men are observing Nature and trying, out of what they call Natural Law, to construct an image of Man.... But before the spirit-eye of Michael, what arises is not Man at all.[537] [Emphasis added.]

This is a perfect premonition by Steiner of what ultimately emerges as sophisticated AI and the transhumanist rationalization that AI engineers give to their dangerous creation. AI creators say that AI is designed on the basis of 'natural law'. Therefore, there is nothing immoral involved in their activity because they are simply following 'natural law'. They do not realize that their 'natural law' is totally created by their ideology of materialism.

... So may one hear the Inspiration which Michael utters in *his dire anxiety*. May not this force of Illusion in men give the Dragon [Ahriman] so much power after all, *that it will be an impossibility for him— for Michael himself—to maintain the balance?*[538] [Emphases added.]

Personally, I am deeply affected by these messages of Steiner. Twice now he speaks about the '*anxiety*' of Micha-el, the fiery spirit of courage. And Micha-el actually articulates this anxiety in Inspiration and Steiner hears it at that level! That is approximately the inspiration one can hear of what Michael says in great anxiety.[539]

Elsewhere, Steiner describes Micha-el as the silent one. He prefers to be silent. He lets humans do their deed and he incorporates these deeds into the workings of the Cosmos if human deeds are worthy for such a dignified transformation of their initiative.

Then I realize that, based on his own integrity, Micha-el will not interfere with what humans do with their freedom. No amount of courage on his part will change the destructive path of humanity unless humans themselves wake up to their situation, ask for spiritual help and transform it with the help of Spiritual Powers that have been guiding humanity for tens of thousands of years.

To even hear of a thought of 'impossibility' in the part of Micha-el is inwardly shattering. This is an indirect way of Micha-el telling humanity through Steiner to take a deep look at what use they are making of their cosmically guaranteed freedom. He seems to be saying that humanity, influenced by a materialistic elite, is taking its technological ambitions too far; that it may not be possible for Micha-el and the other Keepers of Humanity to prevent humanity from jumping to its destruction.[540]

The 'religion of the Gods'—that was how Steiner once described the loftiness and care that the Gods looked upon humans as the creation of the Supreme Logos.[541] And now humans are creating massive artificial idols in their place and rejecting the reverence that the Gods had for humanity. This is absolute blasphemy and humanity will pay for this with its physical extinction by its own hands if it does not wake up and prevent an apocalypse from unfolding.

Steiner continues to systematically describe the situation with Micha-el as he nears his own earthly death.

> . . . eventually, if it [the true image of the human being] be not grasped by the spiritualized power of the Spiritual Soul, this too must end by falling from Michael's range of action into the dominion of Lucifer. That Lucifer might gain the ascendancy in the rocking of the cosmic balance—*this is the other dire anxiety in Michael's life.*[542] [Emphasis added.]

So Micha-el's struggle with Ahriman will not be enough. Depending on human understanding and behaviour, Micha-el will have to renew his battle with another powerful adversary, Lucifer, whom Micha-el had already defeated.[543]

> The preparation for Michael's mission at the end of the nineteenth century rolls on in *cosmic tragedy*. Beneath upon earth, there often reigns the profoundest satisfaction over Man's picture of Nature and its effective working; whilst in the region where Michael is at work there is nothing but tragedy over the obstacles which prevent the true picture of Man [*Mensch*] from finding its way into life.[544] [Emphasis added.]

Now, Steiner intensifies the gigantic stakes that are involved with the materialistic turn of human thinking and doing, a turn that has reached the point of humans replacing themselves with a digital double! And this drastic turn of humanity towards mechanical idols, has its effect on that part of the spiritual world near the earth where Micha-el is active in trying to contain the attacks of Ahriman.

In my opinion, here Steiner gives a hint that Micha-el himself has to deal with the darkening of the Etheric World due to the effects of materialism. This thick darkness as we know from spiritual science resulted in the second 'death' of Christ, this time in the Etheric World, due to the 'suffocation' of the angelic being that carried the Christ.[545]

Fortunately, Christ resurrected from His Deed of consciously taking Evil to transform it and, in this sense, has already cleared that sphere. Forces of illumination and resurrection are present in the Etheric World despite the appearance of the dark clouds of materialism. This, however, does not prevent the phenomenon of darkening. But humans and spiritual beings now have the possibility to see through, live through this darkness and not be overwhelmed by it. This is especially true of Micha-el who has been active in the spiritual world supporting the intentions of Christ.

It is like the temptation of Christ. No matter how pure one is, temptation will come. What is important is how one deals with the temptation when it comes and not to yield to it. It requires precise presence of mind. In the three temptations in the desert, Christ gave an example of how one can deal with these temptations: direct your attention upwards and remember your real nature. And the temptations flit away!

Going back to the quote above, Steiner emphasizes, that this is 'cosmic tragedy'. In addition, the cosmic being that could help deal with this, is faced 'at work there [with] nothing but tragedy over the obstacles which prevent the true picture' of the human being from 'finding its way into life'.

As a result:

> *There was a time* when in the beams of the sun, in the flush of morning skies, in the sparkling of the stars, *there lived the keen, clear spirit-love of Michael. The dominant note this love had now taken, was one of sorrow, aroused on gazing on mankind.*[546] [Emphases added.]

And now here is the most painful 'Leading Thought' of all: the change in the inner mood of Micha-el from his Sun-like sparkle and love to one of 'sorrow' due to the stupidities of humanity and the less-than-fiery enthusiasm and will of his students from his own School to do the best they can to transform the present situation of humanity.

> Michael's position in the Cosmos *became one of tragic difficulty....* Michael was not glad. He was obliged to remain on the far side, *aloof from men*, and carry on the war in his own region against Lucifer and Ahriman. Hence came the great and tragic difficulty; ... *a stormy contest was being waged on Man's behalf*, in the spiritual world next to earth, *by Michael* against Lucifer and Ahriman: *whilst Man himself on earthly territory was busying his soul in opposition to the healing forces of his own evolution.*[547] [Emphases added.]

This is another painful picture that Steiner received from Micha-el through Inspiration. Despite all his preparations, despite his School in the spiritual world, Micha-el's co-workers are mostly asleep to the grand meaning of their task.

And now Micha-el feels isolated from humanity itself. He is 'aloof from men'. This is deeply tragic because Micha-el, after all, is the Time Spirit of present-day humanity. He wants to guide us all. But many of us reject him even among those who have sworn an oath to advance Micha-el's intentions.

He does what he can do but humans not only do not appreciate what Micha-el is doing, but set up 'opposition' to the very force that can heal the great disturbances in human evolution. Talk about aggressive non-gratefulness!

It is difficult not to be shaken by these words. Human beings, especially those who are aware of this knowledge, are making it very difficult and tragic for Micha-el to help humans in their most dire moment of existence. Many are not even aware of the cosmic abyss awaiting humanity should it fail to act properly and in a timely manner.

Steiner sums up all this in a few sentences.

And so Michael, in the time preceding his earthly regency, *can only look with anxiety and sorrow upon mankind's evolution.* For men condemn spiritual contemplation in any direction, and thereby cut themselves off from everything that makes a bond with Michael.[548] [Emphasis added.]

We must view our failures, inadequacies and shortcomings as calls to strive even harder especially now knowing very clearly the inner mood of the Spiritual Being who schooled Steiner to introduce anthroposophy to the world. Marie Steiner, whom Steiner had intended to direct the Second Class of the School of Spiritual Science, has some words of wisdom for all of us to deeply reflect on as we ponder how we can help Micha-el better.

Marie Steiner once said:

Souls who experience themselves as rooted in the spirit, must be tested. When such a trial is sought out by an individual, it always calls forth an accelerated karma; it must also bring to light what otherwise would prefer to remain hidden. Attempts drawn from deep cosmic foundations by spiritual forces with the goal of elevating humanity's development to a higher level have often failed as a result of such trials. This was the case of the French Revolution ...[549]

In plain language, those who have not internalized what failures and trials can mean for one's life, will betray Micha-el just at the very moment Micha-el needs us most for our sake! But those who understand this perspective, are now ready to take THE FINAL STAND with Micha-el and all the spiritual and human powers that have guided and are guiding humanity especially at this unique moment in the history of humanity, the earth, and the cosmos. What we do now will become our individual and collective destiny, for better or for worse.

Chapter 21

The Micha-elic Will and the Future of Humanity

We need to develop Micha-elic Will in us to save a future for the truly human. Let us be inspired by what this could be like by taking a vivid unambiguous picture of this powerful Will. Steiner's direct connection with Micha-el will give us an idea.

> There are two ways of experiencing anthroposophy—many variations lie between, but I am mentioning only the two extremes—and one of them is this: a man sits down in a chair, takes a book, reads it, and finds it quite interesting as well as comforting to learn that there is such a thing as spirit, as immortality. It just suits him to know that with regard to the soul as well, man is not dead when his body dies. He derives greater satisfaction from such a cosmogony than from a materialistic one. He takes it up as one might take up abstract reflections on geography, except that anthroposophy provides more of a comfort. Yes, that is one way. The man gets up from his chair really no different from what he was when he sat down, except for having derived a certain satisfaction from what he read—or heard, if it was a lecture instead of a book.[550]

We must now all be smiling knowingly inside. Most of us will have most likely experienced this kind of relationship to anthroposophy at some point in our life. Unfortunately, many remain at this level. There are groups that study anthroposophy for more than 30 years. But that is it, just study, but no action.[551]

> But there is another way of receiving what anthroposophy has to give. It is to absorb something like the idea of Michael's Conflict with the Dragon in such a way as really to become inwardly transformed, to feel it as an important, incisive experience, and to rise from your chair fundamentally quite a different being after reading something of that sort.

Clearly these are words of action. Have we reached this stage of our relationship to anthroposophy? If yes, then it means that we spend a considerable part of our life trying to bring about Micha-el's mission for the world. And, if not, then let us redouble our efforts and help remove the 'anxiety' of Micha-el and do our part for him.

This ability to rise to the point at which thoughts about spirit can grip us as powerfully as can anything in the physical world, *this is Michael power*. It is confidence in the ideas of spirit . . . leading to the conviction: I have received a spiritual impulse, I give myself up to it, I become the instrument for its execution. First failure—never mind! Second failure—never mind! A hundred failures are of no consequence, for no failure is ever a decisive factor in judging the truth of a spiritual impulse whose effect has been inwardly understood and grasped.

This kind of Micha-el Power in us will be the kind of Will that we need to face the possibility of the impending disaster of humanity. This quotation from Rudolf Steiner actually calls us to take a stand in this situation, a stand that will determine the future of humanity.

As we saw in Part II, from the perspective of the long view of the evolution of consciousness, there is at first a moving 'downwards' away from our original spiritual and unconscious Participation. And now, with our alienated, dual Consciousness we have reached the point where we feel so separated from and have no access to the inner aspects of the world process.

Following this 'downwards' process, because of the emergence of human freedom, there are now two possibilities for humanity and its future.

We can move 'upwards' and forwards to scientific conscious Participation, merged with the directionality of the creative power of the Source of the Universe and do our share of realizing our full humanity in harmony with society, nature, and the spiritual worlds. In this future, humans will be using AI to serve the world and create a more just, sustainable, and flourishing planetary civilization.

The Philosophy of Spiritual Activity of Rudolf Steiner, quoted heavily in many parts of this book, is, in reality, a 'manual' on how to begin this process of Conscious Participation.

Or humanity can take a second path. Some of us can continue to accelerate downwards towards the path of digital Armageddon, tinker some more with artificial super intelligence (ASI) using our alienated consciousness, without any clear idea of how to deal with the Alignment Challenge accompanying ASI.[552]

The bitter pill to swallow here is that most of humanity would naturally prefer the first path. But there are humans, who are in the minority, who have the money, power, and influence to take the risk of accelerating to the cliff of digital Armageddon.

But now humanity has reached a critical decision: whether to continue the descent into sub-nature and Artificial Intelligence or turn in a new direction towards the spiritual. The decision lies with us. Will we use our freedom wisely and decide with the good Gods and Micha-el? Or will we recklessly choose and continue to plunge humanity towards the abyss of extinction?

Here we need Micha-elic power to make the choice and to live our lives in faithfulness to that choice.

If we remain neutral and/or choose non-involvement out of fear or inconvenience, then we are actually making a choice towards the abyss. This is a spiritual battle where one has to take sides actively. By our inaction we, de facto, side with the small segment of humanity, who are dragging billions of humans with them and who have chosen the path to go against the will of the Gods, to put it very pointedly.

Do we really want to place our bets with the dark side of humanity that wants to 'engineer' the next stage of what they prefer to consider as 'natural evolution', where super-intelligent machines, not the human being, are the pinnacle?

Do we, together with the dark side, want to negate 13.8 billion years of earth time that resulted in the creation of the very freedom that small numbers of humans are exercising today to exterminate ourselves?

Or can we awaken to the very loud voice of our Higher Self and join the ranks of Micha-el and the Keepers of Humanity who would battle Ahriman to the end?

This plunge has already begun and it is an accelerating plunge into the abyss. If there are no counterforces from us, then that plunge will be final and executory. Many of us will fail in our first attempts. But with Micha-elic Will we say, 'Never mind. Learn and try again.'

We have to keep on trying. This will be our last stand! We will not be around physically if we fail. The earth will become uninhabitable for the human spirit. That would be a disaster on the cosmic scale. Steiner calls it 'cosmic tragedy'.[553]

Failure is not an option. We have to give our best.

The Anthroposophical Will and 'Sting'

From the Karma lectures, we all know what kind of karma we are carrying as anthroposophists. If we feel a connection to anthroposophy, and if we feel a connection to Micha-el, we have a heavy responsibility to do spiritual battle on behalf of the world.[554]

And, truth to say, despite our doubts and fears stemming from our normal day-to-day self and consciousness, as members of the School of

Micha-el, we have world-shaping powers in our Will. The Micha-elic School was to inspire and train us to undertake the bold task of creating new societal arrangements worthy of the dignity of the truly human. We should not get used to and feel normal that we are very 'small' compared to the larger forces shaping the world. That is not who we truly are. That kind of thought and belief is simply an artifact of our upbringing and social conditioning here on earth.

In other words, because we are part of the Micha-elic School and wake up to this fact that we have the power to change the world and start doing something about it, then we will begin to experience lots of opposition and hardship in our lives.

This is the karmic 'sting' of being an anthroposophist. It follows us like night follows day. The sting comes from the opposing powers that know this civilization-creating power in us. And these dark powers will make sure that we get painful 'stings' in life so we will be afraid to carry out what we can carry out in the world because of who we really are.[555]

A statement by Christ is appropriate in this context.

> Blessed are ye, when men shall hate you, and when they shall separate you from their company, and shall reproach you, and cast out your name as evil. Rejoice ye in that day, and leap for joy: for, behold, your reward is great in heaven: for in the like manner did their fathers unto the prophets. Luke. 6:22–23

The karma of the anthroposophist is a painful one. You are going to be opposed at every direction in your life, especially if you are about to take initiative, and especially if you want to do something out of your enthusiasm for these world ideas.

This 'sting' is the Sword of Damocles over our head: on the one hand we will suffer a lot if we follow our passion to do something constructive in the world; on the other hand, if we do not find that initiative in our life that serves our meaning and purpose, our life would be useless. We will feel useless and we will feel ourselves drifting in and betraying the world.

There is an inner fear in the former case. This is the fear that the moment one incarnates an initiative in the world, one will get all kinds of challenges, all kinds of pain.

This knowledge lives in us unconsciously, making us fearful, sapping our courage to do what we can really do in the world, whether in a local area but with a global consciousness or in a global arena while mindful at the same time of the local.

We need the Micha-elic Power that can endure that sting, and to sacrifice through pain, in the continued service to the world. The Micha-elic Power is the power of courage and the ability to take failure, learn from it and move on, until there is another failure, and then you move on learning all the time, dealing with the pain and the sacrifices involved.

This is what it would take to create a new planetary civilization, and we are at a point in human history where the hour is quite late, the descent into the abyss is accelerating and the forces of good are just awakening.

Final Words of Hope

Taking an overview of the entire AI challenge, I would estimate that more than 90% of the challenges of AI have potential solutions.

We can see these solutions in the headlines of newspapers and articles of magazines plus the buzz in the Internet itself regarding insiders, early investors, geeks, and whistle-blowers from Silicon Valley who, among others, have come together to set up the Center for Humane Technology. There are an increasing number of insiders in Silicon Valley and elsewhere who are stepping forward to blow the whistle at the risk of their careers and lives. They cannot allow, in conscience, for the deleterious and negative side effects of technology to continue.[556]

From the spiritual perspective, this growing groundswell of concern for the direction that modern technology is taking is a symptom of the workings of Micha-el as Time Spirit of the whole of humanity. He continually works to improve the human condition whether humans are conscious or not of his Presence and his Work.

However, the most important challenge, the 'alignment challenge', so far, has no solution. Yet this is the most dangerous challenge as it can wipe out humanity if we do not find a way to make Artificial Super Intelligence (ASI) safe. It seems like a solution to this challenge is impossible.

However, knowing from the facts above about the amazing 'super' potential of the truly and fully human, a potential that has access to the Wisdom and Workings of the Universe, there is a solution out there waiting to be discovered. And this discovery can be done if we all converge together, no matter who we are and what our identities are, and trigger the workings of Collective Human Intelligence in partnership with the spiritual powers that guide the future of human and planetary destiny.

This is not a pipe dream. As we near the end of this book, I want to share a true story of how something considered impossible became possible. This story is familiar among mathematicians but is mostly unknown to the general public. This story gives us hope, that if we really try and continue to try, in a collective way, a solution will emerge.

This is the story of Fermat's Last Theorem. For over 350 years, mathematicians thought there was no solution to this Theorem. But then one day, a mathematician was born into the world. His name is Andrew Wiles. He is still alive today. To the amazement of all, Wiles has the great distinction of providing humanity with a solution to Fermat's Last Theorem. He demonstrated his proof in over 100 pages of complicated mathematics. The impossible became possible.[557]

One is also reminded of Nassim Taleb's book, *The Black Swan*. It is a wonderful documentation of how history is full of 'black swans', the emergence of totally unexpected events and developments when all seems hopelessly the same and a different future looked impossible.[558]

The title takes its cue from the centuries-old belief that there were only white swans until, one day, researchers discovered black swans. Taleb uses this as an example that, if something has been true for a long time, it does not mean the future is always going to be like the past.

In a sense, the rediscovery of spirituality scientifically, will be the 'black swan' of the twenty-first century where the prevailing belief in materialism is the dominant construct of viewing the world. And the harnessing of humanity's spiritual powers will be the 'black swan' of ASI and its 'alignment challenge'.

Today, the 'alignment challenge' is considered almost impossible to solve. There is a solution out there. But it cannot wait 350 years to find the solution. We have only 20 years, maximum, or even less, to solve the 'alignment challenge'.

We know we have to move faster than normal. We need to examine whether we really love humanity, the world, and, for some, anthroposophy. We need to infuse spiritual science into all aspects of life for only a spiritual perspective of the world will solve not only the 'alignment challenge' but the general challenge of AI itself: Be truly human.

If we do not act, then we will have been a party, a passive bystander, to the ultimate destruction of the earth and to the degradation of what the human being can be. Not only do we not want that to be our karma, but, even more important, we surely do not want to have been the generation that blew it, gave up the fight for the Spirit, creating serious consequences for thousands of years to come on a Cosmic scale.

Micha-el has conquered Ahriman. But will humanity and Micha-el succeed if we do not do our part? Our unclear, indecisive, vacillating answer to that question makes Micha-el 'anxious'. If it were up to him the answer would be a resounding 'Yes!' We have to make sure that humanity answers with a resounding yes! When we do, we will join

Micha-el's absolute 'Yes!', go inside the dragon's skin and create an awesome victory and future for humanity.

With this mood, here is a very inspiring picture that Steiner gave to a widow of a Society member. He gave it in the years after 1920. It is as inspiring as the note that Steiner wrote in his notebook: '1888. Ahriman is wrecked'. (See Preface.)

Bernard Lievegoed saw the actual letters of Steiner to this widow. In his book, *Towards the 21st Century* Lievegoed shares the content of the message that Steiner wrote to this widow in one of his letters. Lievegoed describes the situation as follows.

> Steiner told how the one who has gone through the gates of death wakes up, looks down on the earth, and comes to the following Imagination. Ahriman sits in a cave under the earth. He works. He writes things down, counting and counting, calculating and calculating. He tries to build up a whole world out of a new mathematics. [AI algorithms does constitute the new mathematics.] There, Steiner says, Michael stands beside him waiting. For Michael knows that he will make the final addition.[559]

This very inspiring image has one caveat. Micha-el will do the final accounting under one condition. Lievegoed mentions the one condition that determines whether Micha-el will be able to do the final accounting or not. And this condition is what we have been talking about in the entire book.

> ... Michael, with his sword, will make the sum. The moment has not yet come. *Michael is waiting, standing by the side, waiting. He can do this when people on earth are there fighting and going with him.* [Emphasis added.]

In the age of human freedom, Micha-el can only do it if we help him do it. In this book, we have looked at this exciting prospect from many different points of view. And when we help Micha-el, he, in turn, will inspire us on how we can create new worlds from the very extreme technologies that are threatening our existence today. This is the purpose of this book, that we may all wake up and enable Micha-el to do the final accounting!

Let us end with a quote from Rudolf Steiner, the founder of spiritual science, he who enabled us to have the big picture of what is at stake for humanity. He portrays two possibilities. Note the emphasized phrase 'human thing'. It is as if he had a premonition that human beings indeed will become a 'human thing' if they continue believing and actualizing in their technologies that the human being is nothing but a complex biological machine.

> I want with Cosmic Spirit
> To enthuse each human being
> That a flame they may become
> And fiery will unfold the essence of their being.

> The other ones,
> They strive to take from cosmic waters
> What will extinguish flames
> And pour paralysis into all inner being.

> O joy, when human being's flame is blazing, even when at rest.
> O bitter pain, when the *human thing* is put in bonds, when it wants to
> stir.[560]

The bondage of our Spirit will be our destiny if we do not act. Let us do our part! Let our eternal flame burn bright! Let us begin it now! Let us join forces with Micha-el and all other humans of goodwill for the future of the world! Let us awaken, nurture and defend the truly human! Together, let us give humanity a future! So it is.

Dedication

My gratitude to all, spiritual and human, living and dead, who have stood up to defend the truly human. In this book, I have called and identified them as the Keepers of Humanity.

Foremost among these is the Cosmic Christ, as I articulated in this book and as I experience Him in my daily life. This is the Christ beyond all religions, including Christianity. Without Christ, the Creator and Nurturer of the Fully Human, I am truly nothing. Humanity itself would have sunk to the abyss a long time ago.

Special appreciation and thanks goes to all the Knights Templar who were unjustly, treacherously, terribly tortured, by the most inhuman means, for crimes they did not commit. On top of that their sacrifice for humanity was rewarded by slander upon slander of their names and deeds. Nonetheless, the real truth has been publicly revealed and their names cleared as seen above. Their spiritual deeds reach out to all those whose mission is to awaken, nurture, and defend the truly human. Their spiritual strength is especially significant given they were at the merciless receiving end of the spiritual and earthly powers that would violently annihilate the emergence of a truly free, scientific and loving spiritual civilization on earth. Their presence has a special significance for our times.

I would also like to express my gratitude to the late Sergei Prokofieff for his untiring and dedicated efforts to faithfully recast spiritual science in its modern form, with the effect, among others, of making it easier to access the vast corpus of Steiner's spiritual science. He was a dear friend, very helpful with his books, and very illuminating during our personal conversations. I owe him a lot in terms of enabling me to understand spiritual science more deeply.

In my own spiritual journey, I have been inspired by the wisdom and spiritual courage of Christian Rosenkreutz, Parsifal/Mani and Master Jesus. My life would have been very different without their wisdom and guidance as clearly articulated in the works of spiritual science. I am expressing my gratitude to them as they are still truly with and con-tinuously defending humanity, whether they are present on earth or not. This is not speculation.

Last but not the least, this book would not have been possible to write without the works and sacrifices of Rudolf Steiner. For me, he was the fullest expression of what it means to be fully human. And he awakened millions to be aware of their true humanity to the point of nurturing and defending it with initiatives that have benefitted the lives of millions including myself. He truly saved my life in more ways than one, gave it direction and meaning, and inspired all my work through the decades. My debt of gratitude to him is beyond words.

For More Information

I would like to invite all readers to visit two websites for more information.

Foremost among these is www.fully-human.org. It gives an integrated picture of the latest development in Artificial Intelligence.

The second one is www.solutionecosystems.net. It gives the latest on societal threefolding, action in connection with Artificial Intelligence, and information on workshops connected with self-mastery as a preparation for engaging in the process of transforming the world.

For any comments, ideas, initiatives, collective action, research questions, financial support and other responses to this book, you can reach me at: nperlas@protonmail.com. Together we can create a new world!

Notes

1. Nick Bostrom, *Superintelligence. Paths, Dangers, Strategies.* (Oxford: Oxford University Press, 2014). With some exceptions, appropriate references in the Preface will be found in the succeeding chapters.
2. When a machine reaches the level of starting to improve its own software, then the next generation of machines will be smarter than the previous one. The self-improved machine will then improve itself further with accelerating speed. This ever-accelerating self-improving process will then continue under its own momentum until finally sophisticated AI reaches the stage of AGI sometimes called 'ultra-intelligent' machines. This is the 'intelligence explosion'. Shortly thereafter the AGI will produce the ASI. For greater details, see James Barrat, *Our Final Invention. Artificial Intelligence and the End of the Human Era* (New York: Thomas Dunne Books/St. Martin's Press, 2013).
3. Scholars often see three stages in the evolution of AI: narrow AI to AGI and finally to ASI. For reasons discussed above, AGI and ASI will often be discussed together.
4. Chapters 1 to 3 give detailed citations on the impact of AI. Note, however, that this is not the entirety of the problem we are bound to face. I have not yet scratched the surface of possible implications of the wide-scale intrusion in the privacy of billions of people around the world, as well as the addictive, mind-altering technologies introduced by big tech corporations such as Apple, Google, Facebook, and Twitter.

   This is a discussion we will no longer cover here, not because they are less urgent, or less important, but because their impact is so serious, they need to be explored in an entirely different book. In addition, there is a relatively large amount of Internet literature around this topic.

   The same is true with the current Facebook and Cambridge Analytica scandals. The major papers of the world are covering this topic intensely as this book goes to press.
5. The author has directly experienced this mechanical self-image from the participants who have participated in his workshops in different parts of the world.
6. The popular version runs likes this: 'We cannot solve our problems with the same thinking we used when we created them'. Admin, 'Einstein: "We cannot solve our problems with the same thinking we used when we created them".' *Gpaj.*
   http://www.gpaj.org/2016/06/03/14374
7. Chapter 16 elaborates on the many amazing developments in mainstream astrophysics, neuroscience, epigenetic biology, heart science, to name a few.
8. In addressing one particular identity, including its relationship to other identities, I have zero intention of not appreciating the other identities or truth communities of humanity. I have learned from many of them and it is my intention to continue doing so. In due time, because the topic of Artificial Super Intelligence is urgent, I will be writing more books on AI using the language of other identities I will be addressing.

   The situation is much like being in a foreign land, where one does not speak the language of that land. For example, I am Filipino and I do not speak the language of the Hindi, the French, the Germans, the Chinese, or the Spaniards. However, as I have often experienced, and I am sure others also have, the residents of the foreign land deeply appreciate if you try to speak their language. One's delivery of meaning is more accurate, precise, and attuned to the nuances of that language. In addition, the residents of the foreign land also appreciate the attempt to communicate using the categories of reality embedded in their identity.

All identities have a tacit or explicit worldview and value system. Each identity has their specific epistemology, ontology, cosmology, metaphysics, and social hygiene in relating to other identities, and other truth claims. This tacit context guides the actions of those who work out of this specific identity.

In what follows, I will be speaking the language of one particular truth community and identity. This language, understandably will be exotic, or downright strange, and incomprehensible to those not familiar with it, and the reality it contains.

9. As we shall see in the next pages of this book, AI is merely a caricature of what it means to be truly human. Anthroposophists should therefore be among the first to be very deeply concerned about the tragic turn that twenty-first century technology has taken since Rudolf Steiner launched the global anthroposophical movement to awaken, nurture and defend the truly human. Strange as it may seem, the rise of AI and the threat of human extinction can be a potential blessing to anthroposophy itself. Anthroposophy, which has inspired the establishment of tens of thousands of initiatives in various fields such as medicine, education, finance, therapy, art, and agriculture, is a sleeping giant. The existential threat to humanity, including Anthroposophy itself, could awaken this sleeping giant into actively pursuing new ways of birthing innovative global action.

10. This will become clear especially in Chapters 16 and 18. There I encourage anthroposophists to appreciate the work of other scientists as well as civil society activists searching for and advancing the reality of a more sustainable world. I also join spiritual science in appreciating the contribution that appropriate materialism has given and can give to the world. Materialism, within its proper bounds, is important for the evolution of humanity.

11. See Part II for a more in-depth discussion of the evolution of consciousness.

12. That indeed an evolution of human consciousness has taken place is well documented in the works of contemporary thinkers and authors including Ken Wilber, especially in his book, *Integral Psychology*, and, in a more accessible form, in Owen Barfield's *Saving the Appearances*. See Part II below.

13. There are numerous ways this can be done. The Collected Works of Rudolf Steiner, the founder of spiritual science and anthroposophy, has now reached over 350 books. Other anthroposophical authors have added hundreds, if not thousands, of books, and thousands more of articles on the subject. Moreover, there is a vast network of fruitful initiatives in practically all areas of life that anthroposophists have established throughout the planet.

Understanding anthroposophy will require effort on the part of the reader, and a sincere desire to discover the gem that it hides. It may not come so easy in terms of substance and also in terms of difficult anthroposophical personalities who have not walked the talk and therefore have alienated other people who may potentially benefit from spiritual science. But an honest and open effort to explore the substance of spiritual science may contribute valuable perspectives to the current challenge of Artificial Intelligence.

To emphasize this point, even among individuals in the global anthroposophical movement, a significant number still do not understand the distinction between spiritual science and anthroposophy. To clarify, spiritual science is the methodology and process. Anthroposophy is the resulting knowledge of this spiritual scientific process and research.

Anthroposophy can thus evolve into a form, much greater than what it had, when it was first inaugurated publicly in the beginning of the twentieth century. This book is just one tiny facet in the many streams of Spiritual Science that has manifested and developed worldwide in the last 100 years.

14. This book will also have this secondary effect when it becomes available to the public. It will end the tragic reputation of spiritual science as the best-kept secret of the twentieth century. That tragic reputation has to end if humanity will have a much more profound picture of what it means to be fully human in this era of science and technology, and Artificial Intelligence.

15. Cited by Rudolf Grosse, *The Christmas Foundation; Beginning of a New Cosmic Age* (Vancouver: Steiner Book Centre, 1984), p. 119. A discussion of Ahriman can be found in Chapter 4 below. In this sense, it is understandable why Steiner predicted that, of all his works, *The Philosophy of Spiritual Activity*, which is his epistemological and scientific defence of the human being and its capacity for free thinking and loving moral action, would outlive all of his other works.

16. Bostrom, *Superintelligence*, Kindle e-book, Location 51.

17. In this context, and in addressing GAM, I would like to say something about the nature of the title. I had a conversation with Paul Mackay, former Executive Council member of the global Anthroposophical Society. I mentioned to him that the title of this book would be, *The Last Stand. Anthroposophy in the Age of Artificial Intelligence.*

I was surprised when he started speaking about his own experiences with the late Bernard Lievegoed, a renowned and much awarded, public figure in the Netherlands and Chairman of the Anthroposophical Society in that country. Mackay said that Lievegoed told him that some things one had not done properly in the past, can still be changed, but that there were other mistakes that one can no longer change. I took that to mean that he understood the title and intention of this book.

18. I will show evidence of this in later chapters especially Chapter 16.

19. Bernard Marr, 'The Future Of The Transport Industry', *Forbes*, 2017, https://www.forbes.com/sites/bernardmarr/2017/11/06/the-future-of-the-transport-industry-iot-big-data-ai-and-autonomous-vehicles/#60713fd21137; David Freedman, 'Self-Driving Trucks: 10 Breakthrough Technologies 2017,' *MIT Technology Review*, 2017, https://www.technologyreview.com/s/603493/10-breakthrough-technologies-2017-self-driving-trucks/; Omar Abbosh, 'Driverless Trucks Likely to Hit the Roads before Autonomous Cars', *Accenture*, 2017, https://www.accenture.com/us-en/blogs/blogs-moving-business-forward-self-driving.

20. Andrew Tarantola, 'Robot Caregivers Are Saving the Elderly from Lives of Loneliness', *Engadget*, 2017, https://www.engadget.com/2017/08/29/robot-caregivers-are-saving-the-elderly-from-lives-of-loneliness/; Randy Rieland, 'How Will Artificial Intelligence Help the Aging?', *Smithsonian*, 2017, https://www.smithsonianmag.com/innovation/how-will-artificial-intelligence-help-aging-180962682/; Deena Zaidi, 'Meet the Robots Caring for Japan's Aging

Population', *Venture Beat*, 2017, https://venturebeat.com/2017/11/14/meet-the-robots-caring-for-japans-aging-population/.

21. Will Knight, 'This Is the Robot Maid Elon Musk Is Funding', *MIT Technology Review*, 2016, https://www.technologyreview.com/s/601939/this-is-the-robot-maid-elon-musk-is-funding/; David Nield, '5 Ways to Use AI in Your Own Home', *Popular Science*, 2017,
https://www.popsci.com/artificial-intelligence-home-use#page-4.

22. Intel, 'The Future of AI in Healthcare', Intel, 2018, https://www.intel.com/content/www/us/en/healthcare-it/article/improved-diagnosis.html; DeepMind Technologies Ltd., 'DeepMind Develops AI to Diagnose Eye Diseases', *Financial Times*, 2018, https://www.ft.com/content/84fcc16c-0787-11e8-9650-9c0ad2d7c5b5; Megan Moltini, 'Want a Diagnosis Tomorrow, Not Next Year? Turn to AI', *i*, 2017, https://www.wired.com/story/ai-that-will-crowdsource-your-next-diagnosis/; Pallab Ghosh, 'AI Early Diagnosis Could Save Heart and Cancer Patients', *BBC News*, 2018, http://www.bbc.com/news/health-42357257.

23. Guillermo Cecchi, 'IBM 5 on 5: With AI, Our Words Will Be a Window into Our Mental Health', *IBM Research*, 2017, https://www.ibm.com/blogs/research/2017/1/ibm-5-in-5-our-words-will-be-the-windows-to-our-mental-health/; Charlotte Stix, '3 Ways AI Could Help Our Mental Health', World Economic Forum, 2018, https://www.weforum.org/agenda/2018/03/3-ways-ai-could-be-used-in-mental-health/; Megan Molteni, 'WoeBot, The Chatbot Therapist, Will See You Now', *Wired*, 2017, https://www.wired.com/2017/06/facebook-messenger-woebot-chatbot-therapist/.

24. Sébastien Turbot, 'Artificial Intelligence In Education: Don't Ignore It, Harness It!', *Forbes*, 2017, https://www.forbes.com/sites/sebastienturbot/2017/08/22/artificial-intelligence-virtual-reality-education/#4bb5c77b6c16; Ben Dickson, 'How Artificial Intelligence Is Shaping the Future of Education', *PC Mag*, 2017, https://www.pcmag.com/article/357483/how-artificial-intelligence-is-shaping-the-future-of-education; Daniel Faggella, 'Examples of Artificial Intelligence in Education—Current Applications', *TechEmerge*, 2017,
https://www.techemergence.com/examples-of-artificial-intelligence-in-education/.

25. Patrick Thibodeau, 'Internet of Things Brings New Era of Weather Forecasting', *Computer World*, 2016, https://www.computerworld.com/article/3018390/internet-of-things-brings-new-era-of-weather-forecasting.html.

26. Joel Tito, 'Destination Unknown: Exploring the Impact of Artificial Intelligence on Government', 2017, https://publicimpact.blob.core.windows.net/production/2017/09/Destination-Unknown-AI-and-government.pdf;
Emma Martinho Truswell, 'How AI Could Help the Public Sector', *Harvard Business Review*, 2018, https://hbr.org/2018/01/how-ai-could-help-the-public-sector; Ben Miller, 'Automation Beyond the Physical: AI in the Public Sector', *Government Technology*, 2017, http://www.govtech.com/civic/GT-September-Automation-Beyond-the-Physical-AI-in-the-Public-Sector.html;
William D. Eggers, David Schatsky, and Dr Peter Viechnicki, 'Demystifying Artificial Intelligence in Government: Using AI Cognitive Technologies to Redesign Public Sector Work', *Deloitte Insights*, 2017,
https://www2.deloitte.com/insights/us/en/focus/cognitive-technologies/artificial-intelligence-government.html.

27. David H. Freedman, 'Self-Driving Trucks: 10 Breakthrough Technologies 2017'; *PredPol*, 'Predictive Policing Software' *PredPol*, 2017, http://www.predpol.com/; Cynthia Rubin, 'Predictive Policing: Using Machine Learning to Detect Patterns of Crime', *Wired*, 2013, https://www.wired.com/insights/2013/08/predictive-policing-using-machine-learning-to-detect-patterns-of-crime/;
Bernard Marr, 'How Robots, IoT And Artificial Intelligence Are Transforming The Police', *Forbes*, 2017, https://www.forbes.com/sites/bernardmarr/2017/09/19/how-robots-iot-and-artificial-intelligence-are-transforming-the-police/#4420cd175d6l.

28. Michael Kassner, 'AI Stops Identity Fraud Before It Occurs', *TechRepublic*, 2017, https://www.techrepublic.com/article/ai-stops-identity-fraud-before-it-occurs/; Matthew Cochrane, 'MasterCard Is Using AI to Improve Its Fraud Protection', *Business Insider*, 2017, http://www.businessinsider.com/mastercard-artificial intelligence-fraud-protection-2017-1.

29. United Nations, 'Entrepreneur Urges Leveraging Artificial Intelligence for Benefit of All in Second Committee, Economic and Social Council Joint Meeting', *United Nations*, 2017, https://www.un.org/press/en/2017/gaef3477.doc.htm; Daniel Faggella, 'Artificial Intelligence in Marketing and Advertising—5 Examples of Real Traction', *Tech Emergence*, 2018, https://www.techemergence.com/artificial-intelligence-in-marketing-and-advertising-5-examples-of-real-traction/.

30. Sara Loren, 'Analysis of How Technology Is Shaping Consumer Behavior', *Medium*, 2017, https://medium.com/@saraloren506/analysis-of-how-technology-is-shaping-consumer-behavior-607ff9e676be.

31. Rakia Reynolds, 'How Artificial Intelligence Is Changing The Way We Analyze Consumer Behavior', *Forbes*, 2017, https://www.forbes.com/sites/yec/2017/06/29/how-artificial-intelligence-is-changing-the-way-we-analyze-consumer-behavior/#318c1cca741a.

32. Joseph Bennington-Castro, 'AI Is a Game-Changer in the Fight Against Hunger and Poverty. Here's Why', *NBC News*, 2017, https://www.nbcnews.com/mach/tech/ai-game-changer-fight-against-hunger-poverty-here-s-why-ncna774696; Katie Dupere, 'IBM Turns to Artificial Intelligence to Solve Poverty, Hunger, and Illiteracy', 2017, https://mashable.com/2017/06/07/ibm-science-for-social-good/#.VrFaSpHNSqx; Umberto Bacchi, 'Artificial Intelligence Could Now Help Us End Poverty', *Huffington Post*, 2016, https://www.huffingtonpost.com/entry/artificial-intelligence-satellite-images-locate-poverty-research-ers_us_57b71211e4b0b51733a2dd20; Uma Lele, 'How Technology Is Helping India's Rural Poor', *World Economic Forum*, 2017, https://www.weforum.org/agenda/2017/10/india-fourth-industrial-revolution-farming/.

33. Jackie Savitch, Presentation as part of Panel 9, 'Big Data, Big Bang', January 16, 2018, at the global conference on the Congress for the Future, Santiago, Chile hosted by the Senate of Chile.

34. Matt McFarland, 'Elon Musk: "With Artificial Intelligence We Are Summoning the Demon."' *The Washington Post*, 2014, https://www.washingtonpost.com/news/innovations/wp/2014/10/24/elon-musk-with-artificial-intelligence-we-are-summoning-the-demon/?utm_term=.834c61202913.

35. James Titcomb, 'Elon Musk: Become Cyborgs or Risk Humans Being Turned into Robots' Pets', *The Telegraph*, 2016, https://www.telegraph.co.uk/technology/2016/06/02/elon-musk-become-cyborgs-or-risk-humans-being-turned-into-robots/.

36. Stacey Higginbotham, 'Elon Musk, Reid Hoffman, and Amazon Donate $1 Billion for AI Research', *Fortune*, 2015, http://fortune.com/2015/12/11/open-ai/; Andrea Danti, 'Tech Giants Pledge $1bn for "Altruistic AI" Venture, OpenAI', *BBC News*, 2015, http://www.bbc.com/news/technology-35082344.

37. Alex Hern, 'Stephen Hawking: AI Will Be "Either Best or Worst Thing" for Humanity', *The Guardian*, 2016, https://www.theguardian.com/science/2016/oct/19/stephen-hawking-ai-best-or-worst-thing-for-humanity-cambridge.

38. Rory Cellan-Jones, 'Stephen Hawking Warns Artificial Intelligence Could End Mankind', *BBC News*, 2014, http://www.bbc.com/news/technology-30290540.

39. Peter Holley, 'Bill Gates on Dangers of Artificial Intelligence: "I Don't Understand Why Some People Are Not Concerned",' *The Washington Post*, 2015, https://www.washingtonpost.com/news/the-switch/wp/2015/01/28/bill-gates-on-dangers-of-artificial-intelligence-dont-understand-why-some-people-are-not-concerned/?utm_term=.84cb4dd3a67c.

40. Thomas Dietterich, 'Benefits and Risks of Artificial Intelligence', *Medium*, 2015, https://medium.com/@tdietterich/benefits-and-risks-of-artificial-intelligence-460d288cccf3.

41. Natalie Wolcjover, 'Artificial Intelligence Aligned With Human Values: Q&A With Stuart Russell', *Quanta Magazine*, 2015, https://www.quantamagazine.org/artificial-intelligence-aligned-with-human-values-qa-with-stuart-russell-20150421.

42. Bahar Gholipour, 'New AI Tech Can Mimic Any Voice', *Scientific American*, 2017, https://www.scientificamerican.com/article/new-ai-tech-can-mimic-any-voice/; Sercan Arik et al., 'Deep Voice: Real-Time Neural Text-to-Speech', International Conference on Machine Learning, February 24, 2017, 1–17, http://arxiv.org/abs/1702.07825.

43. Tristan Greene, 'Baidu's Voice Cloning AI Adds Gender Swapping and Accent Removal', *The Next Web*, 2018, https://thenextweb.com/artificial-intelligence/2018/02/26/baidus-ai-can-clone-your-voice-and-give-it-a-different-gender-or-accent/.

44. Zhang Huan, 'Chinese Robot Becomes World's First Machine to Pass Medical Exam—People's Daily Online', *People's Daily Online*, 2017, http://en.people.cn/n3/2017/1116/c90000-9293696.html.

45. Adrian Cartland, 'Ailira (an AI) Passes Uni Tax Law Exam', *LinkedIn*, 2016, https://www.linkedin.com/pulse/ailira-ai-passes-uni-tax-law-exam-adrian-cartland.

46. James Vincent, 'Elon Musk and AI Leaders Call for a Ban on Killer Robots', *The Verge*, 2017, https://www.theverge.com/2017/8/21/16177828/killer-robots-ban-elon-musk-un-petition; Ian Sample, 'Ban on Killer Robots Urgently Needed, Say Scientists', *The Guardian*, 2017, https://www.theguardian.com/science/2017/nov/13/ban-on-killer-robots-urgently-needed-say-scientists.

47. Samuel Woolley and Marina Gorbis, 'Social Media Bots Threaten Democracy. But We Are Not Helpless', *The Guardian*, 2017, https://www.theguardian.com/commentisfree/2017/oct/16/bots-social-media-threaten-democracy-technology; Vyacheslav Polonski, 'How Artificial Intelligence Silently Took over Democracy', *World Economic Forum*, 2017, https://www.weforum.org/agenda/2017/08/artificial-intelligence-can-save-democracy-unless-it-destroys-it-first/.

48. Diego Mendez, Ioannis Papapanagiotou, and Baijian Yang, 'Internet of Things: Survey on Security and Privacy', *IOT Security*, 2017, 1–16, https://arxiv.org/pdf/

1707.01879.pdf; Christine Bannan, 'The IoT Threat to Privacy', *Tech Crunch*, 2016, https://beta.techcrunch.com/2016/08/14/the-iot-threat-to-privacy/.

49. Conversation with Gary Lamb, Director of the Center for Social Research at the Hawthorne Valley Association in upper state New York. January 29, 2018.

50. Garett Sloane, 'Sean Parker says Facebook was designed to be Addictive', *AdAge*, November 09, 2017. http://adage.com/article/digital/sean-parker-worries-facebook-rotting-children-s-brains/311238/

51. Tristan Harris, Presentation as part of Panel 20, 'Science', January 20, 2018, at the global conference on the Congress for the Future, Santiago, Chile hosted by the Senate of Chile. Harris was supposed to give his paper the day before but weather problems in the US delayed his flight to Chile.

52. Samuel Gibbs, 'Apple investors call for action over iPhone "addiction" among children', *The Guardian*, 08 January 2018, https://www.theguardian.com/technology/2018/jan/08/apple-investors-iphone-addiction-children

53. Shirin Jaafari, 'Saudi Arabia Has a New Citizen: Sophia the Robot. But What Does That Even Mean?', *Public Radio International*, 2017, https://www.pri.org/stories/2017-11-01/saudi-arabia-has-new-citizen-sophia-robot-what-does-even-mean.

54. BBC News, 'The Humanoid Robot That Can Do a Backflip', *YouTube*, 2017, https://www.youtube.com/watch?v=_bI3jUhPJaU.

55. Tristan Greene, 'This Heavy Metal Music Made by a Machine Will Rock Your Human Face off', *The Next Web*, 2018, https://thenextweb.com/artificial-intelligence/2017/12/02/this-heavy-metal-music-made-by-a-machine-will-rock-your-human-face-off/; Simon Chandler, 'Meet the Artists Using Coding, AI, and Machine Language to Make Music', *Band Camp*, 2018, https://daily.bandcamp.com/2018/01/25/music-ai-coding-algorithms/; Brian Mastroianni, 'Orchestra Music Created with the Help of Artificial Intelligence', *CBS News*, 2016, https://www.cbsnews.com/news/orchestra-music-symphonologie-by-artificial-intelligence-human-composers/; James Vincent, 'This AI-Written Pop Song Is Almost Certainly a Dire Warning for Humanity', *The Verge*, 2016, https://www.theverge.com/2016/9/26/13055938/ai-pop-song-daddys-car-sony; Tom Simonite, 'AI Software Learns to Make AI Software', *MIT Technology Review*, 2017, https://www.technologyreview.com/s/603381/ai-software-learns-to-make-ai-software/.

56. Matt McFarland, 'Popular YouTube Artist Uses AI to Record New Album', *CNN*, 2017, http://money.cnn.com/2017/08/21/technology/future/taryn-southern-ai-music/index.html.

57. James Vincent, 'Can You Tell the Difference between Bach and RoboBach?', *The Verge*, 2016, https://www.theverge.com/2016/12/23/14069382/ai-music-creativity-bach-deepbach-csl

58. Jon Russell, 'Google's AlphaGo AI Wins Three-Match Series against the World's Best Go Player', *Tech Crunch*, 2017, https://beta.techcrunch.com/2017/05/24/alphago-beats-planets-best-human-go-player-ke-jie/.

59. David Silver et al., 'Mastering the Game of Go without Human Knowledge', *Nature* 550, no. 7676 (October 18, 2017): 354–59, https://doi.org/10.1038/nature24270.

60. Dom Galeon and Kristin Houser, 'Google's AI Built Another AI That Outperforms Man-Made Models', *Futurism*, 2017, https://futurism.com/google-artificial-intelligence-built-ai/.

61. Andrew Griffin, 'Facebook's Artificial Intelligence Robots Shut down after They Start Talking to Each Other in Their Own Language', *The Independent*, 2017, https://www.independent.co.uk/life-style/gadgets-and-tech/news/facebook-artificial-intelligence-ai-chatbot-new-language-research-openai-google-a7869706.html.

62. Top500.Org, 'November 2017: TOP500 Supercomputer Sites', *Top 500*, 2017, https://www.top500.org/lists/2017/11/.

63. Ari Levy, 'D-Wave Is Raising Money to Bring Quantum Computing to Public Cloud', *CNBS*, 2018, https://www.cnbc.com/2018/02/23/d-wave-is-raising-money-to-bring-quantum-computing-to-public-cloud.html.

64. CK Media, 'Billionaires on Artificial Intelligence, AI (Elon Musk, Bill Gates, Jack Ma)', *YouTube*, 2017, https://www.youtube.com/watch?v=b08udI6MSR8&feature=youtu.be.

65. Future of Life Institute, 'AI Open Letter', Future of Life Institute, 2018, https://futureoflife.org/ai-open-letter.

66. Ray Kurzweil, 'Beneficial AI Conference Develops "Asilomar AI Principles" to Guide Future AI Research', Kurzweil: Accelerating Intelligence, 2017, http://www.kurzweilai.net/beneficial-ai-conference-develops-asilomar-ai-principles-to-guide-future-ai-research.

67. Machine Intelligence Research Institute, 'The AI Alignment Problem: Why It's Hard, and Where to Start', MIRI, 2016, https://intelligence.org/stanford-talk/.

68. Barrat, *Our Final Invention*.

69. Tom Simonite, 'For Superpowers, Artificial Intelligence Fuels New Global Arms Race', *Wired*, 2017, https://www.wired.com/story/for-superpowers-artificial intelligence-fuels-new-global-arms-race/.

70. Barrat, *Our Final Invention*, pp. 85–86, 91, 135–137. He calls transhumanists, 'singularitarians' or believers in technological singularity where nanotechnology, genetics, and artificial intelligence converge to produce digital super humans or machine-human hybrids.

71. Elon Musk, 'Elon Musk on Twitter: "Probably closer to 2030 to 2040 Imo. 2060 Would Be a Linear Extrapolation, but Progress Is Exponential..."' *Twitter*, 2017, https://twitter.com/elonmusk/status/871886151014940672?lang=en.

72. ABS-CBN News, 'BPOs to Feel Artificial Intelligence "Reality" in Next 3 to 5 Years: Pernia', *ABS-CBN News*, 2018, http://news.abs-cbn.com/business/01/24/18/bpos-to-feel-artificial-intelligence-reality-in-next-3-to-5-years-pernia.

73. Lara Parpan, 'Artificial Intelligence Threatens Jobs in BPO Industry: Trade Department', *CNN Philippines*, 2017, http://cnnphilippines.com/news/2017/09/06/BPO-industry-call-center-Philippines-artificial-intelligence.html; Mirren Gidda, 'Jobs on the Line: New Technology Could Replace Millions of Call Center Workers in the Philippines', *Newsweek*, 2016, http://www.newsweek.com/how-new-technology-automation-ai-take-away-millions-jobs-call-centers-503726; Samuel Medenilla, 'Robots May Soon Replace BPO Workers', *Manila Bulletin*, 2017, https://news.mb.com.ph/2017/07/27/robots-may-soon-replace-bpo-workers/.

74. The estimate comes from the March 12, 2018 Hearings of the Senate Committee of Science and Technology on the effects of the rise of Artificial Intelligence on the BPO industry in the Philippines. Representatives from industry, including the BPO association and the Analytics Association of the Philippines,

government, including the Department of Science and Technology and the Department of Trade and Industry, and an individual from civil society testified during the hearings. The 24 million Filipinos projected to be impacted is a multiplier effect that was not questioned by the representatives from the BPO industry. The multiplier effect coefficient came from the BPO industry and government itself.

75. Roy Stephen C. Canivel, '5-Mo BPO Investments Down 35%', *Philippine Daily Inquirer*, 2017, http://business.inquirer.net/232088/5-mo-bpo-investments-35.

76. Aradhana Aravindan, 'Millions of SE Asian Jobs May Be Lost to Automation in Next Two Decades: ILO', *Reuters*, 2016, https://www.reuters.com/article/us-southeast-asia-jobs/millions-of-se-asian-jobs-may-be-lost-to-automation-in-next-two-decades-ilo-idUSKCN0ZN0HP.

77. John Mauldin, 'Part of Everyone's Job Will Be Automated in the Next Decade', *Market Watch*, 2017, https://www.marketwatch.com/story/part-of-everyones-job-will-be-automated-in-the-next-decade-2017-12-14.

78. Steve Levine, 'McKinsey: Automation May Wipe Out 1/3 of America's Workforce by 2030', *Mauldin Economics*, 2017, http://www.mauldineconomics.com/outsidethebox/mckinsey-automation-may-wipe-out-1-3-of-americas-workforce-by-2030.

79. Daniel Faggella, 'Valuing the Artificial Intelligence Market, Graphs and Predictions', *Tech Emergence*, 2018, https://www.techemergence.com/valuing-the-artificial-intelligence-market-graphs-and-predictions/.

80. The Philippine Senate hearing referred to above demonstrates, for example, that both the BPO industry and the government believe that jobs will increase despite the deployment of AI in the BPO sector.

81. Timothy Revell, 'AI Will Be Able to Beat Us at Everything by 2060, Say Experts', *New Scientist*, 2017, https://www.newscientist.com/article/2133188-ai-will-be-able-to-beat-us-at-everything-by-2060-say-experts.

82. Ben Dickson, 'Why IoT Security Is So Critical', *TechCrunch*, 2015, https://techcrunch.com/2015/10/24/why-iot-security-is-so-critical.

83. Tam Harbert, 'How 5G Will Make AI-Powered Devices Smarter', *IQ Intel*, 2018, https://iq.intel.com/how-5g-will-make-ai-powered-devices-smarter.

84. George Orwell, *1984: Big Brother Is Watching You* (London: Arcturus Publishing, 2013).

85. Osonde Osoba and William Welser IV, 'The Risks of Artificial Intelligence to Security and the Future of Work', *Perspective*, 2017.

86. Bill Joy, 'Why the Future Doesn't Need Us', *Wired*, 2000, https://www.wired.com/2000/04/joy-2.

87. Ralph Nader, 'Why the Future Doesn't Need Us—Revisited', *Huffington Post*, 2016, https://www.huffingtonpost.com/ralph-nader/why-the-future-doesnt-nee_b_8021740.html.

88. Future of Life Institute, 'Asilomar AI Principles', 2017, https://futureoflife.org/ai-principles.

89. Barrat, *Our Final Invention*, 8–9.

90. Nick Heath, 'What Is AI? Everything You Need To Know About Artificial Intelligence', *ZD Net*, 2018, https://www.zdnet.com/article/what-is-ai-everything-you-need-to-know-about-artificial-intelligence.

91. For a more exact and technical definition of these kinds of algorithms and how they

work, see the detailed descriptions of the different kinds of programming in Wikipedia.

92. Andrew Griffin, 'Facebook's Artificial Intelligence Robots Shut down after They Start Talking to Each Other in Their Own Language', *The Independent*, 2017, https://www.independent.co.uk/life-style/gadgets-and-tech/news/facebook-artificial-intelligence-ai-chatbot-new-language-research-openai-google-a7869706.html.

93. Barrat, *Our Final Invention*, 15.

94. Daniel Faggella, 'Valuing the Artificial Intelligence Market, Graphs and Predictions', *Tech Emergence*, 2018, https://www.techemergence.com/valuing-the-artificial-intelligence-market-graphs-and-predictions/.

95. Adam Elkus, 'How to Be Good: Why You Can't Teach Human Values To Artificial Intelligence', *Slate*, http://www.slate.com/articles/technology/future_tense/2016/04/why_you_can_t_teach_human_values_to_artificial_intelligence.html, 2016

96. Ariel Conn, 'When AI Journalism Goes Bad', Future of Life Institute, 2016 https://futureoflife.org/2016/04/26/ai-journalism-goes-bad.

97. Barrat, *Our Final Invention*, 8–9.

98. Matthew Dahlitz, 'Prefrontal Cortex', *The Neuropsychotherapist*, 2017, https://www.neuropsychotherapist.com/prefrontal-cortex/.

99. Robert Naumann et al., 'The Reptilian Brain', *Current Biology*, April 20, 2015, Volume 25, No. 8, http://doi.org/10.1016/j.cub.2015.02.049.

100. Daniel Goleman, *Emotional Intelligence: Why It Can Matter More Than IQ* (New York: Bantam Book, 1995).

101. Machine Intelligence Research Institute, 'The AI Alignment Problem: Why It's Hard, and Where to Start', *MIRI*, 2016, https://intelligence.org/stanford-talk/.

102. Daniel Faggella, 'Valuing the Artificial Intelligence Market, Graphs and Predictions', *Tech Emergence*, 2018, https://www.techemergence.com/valuing-the-artificial-intelligence-market-graphs-and-predictions/.

103. This accounts for out-of-the-box outstanding and seemingly intuitive performance of AlphaGo when it made moves that Go experts did not expect. But as we shall see below in Chapter 6, this is not yet the equivalent of human intuition.

104. Thomas Dietterich, 'Benefits and Risks of Artificial Intelligence', *Medium*, 2015, https://medium.com/@tdietterich/benefits-and-risks-of-artificial-intelligence-460d288cccf3.

105. Barrat, *Our Final Invention*, 61–62.

106. Miriam Diez Bosch, 'Tranhumanism: 5 Characteristics of the Contemporary Race Against Death', *Aleteia*, 2017, https://aleteia.org/2017/03/24/transhumanism-5-characteristics-of-the-contemporary-race-against-death; Mark Harris, 'Inside the First Church of Artificial Intelligence', *Wired*, 2017, https://www.wired.com/story/anthony-levandowski-artificial-intelligence-religion.

107. Barrat, *Our Final Invention*, p.59 plus various pages in the book. Generally, see Chapter 3.

108. Barrat, *Our Final Invention*, p.12, 15.

109. Cheryl Hogue, 'Countries Agree To Ban Geoengineering', *Chemical & Engineering News*, 2010, Volume 88, No. 45, https://cen.acs.org/articles/88/i45/Countries-Agree-Ban-Geoengineering.html.

110. Matt Simon, 'The Future of Humanity's Food Supply Is In The Hands Of AI',

Wired, 2016, https://www.wired.com/2016/05/future-humanitys-food-supply-hands-ai.

111. Katharine Sanderson, 'What You Need to Know About Nano-Food', *The Guardian*, 2013, https://www.theguardian.com/what-is-nano/what-you-need-know-about-nano-food.

112. Adam Withnall, 'Robots Will Be Smarter Than Us All, Warns AI Expert Ray Kurzweil,' *Independent*, 2014, https://www.independent.co.uk/life-style/gadgets-and-tech/news/robots-will-be-smarter-than-us-all-by-2029-warns-ai-expert-ray-kurzweil-9147506.html.

113. Timothy Revell, 'AI Will Be Able to Beat Us at Everything by 2060, Say Experts', *New Scientist*, 2017, https://www.newscientist.com/article/2133188-ai-will-be-able-to-beat-us-at-everything-by-2060-say-experts.

114. Elon Musk, 'Elon Musk on Twitter: "Probably Closer to 2030 to 2040 Imo. 2060 Would Be a Linear Extrapolation, but Progress Is Exponential . . . ," ' *Twitter*, 2017, https://twitter.com/elonmusk/status/871886151014940672?lang=en.

115. Musk predicts AI will be better than humans at everything in 2030. *Teslaratl*. https://teslaratl.com/tesla-model-x-off-roader-imagined-artist-mo-aoun/

116. Timothy Revell, 'AI Will Be Able to Beat Us at Everything by 2060, Say Experts', *New Scientist*, 2017, https://www.newscientist.com/article/2133188-ai-will-be-able-to-beat-us-at-everything-by-2060-say-experts.

117. AI Impacts, '2016 Expert Survey on Progress in AI', *AI Impacts*, 2016, https://aiimpacts.org/2016-expert-survey-on-progress-in-ai/; Katja Grace et al., 'When Will AI Exceed Human Performance? Evidence from AI Experts', *arXiv*, May 24, 2017, http://arxiv.org/abs/1705.08807.

118. Ray Kurzweil, *The Singularity Is Near* (New York: Penguin Books, 2005).

119. Lester R. Brown, *The Twenty-Ninth Day: Accommodating Human Needs and Numbers to the Earth's Resources* (Toronto: W.W. Norton & Company, Inc., 1978).

120. Drake Baer, 'Ray Kurzweil Law of Accelerating Returns', *Business Insider*, 2015, http://www.businessinsider.com/ray-kurzweil-law-of-accelerating-returns-2015-5; Ray Kurzweil, 'The Law of Accelerating Returns', *KurzweilAI*, 2001, http://www.kurzweilai.net/the-law-of-accelerating-returns.

121. Top500.Org, 'November 2015: TOP500 Supercomputer Sites', *TOP500 Supercomputer Sites*, 2015, https://www.top500.org/lists/2015/11/.

122. Top500.Org, 'November 2016: TOP500 Supercomputer Sites', *TOP500 Supercomputer Sites*, 2016, https://www.top500.org/lists/2016/11/.

123. Emerging Technology from the arXiv, 'Google DeepMind Teaches Artificial Intelligence Machines to Read', *MIT Technology Review*, 2015, https://www.technologyreview.com/s/538616/google-deepmind-teaches-artificial-intelligence-machines-to-read/.

124. Abigail Beall and Matt Reynolds, 'What Are Quantum Computers and How Do They Work? Wired Explains', 2018, http://www.wired.co.uk/article/quantum-computing-explained.

125. Karl Freund, 'Arm Chooses NVIDIA Open-Source CNN AI Chip Technology', *Forbes*, 2018, https://www.forbes.com/sites/moorinsights/2018/03/29/arm-chooses-nvidia-open-source-ai-chip-technology/#72d5aa861e50.

126. Christopher Moyer, 'How Google's AlphaGo Beat a Go World Champion', *The Atlantic*, 2016, https://www.theatlantic.com/technology/archive/2016/03/the-invisible-opponent/475611/.

127. Jon Russell, 'Google's AlphaGo AI Wins Three-Match Series against the World's Best Go Player', *Tech Crunch*, 2017, https://beta.techcrunch.com/2017/05/24/alphago-beats-planets-best-human-go-player-ke-jie/.

128. Emerging Technology from the arXiv, 'Google DeepMind Teaches Artificial Intelligence Machines to Read', *MIT Technology Review*, 2015, https://www.technologyreview.com/s/538616/google-deepmind-teaches-artificial-intelligence-machines-to-read/.

129. David Silver et al., 'Mastering the Game of Go without Human Knowledge', *Nature 550*, no. 7676 (October 18, 2017): 354–59, https://doi.org/10.1038/nature24270; Samuel Gibbs, 'AlphaZero AI Beats Champion Chess Program after Teaching Itself in Four Hours', *The Guardian*, 2017, https://www.theguardian.com/technology/2017/dec/07/alphazero-google-deepmind-ai-beats-champion-program-teaching-itself-to-play-four-hours.

130. Samuel Gibbs, 'AlphaZero AI Beats Champion Chess Program after Teaching Itself in Four Hours', *The Guardian*, 2017, https://www.theguardian.com/technology/2017/dec/07/alphazero-google-deepmind-ai-beats-champion-program-teaching-itself-to-play-four-hours.

131. Nick Statt, 'Google's AI Translation System Is Approaching Human-Level Accuracy', *The Verge*, 2016, https://www.theverge.com/2016/9/27/13078138/google-translate-ai-machine-learning-gnmt; Gideon Lewis-Kraus, 'The Great A.I. Awakening', *The New York Times*, April 10, 2016, https://doi.org/10.1002/cne.21974.

132. Daniel Faggella, 'Valuing the Artificial Intelligence Market, Graphs and Predictions', *Tech Emergence*, 2018, https://www.techemergence.com/valuing-the-artificial-intelligence-market-graphs-and-predictions/.

133. Fiona MacDonald, 'AI Just Wrote the Next Book of Game of Thrones for Us', *Business Insider UK*, 2017, http://uk.businessinsider.com/ai-just-wrote-the-next-book-of-game-of-thrones-for-us-2017-8; David Barnett, 'Horror Fiction by Numbers: My Not-So-Shocking AI Collaboration', *The Guardian*, 2017, https://www.theguardian.com/books/booksblog/2017/oct/31/horror-fiction-ai-collaboration-shelley-mit; Natalie Shoemaker, 'Japanese AI Writes a Novel, Nearly Wins Literary Award', *Big Think*, 2017, http://bigthink.com/natalie-shoemaker/a-japanese-ai-wrote-a-novel-almost-wins-literary-award.

134. '6 Ways Retailers Put Artificial Intelligence To Work', *RetailTouchPoints*, May 2016. https://www.retailtouchpoints.com/features/executive-viewpoints/analyze-this-6-ways-retailers-put-artificial-intelligence-to-work.

135. Eliza Strickland, 'Inside an MRI, a Non-Metallic Robot Performs Prostate Surgery—IEEE Spectrum', *IEEE Spectrum*, 2015, https://spectrum.ieee.org/automaton/robotics/medical-robots/inside-an-mri-a-nonmetallic-robot-performs-prostate-surgery; Cancer Research UK, 'Robotic Surgery for Prostate Cancer', *Cancer Research UK*, 2014, http://www.cancerresearchuk.org/about-cancer/prostate-cancer/treatment/surgery/types/robotic-surgery-for-prostate-cancer.

136. BBC, 'Computer AI Passes Turing Test in "World First"', *BBC News*, 2014, http://www.bbc.com/news/technology-27762088.

137. Rudolf Steiner, 'The Remedy for our Diseased Civilization', Lecture, Dornach, 06 August 1921. https://wn.rsarchive.org/Lectures/Dates/19210806p01.html, p. 35.

138. Rudolf Steiner, *Philosophy of Spiritual Activity. Fundamentals of a Modern View of the*

World. Results of Introspective Observations According to the Method of Natural Science
(West Nyack, New York: Rudolf Steiner Publications, 1963). Also known, in
other translations from the German, as *The Philosophy of Freedom.*

139. Rudolf Steiner, *Anthroposophical Leading Thoughts. Anthroposophy as a Path of
Knowledge. The Michael Mystery* (London: Rudolf Steiner Press, 1973), p. 85.

140. Richard Dawkins, *The God Delusion*, (New York: Bantam Press, 2006); Jerry A.
Coyne, *Faith vs. Fact* (New York: Penguin Random House, 2015); Ralph W.
Hood, Peter C. Hill, and W. Paul Williamson, *The Psychology of Religious Funda-
mentalism* (New York: Guilford Press, 2005).

141. Vexen Crabtree, 'A List of All Religions and Belief Systems', *Human Religions*,
2013, http://www.humanreligions.info/religions.html.

142. References to this development are found immediately below in this chapter.

143. Rudolf Steiner, 'Man in the Past, Present, and Future; The Evolution of Consciousness', *RS Archive*, 2004, http://wn.rsarchive.org/Lectures/GA228/English/
RSP1966/19230914p01.html; Jennifer Gidley, 'The Evolution of Consciousness as
a Planetary Imperative: An Integration of Integral Views', *Integral Review*, no. 5
(2007): 4–226, https://www.researchgate.net/profile/Jennifer_Gidley/
publication/228755942_The_Evolution_of_Consciousness_as_a_Planetary_
Imperative_An_Integration_of_Integral_Views/links/
0046351e020db5b604000000/The-Evolution-of-Consciousness-as-a-Planetary-
Imperative-An.

144. Pope John Paul II. 'Message to the Pontifical Academy of Sciences: On Evolution'.
Eternal Word Television Network (1996). Available at: https://www.ewtn.com/
library/papaldoc/jp961022.htm. (Accessed: 14th April 2018)

145. Rudolf Steiner, *Riddles of Philosophy* (Great Barrington, Massachusetts: Steiner-
Books, 2009).

146. Ken Wilber, *Integral Psychology: Consciousness, Spirit, Psychology, Therapy* (Boston:
Shambhala, 1999).

147. Owen Barfield, *History in English Words* (Great Barrington, Massachusetts: Lindisfarne Books, 2007).

148. Owen Barfield, *Saving the Appearances. A Study in Idolatry* (New York and London:
Harcourt Brace Jovanovich, 1965).

149. Ibid., p. 29.

150. Steiner, *Anthroposophical Leading Thoughts*, pp. 81–85.

151. Andrea Falcon, 'Aristotle on Causality', *Stanford Encyclopedia of Philosophy*, 2015,
https://plato.stanford.edu/entries/aristotle-causality/; Aristotle, 'Book 5, Section
1013a', in *Metaphysics*, ed. Hugh Tredennick, Online (Cambridge: Harvard University Press, 1989), http://www.perseus.tufts.edu/hopper/text?doc=
Perseus%3Atext%3A1999.01.0052%3Abook%3D5%3Asection%3D1013a. Sometimes there is confusion between final cause and formal cause. From the understanding of a person without training in philosophy, when one says 'final', one often
has the understanding that this is the 'final' cause, the ultimate source of all causes.
But the Greek word here is 'telos' which is more of an end goal or 'final' in the sense
of ultimate destination, not the ultimate source. And the fact that some commentators on Aristotle point out that the 'final' cause has a related concept called the
'exemplary' cause (connected with the idea in one's mind that guides physical
manifestation) shows the unmistakable link the 'final' cause has with the ideas that
guide the creation of an art. In addition, some commentators link Aristotle's

'formal' cause with Plato's doctrine of 'forms' which latter points to ultimate reasons for the 'why' of things in the world. This connection with Platonic forms points to Aristotle's formal cause as a kind of ultimate cause behind the three other causes.

152. Colin Mcginn, *The Mysterious Flame: Conscious Minds in a Material World* (New York: Basic Books, 1999); John Searle and Rebecca Goldstein, 'The Hard Problem of Consciousness', in *Toward a Science of Consciousness* (Tucson, Arizona: Center for Consciousness Studies, 2014),
https://www.youtube.com/watch?v=vtD-X9MCyVY.

153. Oliver Burkeman, 'Why Can't the World's Greatest Minds Solve the Mystery of Consciousness?', *The Guardian*, January 21, 2015, https://www.theguardian.com/science/2015/jan/21/-sp-why-cant-worlds-greatest-minds-solve-mystery-consciousness; John Horgan, 'David Chalmers Thinks the Hard Problem Is Really Hard', *Scientific American*, April 2017, https://blogs.scientificamerican.com/cross-check/david-chalmers-thinks-the-hard-problem-is-really-hard/.

154. The author is grateful to Fr. Tito Soquino, OSA, Vice-President of the Colegio San Agustin—Bacolod, Philippines, for clarifying the connection between St Thomas of Aquinas and St Augustine of Hippo.

155. R. Dean Peterson, *A Concise History of Christianity* (Belmont, CA: Wasworth Publishing Company, 1999), https://pdfs.semanticscholar.org/4f1b/ca31937de6236a0acb3bf05332f5d47ec94e.pdf; Andrea Borghini, 'Understand the Philosophical Theories of Nominalism and Realism', *ThoughtCo.*, 2018, https://www.thoughtco.com/nominalism-vs-realism-2670598.

156. Rudolf Steiner, *An Outline of Esoteric Science* (Hudson, New York: Anthroposophic Press, 1997).

157. Steiner, *The Philosophy of Spiritual Activity*. Especially Part I of the book.

158. Rudolf Steiner, *Knowledge of the Higher Worlds and Its Attainment* (Hudson, New York: Anthroposophic Press, 1947).

159. Peter Heusser, *Anthroposophy and Science: An Introduction* (Peter Lang. Kindle Edition, 2016).

160. I am using the term 'percept' in line with both Steiner and Heusser to mean the product of both outer and inner perception. The former can be sounds, colour, taste and so on. The latter can be memory, emotions, feelings, concepts, ideas and mental pictures.

161. I purposely inserted the word 'seemingly' because life (seemingly) emerges from matter itself, when observed with the physical senses. However, if one has spiritual vision, one can see that the formative forces of life themselves are responsible for the emergence of the physical form that the life itself would later inhabit. Steiner pointed this out very early in his work. See, Rudolf Steiner, *Theosophy. An Introduction to the Supersensible Knowledge of the World and the Destination of Man* (Forest Row, England: Rudolf Steiner Press, 2005), Chapter 1.

However, advances in mainstream modern science are starting to confirm that life itself, in this case, a snippet of DNA, can organize matter. This is currently known as the 'Phantom DNA Effect' on quanta of light or photons. See Gregg Braden, *The Divine Matrix. Bridging Time, Space, Miracles and Belief* (Carlsbad, California: Hay House, Inc., 2007), pp. 43–46 for the details of the experiment done by Russian scientist, Vladimir Poponin.

Chapter 16 further reinforces this reality of the supersensible affecting and organizing the sensible. In that chapter, for example, I quote Max Planck, co-founder of Quantum Physics, saying that ultimately consciousness is the matrix out of which matter manifests in the world.

162. Heusser, *Anthroposophy and Science*, pp. 172–173.

163. Ibid., p. 173.

164. Steiner, *An Outline of Esoteric Science*. See Chapters 4 and 6.

165. Sergei O. Prokofieff, *Rudolf Steiner and the Founding of the New Mysteries* (London: Temple Lodge, 1994). See especially Chapter 5.

166. Steiner, *Anthroposophical Leading Thoughts*, pp. 216–219.

167. N. Yoshikawa, 'The World I have Seen and the Life I will Live', Plenary talk given at the World Social Initiative Forum 2018, Minobusan University, Japan, March 29, 2018. The theme of the global forum was: 'Knowing Self Through Others: Empathy, A Path toward a Just and Fraternal Society'.

168. Steiner. *Anthroposophical Leading Thoughts*, pp.71–75; 97–102; 118–124.

169. Ed Regis, 'Meet the Extropians', *Wired*, 1994, https://www.wired.com/1994/10/extropians/.

170. T.H. Meyer, *In The Sign of the Five* (Forest Row: Temple Lodge, 2014), p.25.

171. Tristan Greene, 'AI Is Giving the Entire Medical Field Superpowers', *The Next Web*, 2018, https://thenextweb.com/artificial-intelligence/2018/02/05/ai-is-giving-the-entire-medical-field-super-powers/; Abby Norman, 'Your Future Doctor May Not Be Human. This Is the Rise of AI in Medicine', *Futurism*, 2018, https://futurism.com/ai-medicine-doctor/.

172. Scott Galloway, *The Four. The Hidden DNA of Amazon, Apple, Facebook, and Google* (New York: Penguin/Random House, 2017).

173. Ray Kurzweil, *The Age of Spiritual Machines: When Computers Exceed Human Intelligence*, (New York: Penguin Books, 1999); Zoltan Istvan, 'Mind Uploading Will Replace the Need for Religion', Motherboard, 2015, https://motherboard.vice.com/en_us/article/mgbw3v/mind-uploading-will-replace-god.

174. Jamie Bartlett, 'The Online Surveillance Debate Is Really About Whether You Trust Governments or Not', *The Telegraph*, 2015, https://www.telegraph.co.uk/technology/internet-security/11979682/The-online-surveillance-debate-is-really-about-whether-you-trust-governments-or-not.html; David Francis, '5 Reasons Why The NSA's Massive Surveillance Program Is No Big Deal (And 2 Reasons It Is)', *Business Insider*, 2013, http://www.businessinsider.com/nsa-surveillance-prism-phone-nsa-big-deal-2013-6.

175. Nick Ismail, 'The Internet of Things: The Security Crisis of 2018?', *Information Age*, 2018, http://www.information-age.com/internet-things-security-crisis-123470475/; Andrew Meola, 'How the Internet of Things Will Affect Security & Privacy', *Business Insider*, 2016, http://www.businessinsider.com/internet-of-things-security-privacy-2016-8.

176. Mark Harris, 'Project Skybender: Google's Secretive 5G Internet Drone Tests Revealed', *The Guardian*, 2016, https://www.theguardian.com/technology/2016/jan/29/project-skybender-google-drone-tests-internet-spaceport-virgin-galactic; Don Sambandaraksa, '5G, The War on Cash and Big Brother', *Telecom Asia*, 2017, https://www.telecomasia.net/content/5g-war-cash-and-big-brother.

177. Ted Jeory, 'Jesus Christ "May Have Suffered from Mental Health Problems", Claims Church of England', *The Express*, 2012, https://www.express.co.uk/news/uk/341926/Jesus-Christ-may-have-suffered-from-mental-health-problems-claims-Church-of-England; Evan D. Murray, Miles G. Cunningham, and Bruce H.

Price, 'The Role of Psychotic Disorders in Religious History Considered', *The Journal of Neuropsychiatry and Clinical Neurosciences* 24, no. 4 (January 2012): 410–26, https://doi.org/10.1176/appi.neuropsych.11090214.

178. Andrew Welburn, *A Vision for the Millennium. Modern Spirituality and Cultural Renewal from the work of Rudolf Steiner* (London: Rudolf Steiner Press, 1999). Chapter 2.

179. This is my own hypothesis based on a phenomenology of current events. ASI will work with the entire Internet. Combine this fact with the findings of the second scientific and more spiritual revolution (Chapter 16) that consciousness influences the properties and workings of matter. Also bring this together with the spiritual scientific finding that Ahriman is the spiritual being responsible for the workings and spread of materialism, including Artificial Intelligence. (See Steiner, *An Outline of Esoteric Science*.)

180. Elon Musk is pouring his considerable financial resources to create the 'Neuralink'. So the hybrid is a distinct possibility. For Musk's latest venture, see Nick Statt, 'Elon Musk launches Neuralink, a venture to merge the human brain with AI', *The Verge*, 27 March 2017. https://www.theverge.com/2017/3/27/15077864/elon-musk-neuralink-brain-computer-interface-ai-cyborgs

181. Sergei O. Prokofieff, *The Appearance of Christ in the Etheric. Spiritual-Scientific Aspects of the Second Coming* (Forest Row, England: Temple Lodge, 2012), pp. 69–70.

182. Rudolf Steiner, *The Knights Templar. The Mystery of the Warrior Monks* (Forest Row, England: Rudolf Steiner Press, 2007), Chapter 5.

183. Paul Emberson, *From Gondhishapur to Silicon Valley, Vol. 1* (Scotland and Switzerland: The Etheric Dimensions Press, 2009), pp. 41–55.

184. Rudolf Steiner, *Background to the Gospel of St Mark* (London: Rudolf Steiner Press, New York: Anthroposophic Press, Inc., 1968), Lecture 9, Berlin, 13 March, 1911.

185. Steiner, *The Knights Templar*, p.7, Chapter 4 and 5.

186. Ibid., pp. 84–85. This may be a surprising statement given that most people still have the impression that the Templars were demonic heretics. Recent research and actions by the Catholic Church have since restored the integrity and spirituality of the Templars. The proper citations appear below in Chapter 5.

187. Alexander Thomas, 'The Science of Transhumanism: How Technology Will Lead to a New Race of Super-Intelligent Immortal Beings (IF You Can Afford It)', *The Daily Mail*, 2017, http://www.dailymail.co.uk/sciencetech/article-4747174/Transhumanism-lead-immortality-elite.html; Olivia Solon, 'All Aboard the Immortality Bus: The Man Who Says Tech Will Help Us Live Forever', *The Guardian*, 2016, https://www.theguardian.com/technology/2016/jun/16/transhumanist-party-immortality-zoltan-istvan-presidential-campaign; Tim Urban, 'The AI Revolution: The Road to Superintelligence', *Wait But Why*, 2015, https://waitbutwhy.com/2015/01/artificial-intelligence-revolution-1.html; Alexander Thomas, 'Super Intelligence and Eternal Life: Transhumanism's Faithful Follow It Blindly into a Future for the Elite', *The Conversation*, 2017, http://theconversation.com/super-intelligence-and-eternal-life-transhumanisms-faithful-follow-it-blindly-into-a-future-for-the-elite-78538.

188. Steiner, *The Knights Templar*, Chapter 5.

189. For an introduction to all these themes, see Steiner, *An Outline of Esoteric Science*.

190. Prokofieff, *The Appearance of Christ in the Etheric*, pp. 88–89. For his source, Pro-

kofieff cites Steiner's lecture cycle, *Approaching the Mystery of Golgotha*, #152 in the Collected Works of Steiner.

191. Steiner, *Anthroposophical Leading Thoughts*, pp.216–219.

192. Rudolf Steiner, 'The Etherisation of the Blood', Basle, October 1, 1911, GA#130, www.rsarchive.org.

193. Rudolf Steiner, 'Evolution of the Michael Principle throughout the Ages. The Split in the Cosmic Intelligence'. In *Karmic Relationships: Esoteric Studies—Volume III*, 08 August 1924. GA 237. www.rsarchive.org.

194. Rudolf Steiner, *The Mission of the Archangel Michael*, Lecture II 'The Michael Revelation. The Word Becomes Flesh and the Flesh Becomes Spirit', Dornach, November 22, 1919. GA 194. www.rsarchive.org.

195. Rudolf Steiner, *How To Know Higher Worlds* (Great Barrington, Massachusetts: SteinerBooks, 1994). Chapter 5.

196. Michel Foucault, *The Archaeology of Knowledge and the Discourse on Language* (New York: Pantheon Books, 1972).

197. Rudolf Steiner, *The Archangel Michael. His Mission and Ours* (Great Barrington, Massachusetts: SteinerBooks, 1994).

198. Jordan Thomas, 'Silicon Valley could be the next hotspot for SEC whistleblowers', *TechCrunch*, November 19, 2017, https://techcrunch.com/2017/11/18/silicon-valley-could-be-the-next-hotspot-for-sec-whistleblowers/. It is important to note that Jordan Thomas was a former assistant director in the SEC's Enforcement Division and had a leadership role in the development of the SEC Whistleblower Program.

199. The Gospel of St John, Chapter 20, Verse 22.

200. Prokofieff, S.O. *The Heavenly Sophia and the Being Anthroposophia* (Great Barrington, Massachusetts: SteinerBooks, 2006).

201. Rudolf Steiner, *The Anthroposophic Movement*, Lecture 7: 'The Consolidation of the Anthroposophic Movement', Dornach, 16 June 1923, GA258, www.rearchive.org.

202. Rudolf Steiner, *The Effect of Occult Development Upon the Self and the Sheaths of Man*, Lecture 10. 29 March 1913, GA 145, www.rsarchive.org.

203. Rudolf Steiner. 'Preparing for the Sixth Epoch', A Lecture, Düsseldorf, June 15, 1915, GA 159, www.rsarchive.org.

204. The lowest sheath of angels is the etheric body. Rudolf Steiner, 'Perception of the Nature of Thought. Sun Activity in Earthly Evolution', Lecture, Dornach, 10 January 1915, GA 161, www.rsarchive.org. See also, Rudolf Steiner, *The Mission of Folk-Souls In connection with Germanic and Scandinavian Mythology*, Lecture 1, Christiania (Oslo), 7 June, 1910, www.rsarchive.org. And, Rudolf Steiner, 'How Can the Destitution of Soul in Modern Times Be Overcome? Social Understanding, Liberty of Thought, Knowledge of the Spirit', Lecture, Zurich, October 10, 1916, GA 168, www.rsarchive.org.

205. Rudolf Steiner, *From the Esoteric School. Esoteric Lessons 1904–1909* (Great Barrington, Massachusetts: SteinerBooks/Anthroposophic Press, 2007) p. xxv. Sometimes, he also calls them Masters of Wisdom and the Harmony of Feelings. Rudolf Steiner, 'Reading the Pictures of the Apocalypse', Lecture 4. Kristiania, May 13, 1909, GA104a, www.rsarchive.org.

206. T.H. Meyer, T. (Ed.), *Ehrenfried Pfeiffer. A Modern Quest for the Spirit* (Chestnut Ridge, New York: Mercury Press, 2010) p. 167. It is important to note that Pfeiffer indicates that this will happen provided Mani finds a 'suitable body'.

207. Rudolf Steiner., *The Gospel of St Luke* (London: Rudolf Steiner Press, 1975) p. 131–132. See also, Peter Selg, *Rudolf Steiner and Christian Rosenkreutz* (Great Barrington, Massachusetts: SteinerBooks, 2012), p. 4.

208. Rudolf Steiner, *Theosophy of the Rosicrucian* (London: Rudolf Steiner Press, 1966), pp. 8–10.

209. Rudolf Steiner, 'Esoteric Christianity and the Mission of Christian Rosenkreutz', Lecture 1. 'Jeshu Ben Pandira Who Prepared the Way for an Understanding of the Christ Impulse', Leipzig, 4 November 1911, www.resarchive.org.

210. Sergei O. Prokofieff, *Rudolf Steiner and the Founding of the New Mysteries*, Revised Second Edition. Translated by Paul King. (Great Barrington, Massachusetts: SteinerBooks, 2017.)

211. Steiner, *From the Esoteric School, Esoteric Lessons 1904–1909*, p. 132.

212. Bernard C.J. Lievegoed, *The Battle for the Soul. The Working Together of Three Great Leaders of Humanity*, (Gloucester, England: Hawthorne Press, 1994) pp. 64, 81–82. Already, in the fourth century AD, he convened a Council of Masters, including Master Jesus (Zarathustra) and Buddha. Mani himself then initiated Christian Rosenkreutz in his second initiation in the fourteenth–fifteenth centuries. Rosenkreutz later was Steiner's master in the nineteenth century. On the latter, see Peter Selg, *Rudolf Steiner and Christian Rosenkreutz*, pp. 4–8.

213. Richard Seddon, *Mani. His Life and Work, Transforming Evil*, (Forest Row, East Sussex, England: Temple Lodge, 2011) p. vii and the whole book itself.

214. Lievegoed, *The Battle for the Soul*, 'Sixth and Seventh Day' (Chapters 6 and 7).

215. Rudolf Steiner. *Egyptian Myths and Mysteries*, Lecture 10 'Old Myths as Pictures of Cosmic Facts. Darkening of Man's Spiritual Consciousness. The Initiation Principle of the Mysteries'. Leipzig, September 12, 1908, GA106, www.rsarchive.org., This is just one of hundreds of references to this fact in Steiner's lectures. Most of his lectures on the Gospel describe the event from different perspectives.

216. Selg, *Rudolf Steiner and Christian Rosenkreutz*, p. 4.

217. Rudolf Steiner, 'Esoteric Christianity and the Mission of Christian Rosenkreutz', Lecture 1, Neuchatel, 27 September 1911, GA130, www.rsarchive.org.

218. Rudolf Steiner. *The Temple Legend*. Lecture 5 'The Mystery Known to the Rosicrucians', Berlin, 4 November 1904, GA93. www.rsarchive.org. Christian Rosenkreutz is a reincarnation of both Hiram (who knew the technological secret of the Molten Sea and the Golden Triangle) and Count of St Germain who tried to steer the French Revolution with the threefolding goals of Liberté (Freedom), Égalité (Equality), and Fraternité (Brotherhood/Sisterhood or Solidarity).

219. Selg, *Rudolf Steiner and Christian Rosenkreutz*, p. 4.

220. Concerning the spiritual presence of Christian Rosenkreutz in the Christmas Foundation Meeting of 1923, see Sergei O. Prokofieff, *May Human Beings Hear It!* (Forest Row, England: Temple Lodge, 2004), p. 156. For the presence of both in a spiritual altar, see Sergei O. Prokofieff, *The Appearance of the Christ in the Etheric. Spiritual-Scientific Aspects of the Second Coming* (Forest Row, Sussex: England, 2012), pp. 100–103. On the relation of Christian-Michaelic Mysteries and the Christmas Foundation and Rudolf Steiner, see Prokofieff, *May Human Beings Hear It!*

221. Rudolf Steiner, *Rudolf Steiner, An Autobiography*, (Blauvelt, New York: Rudolf Steiner Publications, 1977), pp. 316–318.

222. Rudolf Steiner. 'Buddha and Christ. The Sphere of the Bodhisattvas', a lecture, Milan, September 21, 1911, GA 130, www.rsarchive.org.

223. Ibid.

224. Rudolf Steiner. *The Inner Impulses of Evolution* (Great Barrington, Massachusetts: SteinerBooks). GA171.

225. Steiner, *The Knights Templar*.

226. David van Biema, 'The Vatican and the Knights Templar', *Time*, October 2001, http://content.time.com/time/world/article/0,8599,1674980,00.html.

227. Philip Pullella, 'Knights Templar Win Heresy Reprieve After 700 Years', *Reuters*, 2007, https://www.reuters.com/article/us-vatican-templars/knights-templar-win-heresy-reprieve-after-700-years-idUSL093422320071012.

228. This is my own conclusion when I put the contents of this lecture together with the biography of Steiner as fully expounded by Sergei Prokofieff in his book, *Rudolf Steiner and the Founding of the New Mysteries* cited also above.

229. Rudolf Steiner., *From Symptom to Reality in Modern History* (London: Rudolf Steiner Press, 1976), Chapters 3, 4, 5.

230. See Part II, the section on the evolution of consciousness, especially in connection with the mission of materialism, and the Preface for an appreciation of the value of materialism despite the many problems of post-modern existence due to its out-moded epistemological and ontological assumptions.

231. Steiner, *The Philosophy of Spiritual Activity*, especially Part II.

232. Lindenberg, C., *Rudolf Steiner, A Biography* (Great Barrrington, Massachusetts: SteinerBooks, 2012), p. 546–547.

233. James Gardner, *The Intelligent Universe: AI, ET, and the Emerging Mind of the Cosmos* (Franklin Lakes, NJ: Book-mart Press, 2007).

234. Steiner, *An Outline of Esoteric Science*, Chapter 4.

235. Max Tegmark, *Life 3.0: Being Human in the Age of Artificial Intelligence* (New York: Penguin Random House, 2017).

236. Yuval Noah Harari, *Homo Deus: A Brief History of Tomorrow* (New York: HarperCollins, 2017).

237. Ray Kurzweil, *The Singularity Is Near: When Humans Transcend Biology* (New York: Penguin Books, 2006).

238. Martine Rothblatt, *Virtually Human: The Promise—and the Peril—of Digital Immor-tality* (New York: Pan Books Limited, 2014).

239. Stephen Hawking and Leonard Mlodinow, *The Grand Design* (New York: Random House, 2010).

240. Prokofieff, S.O., *Anthroposophy and the Philosophy of Freedom. Anthroposophy and Its Method of Cognition. The Christological and Cosmic-Human Dimension of the Philosophy of Freedom*, (Forest Row, England: Temple Lodge, 2009), pp. 35–36. See also, Rudolf Steiner. *An Outline of Esoteric Science*, p. 396.

241. Prokofieff, *Anthroposophy and the Philosophy of Freedom*, Chapter 2.

242. Sam Harris, 'An Atheist Manifesto', Sam Harris, 2005, 4–5, https://samharris.org/an-atheist-manifesto/; James E. Taylor, 'The New Atheists', *Internet Encyclopedia of Philosophy*, 2018, https://www.iep.utm.edu/n-atheis/.

243. Rudolf Steiner, 'Gospel of John: Lecture I: The Doctrine of the Logos', Rudolf Steiner Archive & e.Lib, 2018, http://wn.rsarchive.org/Lectures/GA103/English/AP1962/19080518p01.html.

244. Pamornpol Jinachitra, 'Nietzsche's Idea of an Overman and Life from His Point of View', Center for Computer Research in Music and Acoustics, 2018, https://ccrma.stanford.edu/~pj97/Nietzsche.htm; Friedrich Nietzsche, *Thus Spoke Zara-*

thustra: A Book for All and None (New York: Ancient Wisdom Publications, 2015).

245. The nature of the Ahriman and Ahrimanic beings is described in Chapter 4 above.

246. Friedemann-Eckart Schwarzkopf, *The Metamorphosis of the Given: Toward an Ecology of Consciousness* (Bern: Peter Lang International Academic Publishers, 1995).

247. Steiner, *The Philosophy of Spiritual Activity*, Chapter 3.

248. Panu Raatikaine, 'Gödel's Incompleteness Theorems', *Stanford Encyclopedia of Philosophy*, 2015, https://plato.stanford.edu/entries/goedel-incompleteness/; Melvin Henriksen, 'What Is Gödel's Theorem?', Scientific American, 2018, https://www.scientificamerican.com/article/what-is-godels-theorem/.

249. David Bolton, 'Definition of Source Code', *ThoughtCo.*, 2017, https://www.thoughtco.com/source-code-definition-958200.

250. This does not mean, however, that there are no new novel and even dangerous things that can emerge from an AI with an evolving algorithm. This is due to the fact that the details of a paradigm that have not been explored can have new and real, positive or negative, impact on the world. The AlphaGo victory over Lee Sedol demonstrated the seemingly powerful 'intuition' of the Deep Mind's AlphaGo AI. But in fact the machine can only calculate within the rules of the game. This is what scientists call 'narrow AI'. But we need to distinguish between the 'normal' AI science and technology of narrow AI and the real 'revolutionary' science and technology of the fully human. For a distinction between normal and revolutionary science as commonly understood in the scientific community, see Thomas S. Kuhn, *Structure of Scientific Revolutions* (Chicago: University of Chicago Press, 1962).

251. Claus Otto Scharmer, *Theory U. Leading from the Future as It Emerges. The Social Technology of Presencing* (Cambridge, Massachusetts: The Society for Organizational Learning, 2007).

252. Steiner, *An Outline of Esoteric Science* and also *How to Attain Higher Knowledge*.

253. Sergei Prokofieff, *The Michael-Mystery. A Spiritual-Scientific View of the Michael-Imagination and its Representation in Eurythmy* (Sourbridge, England: Wynstones Press, 2015 p. 37).

254. Steiner, *Karmic Relationships, Vol. III*.

255. Rudolf Grosse, R., *The Christmas Foundation; Beginning of a New Cosmic Age* (Vancouver: Steiner Book Centre, 1984), p. 119.

256. Ibid.

257. Rudolf Steiner., *The Knights Templar. The Mystery of the Warrior Monks.* Compiled and Edited by Margaret Jonas (Forest Row, England: Rudolf Steiner Press) pp. 109–110.

258. Steiner, *Anthroposophical Leading Thoughts*, #s 183–185.

259. Rudolf Steiner, 'The Etherization of the Blood', Basel, 01 October 1911, in *The Reappearance of the Christ in the Etheric*, GA 130. https://wn.rsarchive.org/Lectures/ReapChrist/19111001p02.html

260. Oliver Morsch, 'Fast Magnetic Writing of Data', Phys.Org, 2017, https://phys.org/news/2017-09-fast-magnetic.html.

261. Steiner, *Karmic Relationship*, Vols I–VIII.

262. Steiner, *Anthroposophical Leading Thoughts*, #184.

263. Prokofieff, *The Michael Mystery*, 'Chapter III. The Nature of the Michael Mystery', especially the beginning pages of the chapter.

264. I first heard this quote from Peter Senge in one of the leadership workshops that he gave in Vermont, USA, in the early 2000s. However, the documented quote comes from Otto Scharmer, the articulator of Theory U. Claus Otto Scharmer, 'The Blind Spot of Leadership: Presencing as a Social Technology of Freedom', (Massachusetts Institute of Technology, 2003), http://www.ottoscharmer.com/sites/default/files/2003_TheBlindSpot.pdf.

265. Lindenberg, *Rudolf Steiner, A Biography*, p. 736. Steiner gave this figure during the final lecture of his life. This was on September 28, 1924. After that he stopped all lecturing and rested, mostly in bed, but still writing articles and advising people, until he died on March 30, 1925.

266. Sergei O. Prokofieff, *Anthroposophy and the Philosophy of Freedom. Anthroposophy and Its Method of Cognition. The Christological and Cosmic-Human Dimension of the Philosophy of Freedom* (Forest Row, England: Temple Lodge, 2009) pp. 24–25, 47, 173, 213–214, 256–257.

267. There is a huge spiritual challenge translating the results of experiencing the spiritual world directly in higher states of consciousness, into the language of earthly humanity. This includes a lot of sacrifices. But, because Steiner accomplished such a gargantuan task, post-modern, twenty-first century humans can access the thoughts of the Gods communicated by the latter to the spiritual researcher by an intensive, focused, and reverent study of modern-day spiritual science. For a description of this 'translation' process, see Sergei O. Prokofieff, *The Guardian of the Threshold and the Philosophy of Freedom. On the Relationship of the Philosophy of Freedom to the Fifth Gospel* (Forest Row, England: Temple Lodge, 2011) pp. 96–97,100–101. See also, Rudolf Steiner, *The Spiritual Foundation of Morality. Francis of Assisi & The Christ Impulse* (Hudson: New York: Anthroposophic Press, 1995), p. 51.

268. Lievegoed, *The Battle for the Soul*, p. 90.

269. The author has conducted over a hundred workshops, in various context, around the world on 'Courage'. And through an evocative and phenomenological approach, the participants themselves begin to realize that, at this point in their development, and the evolution of humanity in general, they as humans vacillate between their personal, programmed or societally constructed self (a basic premise of the process of socialization in the social sciences) and their creative, True, Higher, Eternal Self, the source of true freedom, love, and courage in the earthly world. Phenomenologically, participants use many other terms for the True Self including Essential Self, Permanent Self, and the Imaginal Self.

There is a national movement in the Philippines called MISSION that is an acronym for the Movement of Imaginals for Sustainable Societies Through Initiatives, Organizing and Networking. MISSION is advocating evolutionary societal transformation on the basis of profound inner change. The word 'Imaginal' refers to the Imaginal Self that has the power to imagine and envision new worlds that it can evolve out of the existing societal arrangements. In this way, this concept is close to Steiner's 'moral technique' as discussed in Chapter 12 of his *Philosophy of Spiritual Activity*, although the latter was not the basis for the Courage Workshops of MISSION. The link between the two emerged organically indicating that the inspirations behind the workshop stems from the same 'source' as Steiner's *Philosophy of Spiritual Activity*.

270. Steiner also spoke of the importance of feelings in dozens of other lectures he gave and books he wrote. The reader can affirm this for himself/herself by searching the

data base of www.rsarchive.org and using the search term 'feeling'. The number of citations that relate to the word 'feeling' will overwhelm the researcher.

271. Joe Dispenza, *You are the Placebo: Making Your Mind Matter* (Carlsbad, California: Hay House, 2014). And Gregg Braden, *The Divine Matrix: Bridging Time, Space, Miracles and Belief* (Carlsbad, California: Hay House, 2007).

272. Meyer, T.H. (Ed.), *The New Cain. The Temple Legend as a spiritual and moral impulse for evolution and its completion by Rudolf Steiner* (Forest Row, England: Temple Lodge, 2013) p. 110.

273. Dispenza, *You are the Placebo*. Importance of feeling one's active imagination is emphasized again and again throughout the book. And it is the same with Braden, *The Divine Matrix*.

274. Prokofieff, S.O., *The Appearance of Christ in the Etheric. Spiritual-Scientific Aspects of the Second Coming* (Forest Row, England: Temple Lodge, 2012) pp. 106–107.

275. One who has used this 'method' knows the truth of this statement.

276. Lynne McTaggart, *The Field: The Quest for the Secret Force of the Universe* (New York: HarperCollins, 2008).

277. Steiner, *Knowledge of the Higher Worlds*, Chapter 1.

278. William Hutchison Murray, *The Scottish Himalayan Expedition* (London: J. M. Dent & Co., 1951). Murray borrowed the last two sentences of this quote from a loose translation of Goethe's work, *Faust*.

279. Lynne McTaggart, *The Intention Experiment: Using Your Thoughts to Change Your Life and the World* (New York: Simon & Schuster, 2008).

280. See Chapter 16 below.

281. George Ellis, a mathematical astrophysicist and a Templeton Awardee (considered more prestigious than the Nobel Prize due the latter's larger financial prize), shared this preference of most astrophysicists for 'deistic design' before his audience in a workshop in Chile as part of the Congress of the Future, 15–21 January 2018. This Congress of the Future was convened by the Senate of Chile, headed by the Chairman of the Senate Committee on Science and Technology and Vice-President of Chile, and has the support of the entire government of Chile, including the President of Chile. Over a hundred scientists, experts, and scholars gave presentations in the Congress. Dr Ellis also confirmed this fact during several hours of personal conversation with him in Chile, 18 January 2018. One can also see his perspective in the book: Murphy, N. and Ellis, G.F.R., *On the Moral Nature of the Universe. Theology, Cosmology, and Ethics*, Minneapolis: Fortress Press, 1996.

282. Rudolf Steiner., *The Philosophy of Spiritual Activity and Truth and Knowledge*, (West Nyack, New York: Rudolf Steiner Publications, 1963) p. 177.

283. Ibid., pp. 195–196.

284. Ibid., p. 264.

285. Prokofieff, *The Appearance of the Christ in the Etheric*, p. 120.

286. Steiner, *An Outline of Esoteric Science*, Chapter 5.

287. Rudolf Steiner., *Knowledge of the Higher Worlds and Its Attainment* (Hudson, New York: Anthroposophic Press, 1947) pp. 260–266. In these pages, Steiner emphasizes the importance of living thinking in all stages of higher knowledge, starting with intuitive thinking. From a different but supportive angle, see also, Prokofieff, *Anthroposophy and The Philosophy of Freedom*, p.181.

288. Albert Einstein, *The Albert Einstein Collection: Essays in Humanism, The Theory of Relativity, and The World As I See It* (New York: Open Road Media, 2016), p.28.

289. Sergei Prokofieff, *The Foundation Stone Meditation. A Key to the Christian Mysteries.* (Forest Row, England: Temple Lodge, 2006). See Chapter 5.

290. C. Otto Scharmer, *Theory U.*

291. Rudolf Steiner., *Background to the Gospel of St. Mark* (London: Rudolf Steiner Press and New York: Anthroposophic Press, 1968), Lecture 8, pp. 132–134.

292. How We Will, 'Healing Our Communities Through Interconnection and New Strategies', in *How We Will: Threefolding Our Cultural Revolution* (Los Angeles, 2017), https://howwewill.blog/.

293. Bernard Lievegoed, *Forming Curative Communities* (London: Rudolf Steiner Press, 1978), Lecture 5.

294. Paul Emberson, *Machines and the Human Spirit. The Golden Age of the Fifth Kingdom* (Edinburgh, Scotland: The DewCross Centre for Moral Technology, 2013).

295. Personal conversation with Dr Michaela Glöckler in Manila during the first decade of the twenty-first century just before she launched ELIANT, the European movement to address the marginalization of anthroposophical initiatives in bio-dynamic agriculture, Steiner education, and anthroposophical medicine. Being a member, at that time, of the extended Executive Council of the global Anthroposophical Society based in Dornach, Switzerland, she had access to the worldwide extent of the influence of the global anthroposophical movement.

296. Alliance ELIANT, 'The ELIANT Alliance', Alliance ELIANT, 2015, https://eliant.eu/en/about-us/.

297. Prokofieff, S.O., *The Michael Mystery. A Spiritual-Scientific View of the Michael-Imagination and its Representation in Eurythmy* (Stourbridge, England: Wynstones Press, 2015) pp. 59–60.

298. Steiner, 'Preparing for the Sixth Epoch'.

299. Rudolf Steiner, 'Prayer', Lecture, Berlin, February 17, 1910, p.25. www.rsarchive.org.

300. Roger Nelson, 'What Is the Nature of the Global Consciousness Project?', The Global Consciousness Project, 2015, http://noosphere.princeton.edu/gcpintro.html.

301. Rudolf Steiner., 'Necessity of Finding the Spirit Again', Lecture, February 27, 1921. www.rsarchive.org.

302. Personal conversation with Rembert Biemond while riding in a car from Jarna to Stockholm, Sweden, October 2017. Biemond has worked in various executive and advisory positions including the global headquarters of the General Anthroposophical Society, Goetheanum, Dornach, Switzerland.

303. Paul Hawken, *Blessed Unrest: How the Largest Social Movement in History Is Restoring Grace, Justice, and Beauty to the World* (New York: Penguin Books, 2008).

304. Plato, *The Last Days of Socrates: Euthyphro, The Apology: Crito [and] Phaedo*, ed. Hugh Tredennick, Revised tr (New York: Penguin Books, 1993).

305. What follows is based on personal experience as an activist at the local, national, and global levels in the past 50 years. It is not a complete articulation of these experiences. But there is enough substance here for the readers to get the gist and essence of what is needed.

306. The general public, including civil society activists, may also benefit from the sharing that will follow.

307. R. Rosenthal and L. Jacobson, *Pygmalion in the Classroom: Teacher Expectation and*

Pupils' Intellectual Development (New York: Rineheart & WInston, 1968), https://doi.org/10.1093/obo/9780199846740-0014.

308. Avil Beckford, 'Margaret Mead: Can a Group of Thoughtful, Committed Citizens Make a Difference? Margaret Mead Thought So', *The Invisible Mentor*, 2009, http://theinvisiblementor.com/can-a-group-of-thoughtful-committed-citizens-make-a-difference-margaret-mead-thought-so/.

309. Luis E. Hestres, 'Tools Beyond Control: Social Media and the Work of Advocacy Organizations', *Social Media + Society* 3, no. 2 (April 12, 2017), https://doi.org/10.1177/2056305117714237.

310. John Arquilla and David Ronfeldt, eds., *Networks and Netwars: The Future of Terror, Crime, and Militancy* (Sta. Monica: RAND Corporation, 2001), https://www.rand.org/pubs/monograph_reports/MR1382.html.

311. Some of the initiatives presented at the World Social Initiative Forum, 29 March to 2 April 2018, Japan. Organized in partnership with the Social Initiative Forum under the leadership of Ute Cramer, co-founder of the Forum, and Joan Sleigh, member of the Executive Council, General Anthroposophical Society.

312. Personal conversation with Dr Christoph Strawe who showed me the relevant item in *Das Goetheanum*, the newsletter of the global Anthroposophical Society. This took place around 2001 in Stuttgart, Germany.

313. Ibid. Strawe conversation. Dr Strawe is one of the foremost authority and exponents on societal threefolding in the European context. His PhD dissertation was on Marx and Steiner, a comparison of their social ideas.

314. Already several initiatives are afoot in the Philippines to provide this safety net. But these initiatives are still in the early stages of implementation.

315. Conversation with Demeter Spain representative at their booth in BioFach, February 2016.

316. Meeting with Ceres Organic, the largest organic wholesale and retail operation in New Zealand, September 2014.

317. Derek Gehl Talk on Digital Marketing, 20 September 2017, Holiday Inn, ADB Avenue, Ortigas, Metro Manila, Philippines.

318. Dr Joseph Mercola, 'Shocking Facts About the Pharmaceutical Industry', *Mercola*, 2008, https://articles.mercola.com/sites/articles/archive/2008/04/19/shocking-facts-about-the-pharmaceutical-industry.aspx.

319. Anna Lappé, 'The Battle for Biodiversity: Monsanto and Farmers Clash', *The Atlantic*, 2011, https://www.theatlantic.com/health/archive/2011/03/the-battle-for-biodiversity-monsanto-and-farmers-clash/73117/.

320. Duncan Geere, 'PayPal Founder Backs Synthetic Meat Printing Company', *Wired*, 2012, https://www.wired.com/2012/08/3d-printed-meat/.

321. Robert Karp and Thea Maria Carlson, 'Biodynamic Farming: A Farm-Forward Approach', *Whole Story*, 2015, https://www.wholefoodsmarket.com/blog/biodynamic-farming-farm-forward-approach.

322. Personal conversation with M.C. Richards in Spring Valley, New York, 1979.

323. Harry Pettit, 'AI will team up with CCTV to predict your every move', *Mailonline*, 09 May 2017, http://www.dailymail.co.uk/sciencetech/article-4488614/New-AI-team-CCTV-predict-move.html

324. Olivia Solon, 'Facebook Says Cambridge Analytica May Have Gained 37m More Users' Data', *The Guardian*, 2018, https://www.theguardian.com/technology/2018/apr/04/facebook-cambridge-analytica-user-data-latest-more-than-thought.

325. Lisa Marie Segarra, 'Mark Zuckerberg Lost $10 Billion in One Week After Facebook's Privacy Scandal', *Time*, March 2018, http://time.com/money/5213181/mark-zuckerberg-lost-10-billion-in-one-week-after-facebooks-privacy-scandal/.

326. Sohini Mitter, 'Facebook has lost over $100 Billion in market cap after the Cambridge Analytica exposé', *Yourstory*, 02 April 2018, https://yourstory.com/2018/04/facebook-has-lost-over-100-b-in-market-cap-after-the-cambridge-analytica-expose/

327. Anna Isaac, 'World's biggest fund BlackRock warns companies to find a social purpose', *The Telegraph*, 6 January 2018. https://www.telegraph.co.uk/business/2018/01/16/worlds-biggest-fund-blackrock-warns-companies-find-social-purpose/

328. Emily Stewart, 'What the Government Could Actually Do About Facebook', *Vox*, 2018, https://www.vox.com/policy-and-politics/2018/4/10/17208322/facebook-mark-zuckerberg-congress-testimony-regulation.

329. I will be basing the statements that follow about Shiva and Rajagopal on my long years of not only associating with them but also converging with them in activist actions and conferences and other global advocacies.

330. Both of these amazing global activists clearly have the Micha-elic Will even if they are not anthroposophists.

331. Hans R. Herren, *How to Nourish the World*, ed. Sue Coles (Bern: Ruffer & Rub Sachbuchverlag, 2016).

332. Lucy Siegle, 'Patrick Holden: "People's Image of Farming Is a Complete Fantasy" ', *The Guardian*, 2014, https://www.theguardian.com/lifeandstyle/2014/aug/20/patrick-holden-peoples-image-of-farming-is-a-complete-fantasy.

333. Goldman Sachs, 'Millennials: Coming of Age', *Goldman Sachs*, 2018, http://www.goldmansachs.com/our-thinking/pages/millennials/.

334. Deloitte. The Deloitte Millennial Survey 2017. *Deloitte* (2018). https://www2.deloitte.com/global/en/pages/about-deloitte/articles/millennialsurvey.html#.

335. Lindenberg, C., *Rudolf Steiner, A Biography* (Great Barrington, Massachusetts: Steiner Books, 2012) pp. 617–618.

336. Lievegoed, *Forming Curative Communities*.

337. Jeremy Jackson, 'Wanna Create A Great Product? Fail Early, Fail Fast, Fail Often', *Co.Design*, 2011, https://www.fastcodesign.com/1663968/wanna-create-a-great-product-fail-early-fail-fast-fail-often.

338. Apple. The future is here: iPhone X. *Apple Newsroom* (2017). https://www.apple.com/newsroom/2017/09/the-future-is-here-iphone-x

339. Peter Senge, Claus Otto Scharmer, Joseph Jaworski, & Betty Sue Flowers, *Presence* (New York: Random House, 2008).

340. Claus Otto Scharmer, Client and Partner List. *OttoScharmer.Com* (2018). http://www.ottoscharmer.com/bio/client-list.

341. Lievegoed, B., *Towards the 21st Century: Doing the Good* (Vancouver: Steiner Book Centre, 1972), p.32.

342. Lievegoed, B.C.J., *Mystery Streams in Europe and the New Mysteries* (Spring Valley, New York: The Anthroposophic Press, 1982), Chapter 4. See also, Rudolf Steiner., *The Spiritual Foundations of Morality. Francis of Assisi & the Christ Impulse* (Hudson, New York: Anthroposophic Press, 1995), Chapter 1.

343. This was the description given by Manfred Schmidt-Brabant of the General Anthroposophical Society in the September 2001 conference on Michaelmas. I was personally present in the 'great hall' when he made this statement.

344. The International Youth Initiative Program. About Us. *YIP. Se* (2018). Available at: http://yip.se/about/. (Accessed: 15 April 2018.)

345. Personal communication from Reinoud Meijer, Program Director of YIP, October 2017.

346. Based on direct experience as one of the faculty members of YIP for the past 10 years.

347. Rudolf Steiner, *The Foundation Stone. The Laying of the Foundation Stone of the Anthroposophical Society* (London: Rudolf Steiner Press, 1979), p. 19.

348. Rajesh Tandon and Mohini Kak, 'Amplifying Voices from the Global South: Globalizing Civil Society', in *Critical Mass: The Emergence of the Global Civil Society*, ed. James W. St. G. Walker and Andrew S. Thompson (Canada: Wilfrid Laurier University Press, 2008), https://www.cigionline.org/sites/default/files/walker_thompson.pdf; Martin Albrow and Fiona Holland, 'Democratizing Global Governance: Achieving Goals While Aspiring to Free and Equal Communication', in *Critical Mass: The Emergence of the Global Civil Society*, ed. James W. St. G. Walker and Andrew S. Thompson (Canada: Wilfrid Laurier University Press, 2008), https://www.cigionline.org/sites/default/files/walker_thompson.pdf.

349. Carole Collins, '"Break the Chains of Debt!": International Jubilee 2000 Campaign Demands Deeper Debt Relief', *Africa Recovery* 13, no. 2–3 (1999), www.un.org/en/africarenewal/subjindx/132debt2.htm; Advocacy International, 'Jubilee 2000', *Advocacy International*, 2018, http://www.advocacyinternational.co.uk/featured-project/jubilee-2000.

350. This has been true for at least one school in the Philippines. And visiting anthroposophists have told me that this is also true in Germany and other places.

351. Tautz, J., *Attack of the Enemy. The Occult Inspiration behind Adolf Hitler and the Nazis* (Forest Row, England: Temple Lodge, 2014). See Publishers Note, p. vii.

352. 'The Gospel According to St Matthew', The Bible, King James Version, p. 1331.

353. Prokofieff, S.O and Selg, P. *The Crisis of the Anthroposophical Society and Pathways to the Future* (Forest Row, England: Temple Lodge, 2013).

354. Conversations with Gary Lamb who has read at least three such books in the past few years, January 29, 2018, New York. Gary Lamb is the Director of the Center for Social Research at the Hawthorne Valley Association and the former co-editor of the *Threefold Review*.

355. See end of Chapter 11.

356. Susan Frey, 'Technology Takes Hold in the Early Grades', *Ed Source*, 2015, https://edsource.org/2015/technology-takes-hold-in-the-early-grades/74465.

357. Beth Gariner, 'Adding Coding to the Curriculum', *The New York Times*, 2014, https://www.nytimes.com/2014/03/24/world/europe/adding-coding-to-the-curriculum.html.

358. Michael Godsey, 'The Deconstruction of the K-12 Teacher', *The Atlantic*, 2015, https://www.theatlantic.com/education/archive/2015/03/the-deconstruction-of-the-k-12-teacher/388631/.

359. Heusser, *Anthroposophy and Science*.

360. Ian Steadman, 'IBM's Watson Is Better at Diagnosing Cancer than Human Doctors', *Wired*, 2013, http://www.wired.co.uk/article/ibm-watson-medical-doctor;

Norman, 'Your Future Doctor May Not Be Human. This Is the Rise of AI in Medicine'; Greene, 'AI Is Giving the Entire Medical Field Superpowers'; Jennifer Kite-Powell, 'See How Artificial Intelligence Can Improve Medical Diagnosis And Healthcare', *Forbes*, 2017, https://www.forbes.com/sites/jenniferhicks/2017/05/16/see-how-artificial-intelligence-can-improve-medical-diagnosis-and-healthcare/#1dfc6ace6223.

361. Conversation with Jim W. Sharman, April 24, 2018. Sharman is the Director of the Gamot Cogon Steiner/Waldorf School in the Philippines. He has attended several of these IPMT trainings in the Philippines.

362. The experience of Sir John Eccles, Nobel Prize Winner for Medicine, is a case in point. See Brian Patrick Casey, *Against the Materialists: John Carew Eccles, Karl Raimund Popper, and the Ghost in the Machine*, Doctoral Dissertation, 2009. http://www.newdualism.org/papers/B.Casey/Casey-AgainstMaterialists.pdf

363. Dr Thomas Cowan, *Human Heart, Cosmic Heart: A Doctor's Quest to Understand, Treat, and Prevent Cardiovascular Disease* (White River Junction Vermont: Chelsea Green Publishing, 2016).

364. In addition, he is receiving a lot of enthusiastic email messages and other forms of responses. Many are thankful that his work has helped them with their heart challenges. Source: Personal conversation with Tom Cowan in San Francisco, USA, 26 January 2016.

365. Dr Joseph Mercola, 'What You Really Need to Know About Heart Disease and Its Treatment', *Mercola*, 2017, https://articles.mercola.com/sites/articles/archive/2017/12/24/stents-heart-disease-treatment.aspx.

366. Alexa, 'Mercola.Com Traffic Statistics', *Alexa*, 2018, https://www.alexa.com/siteinfo/mercola.com.

367. Dr Joseph Mercola, 'Mercola.com Is World's Most Visited Natural Health Site', *Mercola*, 2018, https://www.mercola.com/forms/rankings.htm.

368. For a deeper treatment of this subject matter, see the excellent book on this topic by Pieter van der Ree. The book is full of many examples of this more spiritual form of architecture from different parts of the world. The book also contains dozens of beautiful and amazing pictures of many buildings using organic or living architecture design principles. An exhibit of these buildings was the basis of two International Organic Architecture Conferences in the Philippines. Sarri Tapales, an interior designer, curated the conference with a team in London and the Philippines. Pieter van der Ree, *Living Architecture. Balancing Nature, Culture and Technology*, (Driebergen, The Netherlands: International Forum Man and Architecture, 2017).

369. Lievegoed, *Forming Curative Communities*.

370. Rudolf Steiner, *The Arts and Their Mission*, (New York: Anthroposophic Press, 1964).

371. Tegmark, *Life 3.0* and Gardner, *The Intelligent Universe*.

372. Rudolf Steiner, *Spiritual Science as a Foundation for Social Forms* (Hudson, New York: Anthroposophic Press and London: Rudolf Steiner Press, 1986).

373. Ibid, p. 32.

374. Ibid, p. 27.

375. Rudolf Steiner., *The Christian Mystery* (Hudson, New York: Anthroposophic Press, 1998), p. 176.

376. Steiner, *Spiritual Science as a Foundation for Social Forms*, pp. 35–36.

377. Tom Teodorczuk, 'The Knights Templar: Military Order or the First Financial-Services Company?', *Market Watch*, 2017, https://www.marketwatch.com/story/how-the-knights-templar-became-the-worlds-first-financial-services-company-2017-09-26; Tim Harford, 'The Warrior Monks Who Invented Banking', *BBC World Service*, 2017, http://www.bbc.com/news/business-38499883.

378. For a theoretical elaboration of this point in mainstream society, see Nicanor Perlas, *Shaping Globalization: Civil Society, Cultural Power, and Threefolding* (Manila: Center for Alternative Development Initiatives, 2001). This elaboration can also apply to the global anthroposophical movement.

379. Interview with Gerald Häfner, Head of the Social Science Section at the School of Spiritual Science at the Goetheanum in Dornach, Basel, Switzerland. October 2017.

380. Conversation with Johannes Stuttgen in Frankfurt, Germany, October 2017. Stuttgen was a close student and colleague of Joseph Beuys. Thus he not only gave an overview of Omnibus but also traced its origins to the ideas of Joseph Beuys.

381. For more details, see Perlas, *Shaping Globalization*. This book has been translated into nine languages and have sold over 10,000 copies around the world.

382. Interview with Jude Atilano, then Deputy City Administrator of the government of Bayawan City. February 2018.

383. League of Organic Agriculture Municipalities of the Philippines, 'Mission and Vision', *LOAMC-Ph.Org*, 2017, http://loamc-ph.org/about-us/.

384. National Economic and Development Authority. *Philippine Development Plan 2017–2022*. (Pasig: NEDA, 2017.) Also, the Department of Environment and Natural Resources (DENR), *Memorandum Order on Sustainable Integrated Area Development*, February 2017.

385. Forbes Admin, 'Bill Gates' Creative Capitalism', *Forbes*, 2008, https://www.forbes.com/sites/davos/2008/01/24/bill-gates-creative-capitalism/#6dfdf4287e3d.

386. U.S. Impact Investing Alliance, 'U.S. Impact Investing Alliance Launches to Scale the Practice of Impact Investing', *Cision PR Newswire*, 2017, https://www.prnewswire.com/news-releases/us-impact-investing-alliance-launches-to-scale-the-practice-of-impact-investing-300494435.html.

387. Perlas, *Shaping Globalization*.

388. For the meaning of Masters in this book, see Chapter 5.

389. Meyer, T. (Ed.), *Ehrenfried Pfeiffer. A Modern Quest for the Spirit* (Chestnut Ridge, New York: Mercury Press, 2010) p. 167. It is important to note that Pfeiffer indicates that this will happen provided Mani finds a 'suitable body'.

390. In the Gospel of St John, Christ said: '. . . I am the Way, the Truth and the Life . . .' (John 14:6). True Love is what infuses Life to all things. This is clear from direct experience of many people when they are in the state of true love. And that is why Christ could say that the highest commandment is Love. (Matthew 22:37.)

391. The Filipino language educates Filipinos for empathy. Their notion of democracy is more based on a direct experience of or empathy for the condition of the other person. They mobilize when they perceive gross injustice and inequality not because of the concept of violation of rights but because of '*damayan*' or empathy with the suffering of the other person. The suffering of the other person is one's own suffering.

We see this when hundreds of thousands of Filipinos marched to pay their last respects to Flor Contemplacion, an Overseas Filipina Worker (OFW), unjustly condemned and put to death by the government of Singapore. Filipinos were upset by the pain that Flor Contemplacion suffered, a pain that they also felt within themselves. This created an escalating crisis between the Philippine government and Singapore. It was only solved in a private conversation between the Deputy Prime Minister of Singapore and the National Security Adviser of the former President of the Philippines, Fidel Ramos. In that conversation, the Singaporean government official understood the concept of '*damay*' in Philippine culture and that Contemplacion was not a 'mere maid' but a human being, one whose dignity was grossly violated and which violation Filipinos felt as their pain. Conversation with Dr. Serafin Talisayon, Assistant Secretary, Office of the National Security Adviser, 1998. This capacity for '*damay*' also became the basis of the Philippine revolution and the establishment of the first democratic republic in Asia. See, Ileto, R.C., *Pasyon and Revolution. Popular Movements in the Philippines, 1840–1910* (Manila: Ateneo de Manila Press, 1979).

392. As discussed immediately above, and to be clear, freedom is in the realm of culture, (civil society), equality in the realm of polity (the state), and solidarity in the realm of the economy (business).

393. Alfred North Whitehead, *Process and Reality: An Essay in Cosmology* (New York: The Free Press, 1979).

394. Rudolf Steiner, *Karmic Relationships, Vol. IV* (London: Rudolf Steiner Press, 1983) pp. 149–157.

395. See Chapter 14 above.

396. Meyer, T.H., *Rudolf Steiner's Core Mission. The Birth and Development of Spiritual Scientific Karma Research* (Forest Row, England: Temple Lodge, 2010). In the context of the huge importance of reincarnation research in the Age of Artificial Intelligence, I would recommend individuals to read the entire book.

397. Stefan Nekvapil, 'Moral Technologies: Now and in the Future', *Moral Technologies*, 2018, https://moraltechnologies.com.au/articles/moral-technologies-now-and-in-the-future/.

398. Rudolf Steiner Bookstore, 'MysTech Lecture Series', Rudolf Steiner Bookstore, 2017, http://rudolfsteinerbookstore.com/event/mystech/.

399. Andrew Linnell, 'The Destiny of Humanity with Machines', *Being Human*, 2011, http://www.rudolfsteiner.org/fileadmin/being-human/bh-4-2011-Winter/Linnell-Machines-13-14.pdf.

400. Emberson, P. *From Gondhishapur to Silicon Valley. Vol. 1, Spiritual Forces in the development of data processing and the future of computer technology. Vol. 2, Creating new worlds; The encroachment of the Eight Sphere. Standing against evil* (Switzerland and Isle of Mull, Scotland: Etheric Dimensions Press, 2009 & 2014 respectively).

401. See Chapter 5.

402. For the collapse of the dominance of philosophical materialism in its 'logical positivism' form as well as the 'received' variations of it, see Suppe, F., *The Structure of Scientific Theories* (Chicago: University of Chicago Press, 1977). See the entire Part IV and V. In short, the hegemony of logical positivism is gone and very different views of the nature of scientific theories have emerged. Materialism can no longer be taken as the sole epistemological stance of the world.

403. Carolyn Merchant, ' "The Violence of Impediments": Francis Bacon and the Origins of Experimentation', *Isis 99* (2008): 731–60.

404. June Javelosa, 'Here's How Quantum Gravity Will Change Our Understanding of the Universe', *Futurism*, 2016, https://futurism.com/heres-how-quantum-gravity-could-help-us-understand-the-physics-of-our-universe/; Hans Halvorson, 'What Does Quantum Mechanics Suggest About Our Perceptions of Reality?', *Big Questions Online*, 2015, https://www.bigquestionsonline.com/2015/02/24/what-does-quantum-mechanics-suggest-about-our-perceptions-reality/.

405. Michael Egnor, 'Darwin's Theory, Darwinism, and Eugenics', *Evolution News & Science Today*, 2007, https://evolutionnews.org/2007/05/darwins_theory_darwinism_and_e/; Jack Stewart, 'Self-Driving Trucks Will Kill Jobs, But Make Roads Safer', *Wired*, 2017, https://www.wired.com/2017/05/robot-us-self-driving-trucks-coming-save-lives-kill-jobs/.

406. Alain Aspect, Philippe Grangier, and Gérard Roger, 'Experimental Realization of Einstein-Podolsky-Rosen-Bohm Gedankenexperiment: A New Violation of Bell's Inequalities', *Phys. Rev. Lett.* 49, no. 2 (1982), https://doi.org/doi.org/10.1103/PhysRevLett.49.91.

407. George Musser, 'How Einstein Revealed the Universe's Strange "Nonlocality"', *Scientific American*, November 2015, https://www.scientificamerican.com/article/how-einstein-revealed-the-universe-s-strange-nonlocality/.

408. Zeeya Merali, 'Quantum "Spookiness" Passes Toughest Test Yet', *Nature* 525 (2015): 14–15.

409. John Gribbin, *In Search of Schrödinger's Cat: Quantum Physics and Reality* (Canada: Bantam Books, 1984).

410. Gregg Braden, *The Divine Matrix: Bridging Time, Space, Miracles, and Belief* (California: Hay House, 2007).

411. J.W.N. Sullivan, 'Interviews with the Great Scientists VI: Max Planck', *The Observer*, January 25, 1931.

412. George Wald, 'Life and Mind in the Universe', *International Journal of Quantum Chemistry* 26, no. S11 (March 12, 1984): 1–15, https://doi.org/10.1002/qua.560260703.

413. Andrew Zimmerman Jones, 'What Is the Anthropic Principle?', *ThoughtCo.*, 2017, https://www.thoughtco.com/what-is-the-anthropic-principle-2698848.

414. Ilia Delio, *The Emergent Christ: Exploring the Meaning of Catholic in an Evolutionary* (Maryknoll: Orbis Books, 2011).

415. Jones, 'What Is the Anthropic Principle?'

416. Anil Ananthaswamy, 'Why Our Universe's Dark Matter Mix Is "Just Right"', *New Scientist* 200, no. 2685 (December 2008): 12, https://doi.org/10.1016/S0262-4079(08)63063-8; Simeon Hellerman and Johannes Walcher, 'Dark Matter and the Anthropic Principle', *Physical Review D* 72, no. 12 (December 23, 2005): 123520, https://doi.org/10.1103/PhysRevD.72.123520.

417. Ross, H., *The Creator and The Cosmos. How The Greatest Scientific Discoveries of the Century Reveal God.* (Reasons to Believe: Kindle Edition.)

418. Ed Harrison, *Masks of the Universe* (New York: Collier Books, 1985).

419. Robert Jastrow. 'The Astronomer and God' in *The Intellectuals Speak Out about God* (ed. Varghese, R. A.) 22 (Regnery Gateway, 1984).

420. Jeff Miller, '7 Reasons the Multiverse Is Not a Valid Alternative to God', *Apologetics Press*, 2017, http://apologeticspress.org/APContent.aspx?category=9&article=5396.

421. John B. Arden, *Rewire Your Brain. Think Yourself to a Better Life* (New Jersey: John

Wiley & Sons, 2010)   See also Jean Askenasy, 'Consciousness, Brain, Neuro-plasticity', *Frontiers in Psychology* 4 (2013),
https://doi.org/10.3389/fpsyg.2013.00412.

422. Joseph Chilton Pearce, *Heart-Mind Matrix: How the Heart Can Teach the Mind New Ways to Think* (Vermont: Park Street Press, 2012).

423. Vida Demarin, Sandra Morovic, and Raphael Bene, 'Neuroplasticity, Structural Neuroplasticity, Functional Neuroplasticity', *Periodicum Biologorum* 116, no. 2 (2014): 209–11.

424. John B. Arden, *Rewire Your Brain: Think Your Way to a Better Life* (New Jersey: John Wiley & Sons, 2010).

425. Saurabh Vyas et al., 'Neural Population Dynamics Underlying Motor Learning Transfer', *Neuron* 97, no. 5 (March 2018): 1177–1186.e3,
https://doi.org/10.1016/j.neuron.2018.01.040.

426. Tori Rodriguez, 'Mental Rehearsals Strengthen Neural Circuits', *Scientific American*, September 2014, https://www.scientificamerican.com/article/mental-rehearsals-strengthen-neural-circuits/.

427. Britta K. Hölzel et al., 'Mindfulness Practice Leads to Increases in Regional Brain Gray Matter Density', *Psychiatry Research: Neuroimaging* 191, no. 1 (January 2011): 36–43, https://doi.org/10.1016/j.pscychresns.2010.08.006.

428. Carolyn Gregoire, 'How Stress Changes The Brain', *Huffington Post*, 2014, https://www.huffingtonpost.com/2014/11/18/brain-stress_n_6148470.html.

429. Steiner, *The Philosophy of Spiritual Activity*.

430. Elkhonon Goldberg, *The Executive Brain: Frontal Lobes and the Civilized Mind* (New York: Oxford Press, 2001).

431. Ron McComb, 'Needs, Moral Development, and the Triune Brain', *The Electric Web Matrix of Digital Technology*, 1993,
http://www.co-bw.com/BSC/TriuneBrainFin.pdf.

432. Christoffer O. Hernæs, 'Science and Transhumanism', *TechCrunch*, 26 August 2016, http://www.bibliotecapleyades.net/ciencia2/ciencia_transhumanism62.htm

433. Newsweek Staff, 'All Eyes on Google', *Newsweek*, March 2004,
http://www.newsweek.com/all-eyes-google-124041.

434. Dr John C. Eccles, *Evolution of the Brain, Creation of the Self* (New York: Routledge, 1989), 241.

435. A. Schurger, M. Mylopoulos, and D. Rosenthal, 'Neural Antecedents of Spontaneous Voluntary Movement: A New Perspective', *Trends Cogn Sci.* 20, no. 2 (2016): 77–79, https://doi.org/10.1016/j.tics.2015.11.00. See also, David Pratt, 'John Eccles on Mind and Brain', http://www.davidpratt.info/eccles.htm

436. Benjamin Libet et al., 'Time of Conscious Intention to Act in Relation to Onset of Cerebral Activity (Readiness-Potential)', *Brain* 106, no. 3 (1983): 623–42, https://doi.org/10.1093/brain/106.3.623.

437. Heusser, *Anthroposophy and Science*.

438. Heusser, p. 209.

439. Heusser, p. 209.

440. Roger Nelson, 'The Global Consciousness Project',
http://global-mind.org/index.html

441. The Global Consciousness Project, 'Formal Results: Testing the GCP Hypothesis', *The Global Consciousness Project*, 2018,
http://noosphere.princeton.edu/results.html#alldata.

442. Rahul Dewan, 'Subtle interactions link us with each other and the Earth', *Global Consciousness Project*, June 6, 2017. https://wayofdharma.com/2017/06/06/global-consciousness-project-subtle-interactions-link-us-with-each-other-and-the-earth/

443. Dr Eben Alexander, *Proof of Heaven: A Neurosurgeon's Journey Into the Afterlife* (New York: Simon & Schuster, 2012), 85.

444. Harrari, Y.N., *Homo Deus: A Brief History of Tomorrow* (Harper Collins: Kindle Edition). All the quotes from Harrari can be found in pp. 282–284 of this book.

445. Richard Dawkins, *The Selfish Gene* (Oxford: Oxford Press, 1989).

446. Martine Rothblatt, *Virtually Human: The Promise—and the Peril—of Digital Immortality* (New York: St. Martin's Press, Digital edition. n.d.). From the citations, however, this book came out most likely in 2013 or later.

447. National Institutes of Health, 'The Human Genome Project Completion: Frequently Asked Questions', National Human Genome Research Institute, 2010, https://www.genome.gov/11006943/human-genome-project-completion-frequently-asked-questions/.

448. National Institutes of Health, 'An Overview of the Human Genome Project', National Human Genome Research Institute, 2016, https://www.genome.gov/12011238/an-overview-of-the-human-genome-project/.

449. Dr Lissa Rankin, *Mind Over Medicine: Scientific Proof You Can Heal Yourself* (California: Hay House, 2013).

450. Danielle Simmons, 'Epigenetic Influences and Disease', *Nature Education* 1, no. 1 (2008): 6, https://www.nature.com/scitable/topicpage/epigenetic-influences-and-disease-895.

451. Institute of Medicine (US) Committee on Assessing Interactions Among Social, Behavioral, and Genetic Factors in Health, *Genes, Behavior, and the Social Environment: Moving Beyond the Nature/Nurture Debate*, ed. LM Hernandez and DG Blazer (Washington: National Academies Press, 2006).

452. Nicolaj Strøyer Christophersen and Kristian Helin, 'Epigenetic Control of Embryonic Stem Cell Fate', *The Journal of Experimental Medicine* 207, no. 11 (October 25, 2010): 2287–95, https://doi.org/10.1084/jem.20101438.

453. Ozgun Atasoy, 'Your Thoughts Can Release Abilities Beyond Normal Limits', *Scientific American*, August 2013, https://www.scientificamerican.com/article/your-thoughts-can-release-abilities-beyond-normal-limits/; Fabrizio Benedetti, Elisa Carlino, and Antonella Pollo, 'How Placebos Change the Patient's Brain', *Neuropsychopharmacology* 36, no. 1 (January 30, 2011): 339–54, https://doi.org/10.1038/npp.2010.81.

454. National Center for Biotechnology Information, 'Central Dogma of Biology: Classic View', *NCBI*, 2007, https://www.ncbi.nlm.nih.gov/Class/MLACourse/Modules/MolBioReview/central_dogma.html.

455. *The Economist*, 'Biology's Big Bang', *The Economist*, June 2007, https://www.economist.com/node/9339752; M. B. Gerstein et al., 'What Is a Gene, Post-ENCODE? History and Updated Definition', *Genome Research* 17, no. 6 (June 1, 2007): 669–81, https://doi.org/10.1101/gr.6339607; Patrick Barry, 'Genome 2.0: Mountains of New Data Are Challenging Old Views', *Science News*, September 2007, https://www.sciencenews.org/node/21410.

456. John R. Searle, *The Rediscovery of the Mind* (Cambridge: MIT Press, 1992), 44–46.

457. Ken Richardson, *Genes, Brains, and Human Potential: The Science and Ideology of Intelligence* (New York: Columbia University Press, 2017).

458. Rinske A. Gotink et al., '8-Week Mindfulness Based Stress Reduction Induces Brain Changes Similar to Traditional Long-Term Meditation Practice—A Systematic Review', *Brain and Cognition* 108 (October 2016): 32–41, https://doi.org/10.1016/j.bandc.2016.07.001; Hölzel et al., 'Mindfulness Practice Leads to Increases in Regional Brain Gray Matter Density'.

459. Arthur Zajonc, *Meditation as Contemplative Inquiry: When Knowing Becomes Love* (Massachusetts: Lindisfarne Books, 2009).

460. Mind & Life Institute, 'Biography for Arthur Zajonc', Mind & Life Institute, 2018, https://www.mindandlife.org/arthur-zajonc-bio/.

461. Mind & Life Institute, 'Dharamsala Dialogue Livestream', 2018, https://www.mindandlife.org/mind-and-life-dialogues/dharamsala-dialogue-livestream/.

462. Soren Gordhamer, *Wisdom 2.0: The New Movement Toward Purposeful Engagement in Business and in Life, Wisdom 2.0* (New York: HarperCollins, 2013).

463. Wisdom 2.0, 'Wisdom 2.0: New Leader Summit', Wisdom 2.0, 2018, http://www.newleadersummit.com/; Noah Shachtman, 'In Silicon Valley, Meditation Is No Fad. It Could Make Your Career', *Wired*, 2013, https://www.wired.com/2013/06/meditation-mindfulness-silicon-valley/.

464. Gordhamer, *Wisdom 2.0: The New Movement Toward Purposeful Engagement in Business and in Life*.

465. Dan Seifert, 'Secret Program Gives NSA, FBI Backdoor Access to Apple, Google, Facebook, Microsoft Data', *The Verge*, 2013, https://www.theverge.com/2013/6/6/4403868/nsa-fbi-mine-data-apple-google-facebook-microsoft-others-prism.

466. Soren Gordhamer, 'Google, Facebook, Twitter, and the Wisdom 2.0 Conference', *Huffington Post*, 2017, https://www.huffingtonpost.com/soren-gordhamer/google-facebook-twitter-a_b_495986.html.

467. Solon, 'Facebook Says Cambridge Analytica May Have Gained 37m More Users' Data'.

468. Gordhamer, 'Google, Facebook, Twitter, and the Wisdom 2.0 Conference'; Carole Cadwalladr, 'Wisdom 2.0: It Came For Our Heartbeats, Now Google Wants Our Souls', *The Guardian*, 2014, https://www.theguardian.com/technology/2014/sep/19/wisdom2-mindfulness-meditation-google.

469. Bryan Clark, 'Snowden on Google Allo: "Don't Use It"', *The Next Web*, 2016, https://thenextweb.com/google/2016/09/22/snowden-on-google-allo-dont-use-it/; Tristan Harris, 'How Technology Is Hijacking Your Mind—from a Magician and Google Design Ethicist', *Thrive Global*, 2016, https://medium.com/thrive-global/how-technology-hijacks-peoples-minds-from-a-magician-and-google-s-design-ethicist-56d62ef5edf3; Jeremy Lent, 'The New Mind Manipulators', *Huffington Post*, 2017, https://www.huffingtonpost.com/jeremy-lent/the-new-mind-manipulators_b_9760268.html.

470. Darrin Drda, 'The Selective Awareness of Wisdom 2.0', *Open Democracy*, 2014, https://www.opendemocracy.net/transformation/darrin-drda/selective-awareness-of-wisdom-20.

471. Jayson DeMers, 'This Is How Meditation Could Make You More Successful, According to These 5 Business Leaders', World Economic Forum, 2018, https://www.weforum.org/agenda/2018/04/5-successful-business-leaders-that-have-used-meditation-to-improve-productivity-creativity-and-business-acumen; United Nations, '"A Room of Quiet": The Meditation Room, United Nations Headquarters', United Nations, 2018, http://www.un.org/depts/dhl/dag/

meditationroom.htm; Abigail Somma, 'Mindful Diplomacy: A Pathway to Peace', *Ethics and International Affairs*, 2018, https://www.ethicsandinternationalaffairs.org/2018/mindful-diplomacy-pathway-peace/.

472. Drake Baer, 'Here's What Google Teaches Employees In Its "Search Inside Yourself" Course', *Business Insider*, 2014, http://www.businessinsider.com/search-inside-yourself-googles-life-changing-mindfulness-course-2014-8.

473. Megan Gibson, 'The 25 Most Influential Business Management Books', *Time*, 2011, http://content.time.com/time/specials/packages/article/0,28804,2086680_2086683_2087663,00.html.

474. Shachtman, 'In Silicon Valley, Meditation Is No Fad. It Could Make Your Career'.

475. The New York Times, 'Meditation Archive', *The New York Times*, 2018, https://www.nytimes.com/topic/subject/meditation. Joann S. Lublin, 'Meditation Brings Calm to CEOs', *The Wall Street Journal*, 2017, https://www.wsj.com/articles/meditation-brings-calm-to-ceos-1511960400.

476. Rudolf Steiner, *Background to the Gospel of St. Mark.* (London: Rudolf Steiner Press, 1968), Chapter 9.

477. Kurzweil, *The Singularity Is Near: When Humans Transcend Biology*; Lev Grossman, '2045: The Year Man Becomes Immortal', *Time*, February 2011, http://content.time.com/time/magazine/article/0,9171,2048299-1,00.html; Rothblatt, *Virtually Human: The Promise—and the Peril—of Digital Immortality*.

478. Emberson, P., *Machines and the Human Spirit, The Golden Age of the Fifth Kingdom* (Scotland: The DewCross Centre for Moral Technology, 2013).

479. L.F.C. Mees, *Blessed by Illness* (Massachusetts: SteinerBooks, 1983).

480. HeartMath Institute, 'About Us', 2018, https://www.heartmath.com/about/.

481. Dr Joe Dispenza, *You Are the Placebo: Making Your Mind Matter* (California: Hay House, 2014); Bruce Lipton, *The Biology of Belief 10th Anniversary Edition: Unleashing the Power of Consciousness, Matter & Miracles*, 10th Anniv (California: Hay House, 2015); Braden, *The Divine Matrix: Bridging Time, Space, Miracles, and Belief*.

482. Lipton, *The Biology of Belief 10th Anniversary Edition: Unleashing the Power of Consciousness, Matter & Miracles*.

483. Lipton; Simmons, 'Epigenetic Influences and Disease'.

484. Lipton, *The Biology of Belief*.

485. Howard Gardner, *Multiple Intelligences: New Horizons in Theory and Practice* (New York: Perseus Books, 2006).

486. Albert Soesman, *Our Twelve Senses* (Stroud: Hawthorn Press, 1999).

487. Steiner, *An Outline of Esoteric Science*, Chapter 5.

488. Sascha Cohen, 'Helen Keller's Forgotten Radicalism', *Time*, June 26, 2015, http://time.com/3923213/helen-keller-radicalism/.

489. Jeremy Rifkin, *The Empathic Civilization. The Race to Global Consciousness in a World in Crisis* (New York: Jeremy P. Tarcher/Penguin, 2009). See the entire section on 'What Babies Really Want'. Location 927ff. Kindle edition. Morton Kissen, *Assessing Object Relations Phenomena* (Madison: Intl Universities Pr Inc, 1986).

490. Harry J. Bentham, 'Death, Transcendence and Transhumanism', *Humanity+ Magazine*, December 2014, http://hplusmagazine.com/2014/12/01/death-transcendence-transhumanism/.

491. Gideon Lichfield, 'The Science of Near-Death Experiences', *The Atlantic*, 2015, https://www.theatlantic.com/magazine/archive/2015/04/the-science-of-near-

death-experiences/386231/; Alexander, *Proof of Heaven: A Neurosurgeon's Journey Into the Afterlife.*

492. See Part II.

493. Ernest Valea, 'Reincarnation: Its Meaning and Consequences', *Comparative Religion*, 2018, https://doi.org/A New Vision of the Role of Rebirth in Christian Thought.

494. Prokofieff, *Anthroposophy and the Philosophy of Freedom*, p. 29. Although he cites Steiner as his ultimate reference (Steiner, *From the History and Contents of the First Section of the Esoteric School 1904–1914*) Prokofieff develops a rigorous epistemological consideration of this fact.

495. This is a very short account of Prokofieff's detailed elaboration in Chapter 2 of his book on *Anthroposophy and the Philosophy of Freedom*. Readers who want to get more details should read the entire chapter of this book, which in turn can only be rightly understood by reading the whole book, especially Chapter 1.

496. Florini, A.M. (Ed.), *The Third Force. The Rise of Transnational Civil Society* (Tokyo: Japan Center for International Exchange and Washington, D.C.: Carnegie Endowment for International Peace. See also, Mary Kaldor, 'Civil Society and Accountability', *Journal of Human Development* 4, no. 1 (March 2003): 5–27, https://doi.org/10.1080/1464988032000051469; World Economic Forum, 'The Future Role of Civil Society' (Geneva, 2013), http://www3.weforum.org/docs/WEF_FutureRoleCivilSociety_Report_2013.pdf.

497. What will now be shared is based directly from the more than 50 years' experience of activism in global civil society.

498. John D. Clark, 'The Globalization of Civil Society', in *Critical Mass: The Emergence of the Global Civil Society*, ed. James W. St. G. Walker and Andrew S. Thompson (Canada: Wilfrid Laurier University Press, 2008),
https://www.cigionline.org/sites/default/files/walker_thompson.pdf.

499. Perlas, *Shaping Globalization.*

500. Singapore Management University:
https://www.britcham.org.sg/images/uploads/smu-mtsc-factsheet.pdf.

501. United Nations General Assembly, 'Transforming Our World: The 2030 Agenda for Sustainable Development', in *Resolution Adopted by the General Assembly on 25 September 2015* (New York: United Nations, 2015), http://www.un.org/ga/search/view_doc.asp?symbol=A/RES/70/1&Lang=E.

502. Nicanor Perlas, 'Civil Society—The Third Global Power', *Southcross Review*, 2000, http://www.southerncrossreview.org/4/wto.html; Noah Smith, 'The Dark Side of Globalization: Why Seattle's 1999 Protesters Were Right', *The Atlantic*, 2014, https://www.theatlantic.com/business/archive/2014/01/the-dark-side-of-globalization-why-seattles-1999-protesters-were-right/282831/.

503. World Trade Organization, 'Philippines and the WTO', 2018,
https://www.wto.org/english/thewto_e/countries_e/philippines_e.htm.

504. World Trade Organization, 'Understanding the WTO Agreement on Sanitary and Phytosanitary Measures', 1998,
https://www.wto.org/english/tratop_e/sps_e/spsund_e.htm.

505. United Nations and World Health Organization, 'Codex Alimentarius: International Food Standards', *Food and Agriculture Organization of the United Nations*, 2018, www.fao.org/fao-who-codexalimentarius/en/. The Codex standard for DDT levels in food, for example, is greater than what health experts have considered safe for DDT in mother's milk.

506. International Forum on Globalization, 'About Us', *International Forum on Globalization*, 2018, http://ifg.org/about/about-us/.

507. Stephen J. Kobrin, 'The MAI and the Clash of Globalizations', *Foreign Policy*, no. Fall (1998): 97–109. I was one of around 10 individuals who developed the strategy on how to defeat the MAI. Martin Khor, Executive Director of Third World Network, convened the small meeting of global activists who included Vandana Shiva. This strategy subsequently became the united strategy under the umbrella of the International Forum on Globalization. This took place in a hotel in 1997 in Washington D.C.

508. Perlas, *Shaping Globalization*. See also, Smith, 'The Dark Side of Globalization: Why Seattle's 1999 Protesters Were Right'.

509. 'Field of Tears', *The Guardian*, 2003, https://www.theguardian.com/world/2003/sep/16/northkorea.wto; Immanuel Wallerstein, 'The Battle of Cancun: Anatomy of an Unexpected Victory', *Days of Dissent—Reflections on Summit Mobilisations*, 2004, http://struggle.ws/anarchism/writers/ramor/cancun.html. Najma Sadeque, 'How WTO Kills Farmers', *The Nation*, 2013, https://nation.com.pk/11-Sep-2013/how-wto-kills-farmers; Jonathan Watts.

510. Marc Levinson, 'The Vanishing WTO', *Council on Foreign Relations*, 2009, https://www.cfr.org/expert-brief/vanishing-wto.

511. Tom Lansford, *Old Europe, New Europe and the US: Renegotiating Transatlantic Security in the Post 9/11 Era*, ed. Blagovest Tashev (Hampshire: Ashgate Publishing, 2005).

512. World Trade Organization, 'The WTO and Preferential Trade Agreements: From Co-Existence to Coherence' (Geneva, 2011), https://www.wto.org/english/res_e/booksp_e/anrep_e/world_trade_report11_e.pdf.

513. Hawken, P., *Blessed Unrest. How the Largest Movement in the World Came into Being and Why No one Saw It Coming* (New York: Viking, 2007).

514. The Right Livelihood Award, 'What Is Right Livelihood?', *The Right Livelihood Award, 2018*, http://www.rightlivelihoodaward.org/honour/about-the-right-livelihood-award/what-is-right-livelihood/.

515. The Right Livelihood Award, 'Edward Snowden', *The Right Livelihood Award*, 2014, http://www.rightlivelihoodaward.org/laureates/edward-snowden/.

516. The Local Staff, 'Swedish Politicians Block "Alternative Nobel Prize"', *The Local*, 2016, https://www.thelocal.se/20160608/swedish-parliament-blocks-alternative-nobel-prize.

517. Personal conversation with Ole von Uexküll, Executive Director of the Right Livelihood Foundation, RLF Office, Stockholm, October 2017.

518. Personal conversation with Gina Lopez, former Secretary (Minister) of the Department of Environment and Natural Resources, Philippine Government, July 2016.

519. Deloitte, 'The Deloitte Millennial Survey 2017'; *Achieve*, 'Why Do Millennials Choose to Engage in Cause Movements', 2017, http://www.themillennialimpact.com/.

520. Joel Stein, 'Millennials: The Me Me Me Generation', *Time*, May 2013, http://time.com/247/millennials-the-me-me-me-generation/.

521. Chapter 5 discusses this more thoroughly.

522. Marc Freedman, *The Big Shift. Navigating the New Stage Beyond Midlife* (New York: Public Affairs, 2011) See also, Cal J. Halvorsen and Jim Emerman, 'The Encore

Movement: Baby Boomers and Older Adults Can Be a Powerful Force to Build Community', *Generations*. Winter 2013-2014 (2014), http://asaging.org/blog/encore-movement-baby-boomers-and-older-adults-can-be-powerful-force-build-community.

523. Virginia Sease, *Rudolf Steiner's Endowment. Centenary Reflections on his Attempt for a Theosophical Art and Way of Life, 15 December 1911* (Forest Row, England: Temple Lodge, 2012), p. 25.

524. Personal conversation with David Andrew Schwartz where he referred to an article written by Christopher Schaeffer on the membership challenge of the global Anthroposophical Society, 29 January 2018.

525. Sergei O. Prokofieff and Peter Selg, *Crisis in the Anthroposophical Society and Pathways to the Future* (Forest Row, England: Temple Lodge, 2013), p. 100.

526. Lucifer is the other adversary of humanity. He often works in polar opposite to Ahriman. Although still active today, we have focused more on Ahriman because of the latter's key role in inspiring materialism and the technologies that humans have created on the basis of a materialistic view of the world.

527. See Chapter 12.

528. Three people coined the term 'sustainable agriculture' in 1983 to forge principles of unity that would encourage all these different forms of alternative agriculture to work together. These were Terry Gips, Nancy Hertzberg, and myself. We then went on to form IASA, the International Alliance for Sustainable Agriculture, in the same year. Terry and Nancy are global civil society activists and do not belong to the anthroposophical movement, then or now. I was already a member of the Anthroposophical Society at that time until now. Similarly, the leadership of the bio-dynamic movement, together with key individualities from the other forms of organic agriculture, formed the International Federation of Organic Agriculture Movements (IFOAM) in the 1970s. Today IFOAM influences the global market in organic food as well as legislations of government especially in Europe.

529. See Chapter 16.

530. Rudolf Steiner., *Karmic Relationships, Vol.3* (London: Rudolf Steiner Press, 1977), p. 117.

531. Ibid., pp. 104–105.

532. See Note 15 above.

533. Kevin Maney, 'In Silicon Valley, Failing Is Succeeding', *Newsweek*, August 2015, http://www.newsweek.com/2015/09/11/silicon-valley-failing-succeeding-367179.html; Ryan Singel, 'A Silicon Valley Conference About Failing Is Big Success', *Wired*, 2009, https://www.wired.com/2009/10/failcon-succeeds/.

534. The story of Parsifal, an ignorant teenage would-be knight who eventually became the King of the Grail, the symbol of the highest achievement in esoteric Christianity, is well-known and much-loved within anthroposophical circles. It can also be a description of the modern condition of humanity where each one of us carries a wounded part in our soul, from whatever causes, and the healing of this part of the soul can only come when our spiritual nature purifies and transforms the soul to align the latter in service of the spiritual. For more details on Parsifal and a profound and deep treatment of the mysteries of the Grail, see Stein, W.J., *The Ninth Century. World History in the Light of the Holy Grail* (London: Temple Lodge Press, 1991).

535. Rudolf Steiner, *Karmic Relationships, Esoteric Studies, Vol. III* (London: Rudolf Steiner Press, 1977) p. 169–171.

536. Rudolf Steiner, *Anthroposophical Leading Thoughts* (London: Rudolf Steiner Press, 1973) *The Experiences of Michael in the Course of His Cosmic Mission*. pp.76–80.There is also an electronic version at www.rsarchive.org. The wordings of the translations are slightly different but the message is the same.

537. Ibid., p. 127.

538. Ibid., p. 128.

539. Ibid., p. 128.

540. One can reflect on these statements in two ways. The outcome is the same. The way humanity was and is evolving is of deep concern and anxiety to Micha-el, and for those who understand these things, also for all of us and for humanity. Either Micha-el foresaw what was going to happen in our time, and got concerned. Or, he was already deeply concerned about the extreme theoretical materialism that was starting to become part of everyday culture. If he realized that this theoretical materialism would morph into technological materialism, Micha-el would probably have been more concerned and anxious today.

541. Rudolf Steiner, *The Inner Nature of Man and Our Life between Death and Rebirth* (London: Rudolf Steiner Press, 1994) p. 80.

542. Steiner, *Anthroposophical Leading Thoughts*, p. 129.

543. Rudolf Steiner, *The Fall of the Spirits of Darkness* (Bristol: Rudolf Steiner Press, 1993).

544. Steiner, *Anthroposophical Leading Thoughts*, p.1 29.

545. See Chapter 5 above.

546. Ibid.

547. Ibid., pp. 129–130.

548. Ibid., p. 131 (Leading Thought #136).

549. Sease, *Rudolf Steiner's Endowment*, p. 83.

550. Rudolf Steiner, *Michaelmas and The Soul Forces of Man* (Great Barrington, Masschusetts: SteinerBooks, 1982) Lecture 2. This is also the source of the next few quotes unless otherwise indicated.

551. I had such an experience of one group in the US when I was still living there.

552. The alignment challenge is the current issue that puzzles the AI community all over the world. The key question is how can AI engineers make sure that ASI align their 'behaviour' with human values? One wrong move could mean extinction. Chapter 2 and 3 dealt with this problem in detail. I sincerely hope I am mistaken in my analysis.

553. See Chapter 20 above.

554. See Steiner's 8 volumes on *Karmic Relationships* especially Volume 3 for the karma of anthroposophists.

555. Steiner, *Karmic Relationships*, Volume 3.

556. If the reader takes a look at the various citations in this book, they will begin to get an idea of the 'who's who' in the increasing movement to tame technology for human ends. And there are many more like them. But that would require an entirely new book to document the details of this very promising and hopeful movement.

557. Rishi Iyengar, 'Andrew Wiles Wins 2016 Abel Prize for Fermat's Last Theorem', *Time*, March 18, 2016,
http://time.com/4263916/andrew-wiles-abel-prize-fermat-theorem/

558. Nassim Nicholas Taleb, *The Black Swan, The Impact of the Highly Improbable* (New York: Random House, 2007).

559. Lievegoed, B.J., *Towards the 21st Century: Doing the Good* (Vancouver: Steiner Book Centre, 1972), p. 78. Also the source of the continuing quote.
560. Dr Ernst Katz, a student of Spiritual Science for more than 40 years is the source of this quotation from Steiner. See http://www.rearchive/RelAuthors/KatzErnst/AGM_Address.php

A note from the publisher

For more than a quarter of a century, **Temple Lodge Publishing** has made available new thought, ideas and research in the field of spiritual science.

Anthroposophy, as founded by Rudolf Steiner (1861-1925), is commonly known today through its practical applications, principally in education (Steiner-Waldorf schools) and agriculture (biodynamic food and wine). But behind this outer activity stands the core discipline of spiritual science, which continues to be developed and updated. True science can never be static and anthroposophy is living knowledge.

Our list features some of the best contemporary spiritual-scientific work available today, as well as introductory titles. So, visit us online at **www.templelodge.com** and join our emailing list for news on new titles.

If you feel like supporting our work, you can do so by buying our books or making a direct donation (we are a non-profit/ charitable organisation).

office@templelodge.com

For the finest books of Science and Spirit